DATE DUE

1/27/05	

DEMCO, INC. 38-2931

Globalisation and the Nation-State

Globalisation and the Nation-State

Edited by

Frans Buelens

Faculty of Applied Economics, University of Antwerp (RUCA), Belgium

BELGIAN–DUTCH ASSOCIATION FOR INSTITUTIONAL AND POLITICAL ECONOMY

Edward Elgar
Cheltenham, UK • Northampton, MA, USA

Published by
Edward Elgar Publishing Limited
Glensanda House
Montpellier Parade
Cheltenham
Glos GL50 1UA
UK

Edward Elgar Publishing, Inc.
136 West Street
Suite 202
Northampton
Massachusetts 01060
USA

A catalogue record for this book
is available from the British Library

Library of Congress Cataloguing in Publication Data

Globalisation and the nation–state / edited by Frans Buelens.
    Includes biographical references and index.
    1. International economic relations. 2. Competition, International.
    3. National state. 4. Economic history—1990 –   I. Buelens,
    Frans, 1951– .
    HF1359.G5819   2000
    337—dc21   99–3949
                                                                    CIP

ISBN 1 84064 202 5

Printed and bound in Great Britain by Bookcraft (Bath) Ltd.

Contents

Figures

Tables

Contributors

Jan Annaert
Assistant Professor in Finance at the Erasmus University of Rotterdam, The Netherlands. His research focuses on international finance and financial risk management. Some of this research has been published in international refereed journals and books.

Frans Buelens
Professor at HIVT and researcher at the University of Antwerp (RUCA), Belgium.

Philip G. Cerny
Professor of International Political Economy at the University of Leeds, UK. Author of *The Politics of Grandeur: Ideological Aspects of de Gaulle's Foreign Policy* (1980) and *The Changing Architecture of Politics: Structure, Agency and the Future of the State* (1990).

Paul Hirst
Professor of Social Theory, Birkbeck College, University of London, UK. Author of numerous works including *Associative Democracy* (1994), *From Statism to Pluralism* (1997).

Glenn Rayp
Professor in International Economics at the Faculty of Economics and Business of the University of Ghent, Belgium. He has made several contributions in the field of globalisation, income inequality and social protection.

Maarten Smeets
Maarten Smeets is counsellor at the World Trade Organisation, Switzerland, currently working in the Technical Cooperation Division. Prior to that, he worked for six years at the OECD in Paris, where he held various positions in the Trade Directorate. He has written various analytical and sectoral OECD studies relating to globalisation in world trade.

Grahame Thompson
Senior Lecturer in Social Science, the Open University. Author of numerous works including *Globalisation in Question* with Paul Hirst (1996) and *Economic Dynamism in Asia Pacific* (1998).

Acknowledgements

The editor of this volume, also co-organiser of the Conference on Globalisation and the Nation-State of the Belgian–Dutch Association of Institutional and Political Economy, acknowledges the financial and logistical support of the Department of Economics of the University of Antwerp (RUCA) and the European Commission.

A special message of thanks goes to Professor Julien van den Broeck for his work and support as co-organiser of the conference. Many thanks to the contributors to this volume for complying with the editor's requests and meeting deadlines so efficiently.

Particular thanks go to Anouk Gautreaux for being a mainstay in the editing process and for turning the manuscript into camera-ready copy.

Globalisation and the Nation-State: an Introduction

Frans Buelens

The globalisation of the world economy is one of the most discussed items at the turn of the century and although officially welcomed as a main contribution to world welfare it is held by many to be responsible for job destruction and mass unemployment, and it is feared it will be an even greater threat to jobs, income levels and social security systems in the future: the 'race to the bottom'. These widespread beliefs find their source in such enduring phenomena as mass unemployment in Europe and lowering wages in the United States. The 1997 East Asian Financial Crisis once again confronted the world with its being a 'global village' and the consequences of the globalisation of finance. In the course of the globalisation debate the role of the state has been widely put into question as being a powerless institution in a globalised economy. In short, it seems to these observers as if the world is becoming one big market economy responsible for all of the social evils that are inherent in that market economy. Moreover, as it is taken for granted that this ongoing globalisation process is quickly spreading all over the world it holds two possible attitudes: one of passivity, accepting all the consequences that the globalisation process promises to bring along; the other being a return to protectionism as the only possibility for active protection against the threat of globalisation.

As such, it is not globalisation that is questioned but, in particular, increasing financial instability and the social consequences related to the whole of the globalisation process. As far as this last point is concerned, the underlying 'race to the bottom' hypothesis, although popularised by quite a lot of publications, is only one of many possible hypotheses with regard to globalisation. Others include the upward convergence hypothesis (globalisation bringing rising welfare state spending in all countries) and the globalisation irrelevance hypothesis, putting forward the irrelevance of globalisation or even considering it a myth.

Focusing on the concept of globalisation, the characteristics of the globalisation process and the relationship with the nation-state, four important points can be put forward which will be widely discussed in what follows by international scholars in the field.

Firstly the world economy is, in fact, more open today than it was for instance in the period between the two world wars. This point of comparison is important, as it is widely documented and measured by various statistical measures that the world economy was very open before the First World War, and that the Interbellum was a major interruption to this process. This however does not mean that nothing changed, but a true evaluation must be made. To this end and to make things clear the first two contributions will document international trade, investment and finance. It will be observed from these papers that while trade and foreign direct investment (FDI) are rising, the most explosive phenomenon in the field of globalisation is that of finance. But the bulk of world trade is not with developing countries and as far as FDI is concerned there are only a few companies that are truly transnational. Most operate from their national home base. However, this does not mean there is a standstill in the development of capitalism. Indeed, technology has driven capitalist development in the past and continues to do so today. Ongoing shifts in the capital–labour composition of the production process, increasing returns to scale, the development of oligopolistic structures, production for the world market, intensified competition and fast-growing new emerging markets are some of the characteristics of the process. Moreover, at present free market ideology and practices are more actively promoted, accepted and applied than ever before as they are also institutionalised (World Trade Organisation, WTO) or as institutionalisation is being attempted (Multilateral Agreement in Investment, MAI).

Secondly, the fact that the world economy is more open with regard to international trade, investment and finance does not mean that we can define this as globalisation. The concept of globalisation is indeed 'ill-defined', as Paul Hirst and Grahame Thompson have described it, and most scholars, if not all, agree on this. Clearly, this puts a heavy constraint on the debate and has enormous consequences as far as the state debate is concerned. The world economy is more open but whereas some see this process at a global level, others think that a regionalisation tendency is far more important than this world-wide globalisation process.

Thirdly, many of the so-called consequences of globalisation are in fact not consequences of globalisation but consequences of the economic laws and the functioning of a market economy as such and *laissez faire* government policies. After all, globalisation is rather part of marketisation as Dani Rodrik has put it (Rodrik, 1997, p. 49). With regard to trade the effect of shifts in employment due to international trade with developing countries are rather marginal in general, although for some specific sectors there is a rather greater effect than for others, putting all of the burden on the lower-skilled, all too often specific factors of production. As such, the ongoing globalisation process causes many problems for some people and public policy has, up to now, not really cared about them. But if we consider, for instance, unemployment in Europe, there are other causes which may account for this enormous problem, such as skill-biased technological change, the reduced bargaining power of labour, the persistence of free market ideology.

Finally, globalisation is a concept all too often used within an ideological framework. By over-accentuating its consequences, it can be used by policymakers as an excuse for domestic policy objectives and as an excuse for withdrawal in the light of international events. It is also a dangerous concept as it can lead to protectionism and economic warfare against developing countries. As such, although many scholars stress the ungovernability of the national and international economy, there is an ongoing debate between scholars about the feasibility of extended public governance.

The Belgian–Dutch Association for Institutional and Political Economy decided to adopt 'Globalisation and the Nation-State' as an appropriate theme for its twentieth annual conference which was held at the University of Antwerp (RUCA) in Antwerp, Belgium on 20 November 1998. The chapters in this book offer a selection of the papers presented at this conference.

Maarten Smeets stresses that globalisation has become the catchword of the decade and is likely to influence thinking and policymaking well into the next millennium. In the field of trade, he says, trade liberalisation has always had some negative effects in certain sectors of the economy and requires adjustment measures, while at the same time it is proven that the benefits of trade liberalisation largely outweigh the costs. In his view, governments have little choice as there is no alternative to the road of progressive liberalisation of markets and enhancing competition. He argues that the WTO multilateral trading system currently provides the framework for addressing a large number of issues and is moving increasingly in the direction of providing global responses to global issues.

Jan Annaert discusses the globalisation of finance. As the author states, during the 1980s and especially during the 1990s, financial markets world-wide experienced an internationalisation process, witnessed before only in the late nineteenth and early twentieth centuries. In the first section he illustrates this process using financial data. The second section identifies the underlying reasons of this process. The technological developments and the deregulation tendency experienced in most countries are not the only reasons for the globalisation of financial markets. The institutionalisation of savings has also dramatically increased demand for more sophisticated global products. In the third section the implications for capital markets are investigated. More specifically, he reviews the empirical literature studying the integration of capital markets. This literature is divided into four parts: studies focusing on price equalisation, on portfolio diversification, on international risk-sharing and on the savings–investment relationship. The advantages and disadvantages of globalisation are discussed in the fourth section. Besides the traditional advantages of more opportunities for diversification and lower financing costs, attention is also paid to indirect advantages such as the increasing efficiency of domestic markets and the disciplining effect of financial markets. Among the disadvantages are the potential social consequences for developed countries, the loss of policy autonomy, and the inherent instability of deregulated financial markets. In the fifth section some policy guidelines are provided, both from the macroeconomic and the regulatory point of view.

Glenn Rayp tries to show how an EMU may limit the social protection level in some or all member states because of the use of social security taxation as a strategic instrument in the international competition in imperfect substitutable consumer goods. In his model each country has a private interest in low domestic but high foreign social protection. In these circumstances the absence of co-ordination between countries may result in a global downward pressure on social protection to a sub-optimally low level. He arrives at the conclusion that a global position on globalisation might not be a good idea and that 'socially oriented' countries need to differentiate their attitude and claims, in accordance with the origin of the constraints on their policy.

Philip Cerny discusses the modern nation-state. He posits that the state as we have known it represents one particular kind of institutionalised governance structure among many possibilities. Its structural predominance and durability have reflected a combination of two factors. The first involves a calculus of institutional efficiency, the second involves the embeddedness of social practices. In his chapter he argues that globalisation creates profound paradigmatic structural changes to the nation-state. However, because of actors, embedded expectations and the complex, diverse and additive character of globalisation processes themselves, effective strategic political responses to globalisation have not yet emerged.

Paul Hirst and Grahame Thompson in their chapter test the concept of globalisation against the available evidence. Conventionally globalisation is seen as a recent change in the nature of the international economy in which world markets and transnational companies have replaced national economies. They argue that instead there are now three major trade blocs, the EU, NAFTA and Japan, and that trade within the blocs is more significant than that between them. FDI is similarly concentrated within rather than between the union blocs. Capital markets are far less internationalised than supposed. The welfare state in advanced countries is not crumbling under the pressure of international competition. They are therefore looking at a system in which the two main forces, the EU and the USA, have become increasingly dominant.

REFERENCES

Bowels, Paul and Barnet Wagmans (1997), 'Globalisation and the welfare state: four hypotheses and some empirical evidence', *Eastern Economic Journal*, **23** (3), Summer, 317–36.
Rodrik, Dani (1997), 'Has globalization gone too far?', *California Management Review*, **39** (3), Spring, 29–53.
Strange, Susan (1996), *The Retreat of the State: The Diffusion of Power in the World Economy*, Cambridge: Cambridge University Press.

1 Globalisation of International Trade and Investment

Maarten Smeets[*]

INTRODUCTION

Globalisation has become the catchword of the decade and is likely to influence thinking and policymaking into the next millennium. For some it simply is a buzzword, globalisation being no more than a continuation of integration of markets and economic interdependence, a development that has been characteristic of international trade for several decades. Those who reject the notion that globalisation represents a new development argue that the trade interlinkages and interdependence were stronger last century than today. Those who disagree with this hold that trade liberalisation has led to unprecedented specialisation, with production patterns changing to exploit on a world-wide scale comparative advantages in all stages of the production process. Moreover, they argue, through the high degree of economic integration, the surge in foreign direct investment flows, technological developments and innovations, financial and domestic market liberalisation and deregulation, globalisation is unprecedented and shaping a new environment that has a direct bearing on consumption patterns, business behaviour and overall levels of welfare. What is myth and what is the reality? Who is right and who is wrong?

Unfortunately, there is no definition of globalisation and there are no quantitative indicators readily available that would allow measurement of the degree of globalisation, its relative increase or decrease, its impact on production, trade and consumption patterns and the establishment of causal relations. Thus, the debate between protagonists and antagonists is likely to continue unabated. The process underlying globalisation should be better understood and the policy options that allow us to address the consequences of it be considered. Globalisation cannot simply be held responsible for job destruction and unemployment in the developed countries. Trade liberalisation has always had side-effects in certain sectors in the economy and required adjustment measures; there is little news there. No pain, no gain! The economic benefits to be derived from trade liberalisation are uncontested and well documented: economic decisions should be based on sound, rational market principles. On the aggregate level, the benefits of trade liberalisation largely outweigh any costs that may be associated with the process.

Globalisation offers new opportunities and challenges for the new multilateral trading system. It is a dynamic process, with trade and investment flows moving more freely than at any previous time. It is a process driven by the market that cannot be 'dosed', with governments deciding to freeze it for a while, or have more or less of it. Any attempt to steer globalisation or halt it by resorting to protectionism would have detrimental effects on overall levels of welfare. Liberalisation equals inclusion: protectionism exclusion. This leaves policymakers with little choice: if governments stick to the common determination to raise overall levels of welfare, which has been the basis of the very success of the GATT/WTO multilateral trading system, there is no alternative to the road of progressive liberalisation of markets and enhancing competition in goods and services alike. How can it be ensured that all countries participating in international trade take advantage of this process and participate in globalisation? The answer to this question extends much beyond the trade policy domain and would require the analysis of other macroeconomic factors, fiscal and monetary policies, as well as structural adjustment policies, the operation of domestic infrastructures and so on.

This chapter will address some determinants and features of globalisation, and try to better understand the process of globalisation of production and international trade. What are the key features? It will cover the patterns of trade and investment that have rapidly evolved in the 1980s, mostly as a result of opportunities created through the opening of markets and the trade policy response to globalisation that can be provided through the multilateral trading system. It will be argued that the WTO currently provides the framework to address a large number of issues that are one way or another related to globalisation and is strengthening its efforts to keep abreast of ongoing developments and to adapt its rules to new trading requirements. The WTO is moving increasingly in a direction to provide global responses to global issues. The trade agenda of the WTO thus covers both the traditional trade instruments that have been in operation for the past half century, including tariffs and other measures restricting imports to safeguard the domestic industry from either unfair or fair competition, under conditions defined in the agreements, as well as for balance-of-payments purposes. At the same time, the trade policy agenda is increasingly moving to cover policy issues within the domestic boundaries, often referred to as the 'new' trade policy instruments.

The WTO takes a forwardlooking, dynamic approach that allows the incorporation of new elements into the trading system as the need arises and as its members see fit. The agenda of the WTO foresees further negotiations in areas that are directly and indirectly related to trade and that often were considered uncharted waters just over a decade ago. It is recalled that the Uruguay Round negotiations broke new ground by including rules on trade in services and by members committing themselves to opening domestic markets to competition in services sectors. In addition, an Agreement was concluded on the trade-related aspects of intellectual property rights (TRIPS), which aims to promote effective and adequate protection of intellectual property rights. Following the conclusion of the Uruguay Round, negotiations continued in various areas and impressive results were archieved in basic telecommunications and financial services, as well as a recent agreement in a broad range of information technology goods, the Information Technology Agreement. Today, trade negotiators address issues relating to electronic commerce, foreign direct investment (FDI), competition policies and, last but not least, the environment.

Given the major challenges the WTO is facing in preparing for the next millennium, institutionally it requires a solid architecture and a broader public understanding of what the WTO's contribution can be to solve international problems. It would seem that it is not always well understood by the public at large what the WTO stands for and what its boundaries are in offering solutions to broader economic problems. There may be shortcomings in communication, which could explain why trade liberalisation through the WTO multilateral trading system and globalisation are often held responsible for economic problems in societies that in reality find their origin in other factors. Improving this interaction with the producer and consumer alike, to enhance understanding of the issues at stake, is a main objective of the WTO.

GLOBALISATION DRIVEN BY TRADE AND INVESTMENT

Foreign direct investment: from substitute to complement

FDI is an essential instrument to penetrate foreign markets, both for the production and sales of goods, after sales service and establishing a close customer–producer relation. It is a vehicle for establishing foreign production facilities and has often been seen as a substitute for trade. In a globalising world FDI increasingly complements trade flows. Trade and investment are increasingly intertwined but, more importantly, financial market deregulation and integration and the growing mobility of capital as a production factor have contributed to strong financial interlinkages between economies. Many firms have developed strong links with foreign markets and adopted global approaches in outlook, strategies and operations. While this is not new, the process seems to have accelerated in the 1980s with companies increasingly looking beyond their national borders for new products, customers and inputs.

Globalisation has gained importance during the 1980s through FDI, the aim of the multinational firms being to find a balance between reaping some of the scale advantages of global markets yet exploiting the often geographically determined diversity of consumers and production factors. There are now some 53,000 transnational corporations (TNCs) in the world, with some 450,000 foreign affiliates. At the same time, FDI flows seem to be fairly concentrated: the world's 100 largest TNCs, one-third of whose assets are located abroad, are estimated to account for 17 per cent of world FDI (outward) stock. The large multinational firm's organisational structure as well as production and information technology give it the necessary flexibility to confront this diversity. In fact, modern communication techniques allow instant interaction between geographically dispersed entities (affiliates) and provide access to the same information, for example, through satellite systems. The decentralisation of production units, marketing and even research, together with a diversification of subcontractors, enables it to take full advantage of this diversity. Contrary to the past, companies are no longer bound to geographical proximity for the purpose of centralising activities: geographical distance hardly matters any more.

While there is no agreed definition of globalisation, the view is generally held that globalisation of production is reflected in a new organisational structure of companies and business behaviour. Globalisation refers to the stage now reached and the forms taken today by what is known as 'international production', namely the value-adding activities owned or controlled and organised by a firm (or group of firms) outside its (or their) national boundaries. It pertains to a set of conditions in which an increasing fraction of value and wealth is produced and distributed world-wide through a system of interlinking private networks. Large multinational firms operating within concentrated world supply structures and capable of taking full advantage of financial globalisation are at the centre of this process. The result is that borderlines between previously fairly distinct channels and processes of international relationships have become increasingly blurred.

It is well recognised that FDI today takes many forms. Besides the traditional green field investments of take-overs, modern operators more and more resort to forms of business co-operation, for example. in joint ventures, strategic alliances or pooling of research and development resources. These developments underline that the general attitude towards FDI has changed. While in the 1970s, the debate was largely dominated by the concern that globally operating multinational enterprises (MNEs) would interfere with the independent development of states, today it is now almost generally accepted that FDI is a beneficial phenomenon – not only for the host, but also for the source country.

The OECD lists the injection of extra investment capital into the economy, the contribution towards a healthy external balance, increased productivity, additional employment, stimulation of competition and rationalisation of production as well as a significant transfer of technical and managerial know-how as positive effects for the host economy. Recognising this, the developing countries have given up much of their restrictive attitude against the inflow of FDI. They are often willing to allow free transfers without restrictions for balance of payments reasons, have shown that they accept global disciplines on trade distorting investment matters in the Uruguay Round and are even generally starting to compete for investment from abroad. Since the dramatic change in East–West relations it has become more evident that foreign investment is a scarce resource which no one can afford to penalise.

The surge in investment during the last decade is closely related to strong growth in economic output in the OECD. FDI was strongly pro-cyclical during that period, affected by macroeconomic swings and responding during recovery with greater vigour than either domestic investment or world trade. The macroeconomic conditions and environment thus are particularly important, as economies are rapidly integrating and becoming strongly interdependent. Most OECD economies in the recent past witnessed an acceleration in deregulation and privatisation, thus creating new incentives to expand economic activities under free market conditions. In addition, the liberalisation of capital markets has probably been one of the main factors in the rapid growth of FDI.

Flows of FDI have surged dramatically in recent years and outpaced the growth in gross domestic product and exports. In the past decade, the stock of FDI in the OECD has almost tripled. World FDI inflows increased by 19 per cent to reach $400 billion in 1997, whereas outflows reached an estimated $424 billion. The number of bilateral investment agreements grew from more than 370 at the end of 1980s to some 1600 today, between 150 countries. The majority of these have been concluded since 1990.

Geographically, however, FDI flows remained mainly concentrated in the industrialised world, which can partly be explained by the existence of large consumer markets and partly by the liberalisation of capital markets, mainly within OECD. Indeed, about two-thirds of FDI inward stock and 90 per cent of FDI outward stock are taking place in developed countries. The Triad (the EC, Japan and the United States) accounts for some 70 per cent of world-wide inflows. The five major home countries (France, Germany, Japan, United Kingdom and United States) account for two-thirds of outward FDI.

European and Japanese multinationals are the major direct investors in the United States, but Japan also directs important flows of FDI to Europe and South-East Asia. Japan notably performs much of its production of parts and components (for example, in consumer electronics) in neighbouring Asian countries. Of particular note is the EC's attraction as a destination of FDI. The EC's share of OECD inward investment has climbed to over 45 per cent. FDI flows from newly industrialising countries, in particular from a number of South-East Asian countries, such as. South Korea, towards the OECD have become more important, too. While the volume remains small, the development is significant. The motivations often relate to gaining effective market access, scale economies (EC Single Market) or overcoming trade barriers (for example, the application or threat of quotas (official and unofficial), anti-dumping measures, local content requirements).

Developing countries improved their situation and have become more important host regions to FDI, accounting for 37 per cent of world FDI inflows in 1997, compared to shares of 17 per cent during 1986–90 and 32 per cent during 1991–93. FDI flows to these countries continued to increase during the period when world flows declined (1991–93). It is true, however, that FDI is concentrated among a small number of developing countries. The ten largest host developing countries account for about four-fifths of FDI inward stock in developing countries, a unique feature that does not appear in their share in other economic variables (about 40 per cent of developing-country GDP and one half of developing-country exports). At the same time, developing countries have become important home countries for FDI. About 10 per cent of TNCs in the world are from developing countries, which also accounted for 10 per cent of FDI flows during 1990–94, compared with 5 per cent during 1980–84 and 6 per cent during 1985–89. In some areas, intra-developing country FDI is significant. In nine major host countries in South, East and South-East Asia, intra-regional FDI accounted for 37 per cent of FDI stock in 1993.

Globalisation of markets and customisation of production

Key questions as to what exactly triggers FDI, and what factors determine the nature, location and timing of the investment, remain largely unanswered. Each decision is driven by different factors. The choice of location is well known to play an important role in companies' decisions to invest and then sell in foreign markets, rather than limit themselves to exports. Companies want to benefit from advantages related to market access, that is, to have a presence in the market for economic or purely strategic reasons, including potential economies of scale, or to benefit from comparative advantages in the host countries, including the availability of highly skilled labour, technology, know-how and infrastructure. Government policies geared towards attracting foreign companies through fiscal incentives, local or regional subsidies, as well as other support measures promoting research and development can equally play a decisive role.

Porter (1990) used the term 'competitive advantage' to indicate that a country has – or more specifically, local firms of a country have – the ability to use location-bound resources in a way that will enable it (them) to be competitive in international markets. A country possesses a set of attributes which shape the environment in which local firms compete, that promote the creation of a competitive market. The strength, composition and sustainability of a nation's competitive advantage will be revealed in the value of its national product (more particularly, the part that enters into international transactions), and/or the rate of growth of that product, relative to that of its leading competitors.

The need for companies to be closer to the customer, in order to adapt the product to local taste and the particular conditions of the local market, often referred to as 'customisation', implies that trade and investment more than ever are two sides of the same coin, reinforcing each other, rather than being substitutes. As mentioned before, the choice no longer is between trade or investment, but investment is a vehicle to enhance productivity and complement trade. Trade requires investments in order to market the good, but also tailor it to the need of the customer. FDI is only the initial vehicle through which firms establish themselves in their target market, but which at the same time triggers off new trade flows. It is the local purchases from suppliers and sales to customers in their host markets that are analogous to imports and exports. Not only are these much larger than the initial FDI flow, but they generally continue for many years after the investment takes place. This has been particularly noticeable in the automobile industry, where both intra- and inter-regional trade in parts and components has largely outpaced trade in assembled cars. In addition, it can be observed that investments increasingly spread out to related activities, including R&D and design, but also investments in sales distribution systems, after-sales service as well as related activities. This explains the rapid surge in investments in services, too, often related to the sales of goods. In fact, the financial sector itself became the object of extensive investment activity. This gave a new dimension to FDI. The United States, in the early 1970s, noted a strong influx of foreign banks and securities firms, which were attracted to the United States by their multinational clients who had already settled there. The growth of Japanese banks has been particularly important, keeping pace with the spread of Japanese business and foreign investment.

The explosive growth of FDI in the last decade has led to changes in the structure of MNEs and the organisation and dispersal of economic activities and siting of firm operations. Many companies now have become global operators. Nevertheless, the strategies of firms largely vary in the way they internationalise production. There is not one single mode of operation: some MNEs take the world market as their field of action, others continue concentrating on individual markets, or, alternatively some MNEs concentrate their activities regionally. This depends largely on the nature of the product, but also the barriers companies may face in obtaining market access. Some products, such as consumer electronics, can easily be marketed worldwide, with minor adaptations to conform the product to local standards or consumer preference. Also, certain foodstuffs can be found worldwide, with adaptation occurring mainly at the level of packaging and sometimes taste, to adapt it to local customs and preferences. Other products, which can be considered global in their very nature, such as pharmaceutical products (drugs with a very specific curative effect), require more specific adaptation to local market conditions, given the high degree of government regulation that is characteristic of this industry.

Porter's (1986) studies on competition in global industries suggest that the pattern of international competition differs markedly from industry to industry, as they vary along a spectrum from 'multi domestic' to global in their competitive scope. A multi domestic industry is one that is present in many countries, but in which competition occurs on a country-by-country basis. The competitive advantages of the firm are largely specific to the country in which it operates. A 'global' industry consists of an industry in which a firm's competitive position in one country is significantly affected by its position in other countries or vice versa. A global strategy consists of integrating activities within a global framework, implying increased interdependence between the geographically separate activities of subsidiaries and the parent company. At the same time it includes optimising the local advantages of each subsidiary and satisfying local demand conditions, in other words 'think global, act local'. A global strategy combines integration, co-ordination, segmentation and differentiation with a view to promoting flexible adaptation to changes in technology and demand. The trend is towards specialisation by subsidiaries in types of production which make use of the comparative advantage of the host country. Labour-intensive manufacturing is located in cheap labour areas; R&D laboratories are built close to major universities in countries with the strongest science and technology potential. In a way, the globalisation process could be compared with international trade specialisation but on the micro level, that is within the MNE.

The globalisation of the goods market is also reinforced by the shortening of the product cycle, which requires firms that wish to remain successful to access the world market rapidly in order to amortise the considerable investments required by the development of the highly sophisticated systems that make this possible. Companies may face constraints in expanding due to geographical, financial, technological or other factors which limit the optimal size of the firm. In those instances, the company can decide to find appropriate control through strategic alliances, networking, joint ventures and so on, in order to gain access to markets, to exploit complementary technologies and to reduce the time required for innovation. Globalisation thus is not strictly confined to the largest and strongest MNEs, but small and medium-sized companies have access to this mode of operation: a single firm – operating at the national level and which may not have all relevant, complex technological knowledge, and which does not wish to go the road of mergers and acquisitions – must seek collaborative arrangements or alliances at the international level, thereby also spreading the risks involved. It now is a rather common way of getting access to the international market. Some sectors are less likely to globalise, as they are sometimes bound by strict national rules and regulations, as is the case in certain service industries; while on the other hand, constraints posed by domestic markets, may give companies an additional incentive to turn global.

Globalisation is directly affecting the traditional paradigm which based a country's comparative advantage on the relative availability of production factors, such as natural resources, labour and capital input. Today, the world's largest corporations look to all nations to gain advantage in production, marketing and research, in effect reducing the comparative advantage of a country to its contribution to their global strategies, for example through international sourcing. Specialisation now more than ever can occur in one segment of an industry, thus making a country a preferred location for making parts and components for automobiles, semiconductors in electronics or other specialised products. While companies often co-operate with their competitors to gain technological advantages, particularly in the intermediate components stage, they still compete keenly in final markets. These new developments have had an important effect on trade and investment flows and influence the current debate on rules that should be designed for governing FDI.

THE ROLE OF THE STATE: DOES NATIONALITY MATTER?

Strategic trade policy and targeting

Over the years, host country governments have become more concerned about the quality of investment, as they are keen to promote certain forms of investment that can best contribute to the development of the economy. While nearly all countries try to attract FDI as a means to stimulate economic growth and welfare, the concern of developing country host governments is particularly related to transfer of capital, technology and the creation of employment, with a view to creating a competitive position in world markets which leads to exports and thus to income. Special incentives are often provided in the form of fiscal advantages, including direct or indirect subsidies, tax breaks, often directly linked to performance requirements imposed on or negotiated with the foreign investor. Such policies are not only confined to developing countries;

developed countries, too, have become increasingly concerned with the value-added of FDI and its contribution in terms of technology for the local economy. Governments can play a pro-active role in attracting FDI, by reducing the costs of market deficiencies, remove entry barriers and other obstacles, thus encouraging competition in the domestic market and by reducing transaction costs for MNEs, thus influencing their decision in choosing their location abroad. They can encourage the creation of tangible and organisational capabilities that may influence the MNE's decision where to invest. Direct incentives are often provided through subsidies or by providing locational advantages.

This concern of governments has triggered targeting policies, in support of so-called 'strategic' industries, which are considered to be those industries that are of fundamental importance to the development of the economic potential of a country, because of their technology intensity and/or the spin-off the activities of a particular industry can have to related industries. Investments should generate activity in value-adding or 'high tech' industries, which add to the economy's competitive strength in world markets in leading products. Competition is particularly fierce in knowledge-intensive goods, including consumer electronics, computers and telecommunication, as they often have rather short product cycles but are generally believed to contribute most to the economy's overall performance, through backward and forward linkages, as they often embody the latest state of the art technology. Supporting strategic industries often entails the implementation of a set of complementary measures, aiming at protecting markets, attracting multinationals, securing a competitive environment, but most of all, attracting technology.

While the objective seems quite legitimate from a domestic perspective, that is, supporting industries that are likely to bring the biggest contribution to the national economy, the way in which this objective is achieved can be objectionable. Obviously, the advantages that governments may decide to grant to attract one type of investment to stimulate an economic activity over another is likely to distort competitive conditions both for domestic and foreign competitors. The domestic competitive effects of the investment incentives are not necessarily limited to producers of the like products, but can and are likely to extend to the supplying industries of intermediary products.

Certain trade policy instruments have been used to ensure that the investment is qualitatively substantial and that inward investment is not merely to circumvent trade measures, but that high-value, high technology operations be transferred or fostered in the host country. Sometimes these objectives are achieved through trade-related investment measures (TRIMs), which are distortive in their very nature. Trade related investment measures are covered by the WTO rules, as part of the Uruguay Round Agreements, which do not cover investment *per se*. The most frequently encountered TRIM relates to local content requirements in the value-added, an export requirement of part of the total output, or conditions with regard to the recruitment of local senior staff as well as, for example, setting aside part of the capital for local shareholders. Local content is variously defined but is a measure of local value-added, that is, the sum of the value of parts and materials procured from domestic sources plus the value of domestic assembly, labour, overhead and mark-ups. Rules relating to local content requirements imposed on foreign investors have been controversial and most OECD countries do not have mandatory local content requirements, but some negotiate commitments from foreign assemblers in return for location and other assistance.

Economically, performance requirements create distortions in the investment and trade decisions and thus are undesirable. They imply a misapplication of economic resources, but at the same time create distortions within the host country that can also work to the detriment of competing local firms, by bidding up asset and factor prices beyond what they would have been if the trade/investment choice were a policy-neutral one. They tend to generate economic inefficiencies in the economy and reduce the overall welfare level. Trade policy measures may also be counteracted by the global strategies of enterprises and have unforeseen effects. Trade protectionism can cause firms to substitute investment for exports, thereby creating additional competitive pressures and even excess capacity. Bilateral arrangements to modify flows of imports and exports may encourage collusive behaviour among firms and raise barriers to entry in certain sectors.

Does nationality matter and is sovereignty of the nation-state undermined?

What is the meaning of nationality and can governments still conduct a national industrial policy in the presence of MNEs that take the globe as their field of action? What is at stake in the negotiations for international rule-making? While the consumer often expresses strong feelings about this, the reality is that when you think you buy an American product, like Nike shoes or Toys 'R Us children's toys or various brands of consumer goods, it may appear that only the brand name is American, the inputs foreign and the production process also taking place abroad. If you buy what you think is a Dutch Phillips TV, chances are that it is manufactured or rather assembled in Mexico or in Austria, with inputs from all over the world. What then is Dutch about the product, other than that the company is Dutch and has its headquarters in the Netherlands? The same goes for some Japanese cars manufactured in the United States, where in some instances careful analysis to determine the origin of the good revealed that, after the car was broken down into small parts and pieces, the Japanese make manufactured in the US contained more American local content than the

American car, which was assembled in the US with parts and components coming from abroad. So what does nationality mean and to what extent does it matter?

Robert Reich (1990) posed the question in this very direct manner: 'Who is Us'?' The question has direct policy implications: can one still define the national interest in a context where MNEs site main parts of their economic activities in different parts of the world. What policy should be conducted by the host country? Does an American company conducting most of its R&D and product design and most of its complex manufacturing outside the US, thus employing more people outside the US than within the American market, reflect more the American national interest than a foreign company headquartered abroad but employing more Americans in the US through its affiliates than foreigners? Are the employment criteria decisive or is it control? Whatever the answer is, it raises the very pertinent question of multinational corporations versus national authority.

The policy implications, however, are not negligible. To what extent should affiliates be able to benefit from subsidies and national or regional support or R&D programmes aimed at strengthening competitiveness of the domestic industries, or those of the region, such as those provided under European Communities legislation? Can the foreign producer in the domestic market claim the same rights as the domestic producer on the grounds that it represents a vital interest to the domestic producer, that is, that of the host country where it is located? Can it and should it be allowed to represent the domestic industry and can it then follow the same procedures in launching complaints against third parties? Yes, why not? In 1993, the USITC (US International Trade Commission) determined that imports of certain electronic typewriters from Singapore, produced by an American affiliate, were causing injury to the US industry. Ironically, the case was put before the USITC by a Japanese-affiliated company in the US, which was recognised as representing the US industry. This implies the recognition that there are limits to the concept of nationality. What really matters is the contribution the production can make to the economy of the host country, to employment and to creating new competitive opportunities for the domestic and related industries.

As a result of closer economic integration of national economies, boundaries between economies are gradually blurring, and the scope for governments to confine a domestic policy to national firms is becoming limited. This does not only apply to those countries formally engaged in regional arrangements, but to all economies that have developed close economic ties. Policy instruments themselves become more closely interrelated. In some cases, the distinction between border policies versus domestic policies is becoming artificial; industrial and trade policies, for example, cannot always easily be separated and their impacts not easily isolated. In addition, FDI flows easily jump over borders, thus circumventing the intended protection and undermining the conduct of isolated domestic policies.

The question of multinational corporations versus national authority is often addressed from the angle of responsibilities of the host government towards their citizens, which include ensuring economic activity and national security, the latter argument being invoked to justify the prohibition or regulation of certain types of FDIs. To what extent can foreign subsidiaries of MNEs contribute to the objective of the government in the host country or undermine achieving domestic policy objectives? Related to this: should they be treated on an equal footing with national firms? While the question is certainly not new, it becomes more pressing, as host countries are faced with the prospect of a growing role for non-national firms in their economies, given the rapid surge in FDI in recent years; home countries, too, must deal with the challenges that are posed by outward FDI.

Does globalisation erode national sovereignty? Arguments can easily be presented in support of and against this idea. The issue is quite complex and the position one takes directly relates to the definition of sovereignty. Most of the developed countries are consensus societies in which domestic policies to a larger or smaller extent depend on other countries' policies. There is a movement towards harmonisation and co-ordination of policies between nations in most areas of policymaking, without the sovereignty of the nation-state being questioned. This applies both to political and economic issues. Economic and other summit meetings are held continuously to ensure policy co-ordination; countries thus implicitly and/or explicitly reduce scope for conducting autonomous policies. Moreover, it would seem that many countries are ready to give up at least part of their sovereign policymaking through regional integration arrangements. Most WTO members are part of a regional arrangement. While these arrangements differ widely, some being 'deep', others being 'shallow', they all require giving up some degree of sovereignty.

Some currencies in international markets are directly pegged to other major currencies (the US dollar) or closely follow the movement of other currencies without being pegged, because the economies are closely intertwined, without the constituency arguing that this undermines the sovereignty of the nation-state. It would seem, though, that a main difference between the present and the past is the increased level of co-ordination, harmonisation and sharing of responsibilities between nations. The more interdependent the elements of the global economy become, the more co-ordination is needed to bring together in a positive synergy the various governments and international institutions. More and deeper co-ordination is required at the policy level to reflect deeper integration at the economic level. This is part of the new reality.

The notion of sovereignty and the significance given to it by nation-states seems to have evolved over time. It had a more individual connotation in the

once adopted by members through a negative consensus rule; that is, panel reports will be automatically adopted, unless a consensus is reached to not adopt the report. Rulings are made within fixed time frames and the party found 'guilty' cannot escape the consequences of non-implementation of the recommendations. The mechanism is designed in such a way that the offending party will have to modify its practices and legislation, to the extent necessary to end the malpractice or, alternatively, it will face retaliatory measures. Retaliation can be authorised to be taken in any sector and is not limited to the area of dispute.

2 Since the creation of the WTO to date, there have been over 150 consultation requests covering some 120 distinct matters. A fifth of these cases have been settled without going through the full procedures. In 18 cases, which have gone through the full procedures, including the appellate stage, the verdict has either been implemented or is in the process of being implemented. Several of these cases have involved developing countries in which the practices of developed countries were challenged. Equally, developing countries have invoked the dispute settlement system against each other. The extent to which the dispute settlement system is used is generally seen as a measure of the success of the operation of the system itself.

3 Some of the fundamental principles that are enshrined in the WTO trading system relate to non-discrimination, through most favoured nation treatment and national treatment. The principle of most favoured nation means that any benefit or particular treatment granted to any one country will automatically be extended to the other WTO members. This has proved to be a valuable approach to ensure that all benefits negotiated between a limited number of parties get automatically multilateralised, thus extending these benefits to all parties alike. Together with the principles of national treatment, which implies that any foreign product that has entered a market should obtain the same treatment as the domestic like product (national treatment), non-discrimination is ensured. Also, prior to entering the market, products cannot be discriminated against at the border if they originate from any WTO member country. These principles have been reinforced for all areas now covered in the multilateral trading system and apply to goods and services alike.

4 The system is gradually extending and becoming truly universal through the expansion of its members. Currently the WTO comprises 133 members and 31 more countries are in different stages of their accession negotiations. All major players in the world economy, with the exception of China and Russia, are part of the system, representing some 90 per cent of world trade in goods and services. The vast majority of the members are developing countries and least-developed countries. China and Russia are currently

negotiating the terms of their WTO Membership.

5   Trade liberalisation has been unprecedented both in the area of tariffs and non-tariff measures. If one disregards the preferential treatment given by developed countries to the import of goods originating from developing country members through autonomous trade regimes and which mostly are zero, the most favoured nation treatment duties applied by developed countries for the access of industrial goods to their markets are 3.8 per cent on a trade weighted average. This compares with nearly 50 per cent at the origin of the GATT system. The advantage of this can be seen in everyday life, with a wider choice in consumer goods at lower prices. According to the OECD (1998), the case for open markets rests on a few simple, common-sense premises. One of them relates to the natural preference of people the world over for more, rather than less, choice and freedom. A world without trade or investment – or with less of it – is a world with less choice. And a world with less choice is quite simply a world with less freedom. The power of the free trade ideal lies to a great extent in the freedom individuals and societies gain from exercising greater choices: over what to buy and to sell and at what price; where to obtain inputs; where and how to invest; what skills to acquire; or what regulatory approach to pursue. At the same time, the OECD report recognises that, while trade and investment liberalisation raises world welfare in aggregate, the gains will be distributed unevenly across countries and between different sectors and groups within countries. Workers do not move easily from shrinking sectors and transitory adjustment problems will appear. Politically these problems get a lot of public attention, which cannot be ignored. While calls for protectionism under these circumstances are well understood, it is the role of politics to explain the broader overall gain for society that is achieved through liberalisation, as opposed to protectionism. While this is generally well accepted, the short-term political gains that can be achieved by responding to calls for protection conflict with the long-term economic welfare gains. The costs of protectionism are generally well documented, the benefits of free trade less so. As a result of the reduction in trade barriers, trade flows increased fifteen-fold since the establishment of the GATT in 1948.

6   The trading system has been made more transparent, secure and predictable because, in addition to the trade liberalisation, almost all duties are 'bound'. This implies that the duties that are reflected in each of the member's Schedules of Concessions cannot automatically be increased at any time in the future. Any change in tariff concessions will require formal renegotiations, which means that to the extent that the value of a tariff concession is eroded, compensation will be provided through tariff reductions in another good or service. This is a key element for any business

involved in investment and trade. When it comes to trade and investment decisions, entrepreneurs want to know what their rights and entitlements are today, but also tomorrow and the day after. FDI implies long-term engagements and thus requires a stable and predictable host environment.

Finally, the system has become more transparent through the introduction of various mechanisms. One relates to the periodic reporting and notification requirements that are mandated in most of the Agreements. While this turns out to be a cumbersome and tedious exercise for most WTO members, the underlying principle is that all members should have access to any information regarding another member's trade policies, both in terms of legislation and practices. Separately and in addition, a country's trade policies and practices are periodically reviewed by the WTO Secretariat and by other embers through the Trade Policy Review Body. This Body is part of the institutional basis of the WTO and foresees the collective appreciation of a country's trade policy regime and practices. These reviews provide a very detailed review of all aspects of a country's trade policy's regime and the outcome of the process is one that greatly facilitates a better understanding of all trade policies that relate to that country. The information thus provided contributes to enhancing overall transparency.

Main instruments to fend off competition and/or to protect domestic markets

While markets have gradually opened up to foreign competition as a result of liberalisation initiatives, the predominant wish of governments to protect domestic markets from undesired market penetration has remained a central aspect of policymaking. There are obviously conditions attached to the degree to which this right to protect an industry or a market is exercised, as the rules mainly serve to avoid discrimination in trade, thus securing the respect of such fundamental principles as non-discrimination and most favoured nation. Tariff protection aims at protecting the domestic producer by way of applying a duty or 'surcharge' on the importation of a product, thus making it more or less expensive, depending on the level of the tariff. There is a variety of other instruments that aim at fending off 'unfair' competition (for example, dumping, subsidies that distort trade), or 'fair' competition, that is, when the importing country can simply not absorb the surge in imports, which would justify applying safeguard measures. While these areas were already covered in the GATT, they have been adjusted and refined in the course of several rounds of negotiations to make them applicable to changing practices and new realities.

Some of the adjustments still under discussion are meant to explicitly take into account the effects of globalisation of markets. During the negotiations of the Agreement on dumping, which covers situations of price undercutting, that is, the sale of a product below the normal value, much time and effort was devoted to the question of preventing circumvention of anti-dumping duties. In the last decade, several cases where circumvention of anti-dumping duties was suspected have come to the fore. Companies were suspected of relocating parts of the production process or assembly operations to other countries than where the production initially took place, with a view to affecting the origin of the good and thus escaping anti-dumping duties. The question then was how to determine the origin of the good and the criteria to be used, for example, substantial transformation, change of tariff classification and so on. These questions have led to a complex and lengthy technical process of negotiations to determine for all goods the basis of conferring origin to goods. The main purpose of this exercise is to prevent what are considered to be simple 'screwdriver operations' to be sufficient to change the origin of the good and thus influence the treatment the product will receive at the point of importation. The tedious technical work carried out in this regard mainly by customs officials of the WTO members in the World Customs Organisation has turned out to be much more complex than was initially anticipated and the three years that were allocated to accomplish this task of harmonising the widely differing practices applied by countries in determining the origin of goods turned out to be insufficient. The reason for this is not only related to the technical complexity of the issues, but also to the economic and trade impacts directly related to the decision as to the requirements that need to be fulfilled to confer origin to a good. It goes without saying that any such decision can have direct repercussions for an industry as a whole. Once the task is completed, this should facilitate the process of determining the origin of a good and reduce the risk of arbitrary judgements.

While it has not been possible during the Uruguay Round negotiations to devise rules for the situation where producers are suspected of circumventing anti-dumping duties by relocating parts of the production process, the issue has remained on the agenda of the committee that oversees the implementation of the Agreement. Again, the issue is not only technically rather complex and politically sensitive, it is a difficult task to devise language to address the situation of circumvention, while at the same time preventing abuse of the rules.

Safeguard measures are part of the rules that are meant to cover fair 'trade': safeguard measures can be invoked when the domestic industry can simply not cope with foreign competition of the like product. The reasons for this may differ and can include situations in which a country has a domestic industry producing a good that competes with the like imported good, but the domestic producer has mainly produced for the domestic market (no exports), which is too small to generate economies of scale, thus putting the domestic industry at a disadvantage against the foreign producer located in a larger market. The domestic producer, which may be in its nascent stage, is not ready to face this competition and may itself turn to the government to ask for relief measures. When so requested, the government of the importing country can decide to take safeguard measures for a temporary period, thus providing a breathing space for the domestic industry. In order to do so, it will have to provide evidence that the surge in imports is such as to cause or threaten to cause serious injury to the domestic industry. The Safeguard Agreement spells out in detail the conditions that need to be met. The type of import restrictions may vary, preference being given to tariffs, but in any case the Committee on Safeguards will exercise its monitoring function, which is to ensure that any measure is taken in accordance with the rules and disciplines laid down in the Agreement.

The Safeguards Agreement is a totally new Agreement, as this area was not well covered previously in the GATT through Article XIX, which was meant to provide the legal basis for safeguard actions but in practice was hardly used, given the conditions attached to its use. The necessity to devise rules has become increasingly apparent with the mushrooming of all kinds of measures that escape multilateral surveillance, including orderly marketing arrangements (OMAs) and voluntary export restraints (VERs), which effectively escape multilateral surveillance and have seriously contributed to undermining and eroding the multilateral trading system. Such arrangements became quite popular in the 1980s, as they provided a quick fix to a sudden problem. They thus facilitated responding to undesired trade flows, but are the worst of evils for those who support the market for trade and investment decisions. The main feature of OMAs and VERs is that they effectively discriminate in trade between suppliers through bilateral deals and thus undercut the free functioning of the market, in particular the price mechanism. While this had long been recognised, until the conclusion of the Agreement no effective way of dealing with these arrangements had been found. At the same time these measures generate economic rents through the application of quotas, thus artificially raising prices consumers. Moreover, their very anti-competitive bias is economically harmful to other producers. With the conclusion of the Safeguards Agreement, members have agreed to abandon the use of these types of market restrictions.

The General Agreement on Trade in Services (GATS)

Rules have been extended to such areas as trade in services, which has taken an increasingly important share in international trade. The ways in which services can be provided have required much creative thinking by negotiators to ensure that the rules have direct significance for trade flows. While much time has been devoted in the negotiations to the question of how to define a service, negotiators have adopted a very pragmatic approach in the General Agreement on Trade in Services (GATS), recognising the various ways by which services transactions can be concluded. One of the distinguishing features of services as compared to goods is that services are intangible and the production and consumption of services takes place simultaneously. A service cannot be stored, for example.

Services are not only traded in their own right, but the services component in industrial goods has grown fast. Also, the services that are directly related to the sale of a good have come to take a predominant place in transactions, that is, the consumer wants to be sure that following the acquisition of the good there is an adequate guarantee of after-sales services. This explains the explosive growth in FDI in service-related activities in most developed countries.

Acknowledging one of the defining characteristics of trade in services, namely the frequent need for proximity between suppliers and consumers, hence for commercial presence, the GATS contains the single largest number of investment-related provisions found in the Final Act of the Uruguay Round. Such provisions relate both to matters of investment liberalisation and to investment protection, albeit with differing degrees of comprehensiveness.

The Agreement defines trade in services as consisting of four modes of supply, one of which is the supply of a service by a service supplier of one member through commercial presence in the territory of another member. This mode of supply is recognised as Mode 3 in the GATS. Commercial presence is defined as consisting of any type of business or professional establishment, including through the constitution, acquisition or maintenance of an enterprise or the creation or maintenance of a branch or representative office. Because of the very nature of services transaction, the agreement contains more than any other WTO Agreement provision on investment. Examples of areas in which FDI has played an important role are the banking and insurance sectors. For banks to be competitive on international markets, they will be required to operate in foreign markets. There is a mutual interest, both for the service provider, who wants to be close to the consumer, and for the host government, which wants to apply its prudential regulations and enforce its banking laws and regulations to the foreign operator. It will only be able to exercise those powers when the foreign bank or insurance company is physically present in the territory of the host country.

Other means of trading services is by way of export of the service *per se*, that is, when the service takes the characteristics of a good. This mode of supply, which is the first one recognised in the services agreement, applies *inter alia* to postal and telecommunication services, whereby the postal package or telephone call/fax and so on is directly delivered from one country to another. The service crosses the border, as if it were a good.

The second mode of supply relates to the movement of the consumer to the country where the service is 'consumed'. This type of service transaction applies to tourism, where the tourist needs physically to go to the country to enjoy the attractions that the country has to offer, or the consumer wants to benefit from medical services (health care) provided in the host country.

The last (fourth) mode of supply relates to the movement of natural persons, whereby a person will be required to move to a country to provide a service. An example relates to professional services provided by consultants, accountants, architects. They will only be able to provide their expertise by temporarily residing in the country where the service needs to be provided. The GATS provides for the conditions that can be attached to the presence of foreign services providers, for example the time they can be allowed to stay.

It would go beyond the purpose of this contribution to detail the provisions of the GATS, but the main point is that the rules in the new trading system were adapted to recognise new ways of trade, particularly through services transactions. This area is one in which negotiations have continued almost unabated following the conclusion of the Uruguay Round to complete negotiations in some areas and/or improve the offers. Two main areas come to mind, including financial services and basic telecommunications, for which negotiations were concluded in 1997 and 1998 respectively.

Recent initiatives to further trade liberalisation

Trade negotiators have been largely driven in recent times to open up markets, not only for traditional industrial products, but increasingly in sectors which have significantly gained importance in international trade. At the first Ministerial Meeting of Trade Ministers, held in Singapore, December 1996, the so-called Information Technology Agreement (ITA) was concluded. Efforts to liberalise trade in information technology products have gained ground as more countries become aware of the vast market potential in this sector. Exports of information technology products amounted to more than $595 billion in 1995. Trade in this sector is now larger than world exports of agricultural products. It is currently the fastest growing industry and concerns a wide range of items, from computers and semiconductors to telecommunication equipment and integrated circuits. Broader categories include some of the following: computers, computer parts and computer software; semiconductors and integrated circuits; and telecommunications equipment, including opto-electronic and radio-based network equipment. The seven leading countries that contribute the bulk of imports and exports in this sector, including Japan, the United States, the European Union, Singapore, Korea, Malaysia and Chinese Taipei, agreed to eliminate duties on all information technology products, including telecommunications equipment by the year 2000. The elimination of duties follows a timetable and these will be applied on a most favoured nation basis, thus extending the benefits of these discussions to all members of the WTO. In February 1998, the same countries plus another seven decided to extend the list of products on which duty-free treatment should be provided with several hundreds of IT products, thus further broadening the scope of the Agreement. These include printed circuit board manufacturing equipment; flat panel display manufacturing equipment; capacitor manufacturing equipment; audio, radio, television and video apparatus; telecommunications products; electrical/electronics machines; instruments; and parts and inputs for IT products. Negotiations continued through 1998 and were due to be concluded in the beginning of 1999.

In the area of electronic commerce, which again is a booming market, with several millions of transactions taking place at high speed through the internet or in any other high tech way of data transmission, no trade restrictions are currently in place. From a trade policy perspective, it basically is an open market, where domestic regulations apply but no customs duties or other charges are applied at the border. There is a free movement of information and data transmission, rendered possible through the development of new technologies. In May 1998, members adopted a US proposal which effectively amounts to a work programme for the General Council in the area of all trade-related issues relating to global electronic commerce in the year ahead. Without any prejudice to the outcome of the work programme, members agreed to continue the current practice of not imposing customs duties on electronic transmissions.

These initiatives underscore the importance that is given by policymakers to liberalise markets, rather than erecting new trade barriers in products in which competition has just started and which can generally be considered as fairly sensitive and certainly of strategic importance. It is by keeping momentum in the movement of trade liberalisation that economic gains can be obtained. This notion is increasingly well understood by policy officials, but not always sufficiently well explained to the public at large.

Market integration, harmonisation of policies, coherence

The Uruguay Round negotiations have been guided by the principle of 'Single Undertaking', which meant that no agreement could be reached until agreement had been achieved in all policy areas. This effectively meant that the negotiations could not be concluded leaving out agriculture, services or any other area on the agenda, thus ensuring that all parties would obtain results in areas of importance to them. Through the Single Undertaking approach, all members subscribe to all agreements. This is in sharp contrast to the GATT system, where an *à la carte* approach was introduced in the Tokyo Round, with countries being encouraged to subscribe to those agreements that they were interested in. While it was hoped that the initial approach (*à la carte*) would allow the system gradually to multilateralise by enlarging the number of subscribers, it led to a fragmentation of the trading system. This has now been corrected, with all members having the same rights and obligations, except for developing and least-developed countries as well as countries in transition, which benefit from longer phase-in periods. This approach has contributed to the harmonisation and coherence of policies.

In addition, the Marrakech Agreement explicitly recognises the increased interdependence in policymaking and includes a decision that provides for strengthening coherence in policymaking. This has the particular attention of the Director-General of the WTO, who is in discussion with the heads of other organisations, including IMF and the World Bank, to substantiate this particular provision. The main purpose of policy coherence is to insure that policy prescriptions of the various organisations go in the same direction and do not conflict. Furthermore, the agencies co-operate actively in providing technical assistance to developing countries to integrate in the multilateral trading system, to build capacity and strengthen their knowledge base in trade and trade-related areas. Increasingly programmes are designed in a co-ordinated fashion, ensuring complementarities and making best use of each organisation's expertise.

The need to ensure policy coherence is also reflected in the large number of initiatives by WTO members to integrate regionally. Regional co-operation and integration can be considered in part a response to the new reality of global markets. It reflects a degree of recognition by national governments of the limits to their effective sovereignty and that co-operation is necessary in order to deal more adequately with the policy issues they have to face. Regional liberalisation can generally be achieved easier than multilateral liberalisation, because it involves fewer participants, who often share a common interest. Moreover, it is more likely to achieve policy convergence on a regional than on a multilateral level, particularly when the economies have a similar level of economic development and are characterised by high levels of intra-industry trade. Contrary to what is often felt, the WTO recognises regional integration as a step towards multilateral trade liberalisation, provided that a number of WTO provisions are met. These rules are partly reflected in the GATT 1994 Agreement, partly in a Decision adopted in 1996 to look again at the procedures on reviewing regional integration.

The WTO challenge to provide global answers to global problems

Because of the success of the multilateral trading system over the past 50 years in the field of trade, more and more issues are being put before the WTO and more and more answers expected from its members. The success of the WTO as judged by the public, however, is largely measured by the extent to which it is able to address the issues that are of common concern to the public at large, whether they fall within the competence of the WTO or not. There is a lot of misunderstanding in that respect, as the WTO's competence is confined to trade policies *per se* and to some extent covers related policies, but the WTO does not pretend to offer solutions in areas that are not directly part of its mandate. Pressures are put on the WTO to offer solutions in areas like employment, marginalisation, environment, labour standards, cultural diversity and financial stability. The WTO has to follow with great care all issues that are put before it and recognise the boundaries within which it operates. This implies, for example, that global environmental problems will not be solved by applying trade measures, including sanctions and trade remedies, if a solution cannot be found by those who are responsible for environmental policies in the first place. Trade sanctions and remedies should strictly be confined to areas where the rules of the game have clearly been defined.

The same could be said on labour standards. While this is a very sensitive issue and has given rise to very intense debates in the preparation of the Singapore Ministerial Meeting (December 1996), it is recognised that the use of labour standards should be rejected for protectionist purposes and that the comparative advantage of countries, particularly low-wage developing countries, must in no way be put in question. The WTO and the ILO (International Labour Organisation) Secretariats will continue their existing collaboration. The Ministerial Declaration explicitly states that members recognise the commitment to the observance of internationally recognised core labour standards. It states that the ILO is the competent body to set and deal with these standards and the WTO supports its work in promoting them. It is furthermore stated that members believe that economic growth and development fostered by increased trade and further liberalisation contribute to promoting these standards.

There are areas where it is more likely than others for the WTO to make progress and which are currently not covered under WTO rules. This includes necessarily rules on investment, as it is one important area that affects trade in goods and services alike, for which no international disciplines exist. As has been shown throughout this chapter, the interrelation that exists between trade and investment would justify giving more direct attention to investment rules in the WTO. Since no single comprehensive set of rules on investment exists, there are some 1600 bilateral investment agreements currently in existence, which produce a fragmented, non-transparent picture for FDI. Growing awareness of the present shortcomings have led to attempts to remedy this situation. When in the framework of the Uruguay Round some first steps were made to address traderelated investment issues, focusing on trade distortions created by imposing conditions on inward FDIs, the intention was not to liberalise investment flows. Separately, the GATS contains provisions that directly touch upon investments as a way to deliver services in foreign markets. The GATS sets standards for the commercial presence of a service provider in another GATS member state and therefore covers a substantial part of FDI. The OECD codes of liberalisation and the non-binding OECD National Treatment Instrument relate directly to some investment matters, but the OECD instruments apply to OECD members and lack stringent dispute settlement procedures.

This patchwork of rules is unsatisfactory and is being increasingly seen as a very inefficient and non-transparent way of liberalising investment regimes and protecting investments abroad. This lacuna implies a need for international investment rules. On an international level, the most developed rules on investment are those embedded in the OECD Instruments. Although negotiations in the OECD on a Multilateral Investment Agreement were scheduled to be concluded in 1997, a new deadline was set for May 1998, but negotiations seem to have failed altogether. Should the WTO now fill the vacuum and negotiate multilateral rules on investment?

Both policymakers and the business community see a need for adapting national and multilateral rule making to better reflect the new realities and to ensure all policies pull in the same direction. Currently, rules are largely based on traditional concepts such as nation-states, national industries, national interest and so on, whereas the new reality requires a more open and transparent approach, offering global solutions to global problems. The globalisation of industrial activities and overlaps between industrial and trade policies necessitate a broader multilateral framework for harmonisation of industrial policies. A good example relates to competition policy rules. Whereas competition policy is strictly confined to the national economy, the application of competition law can have a direct bearing on trade policy, and the other way round. While both policies share a common objective, that is, the use of the market place competition to achieve an efficient allocation of resources and maximum economic growth and welfare benefits, their respective instruments differ and may be conflicting in achieving this objective. A new approach thus requires dealing with the issues in an interrelated fashion.

CONCLUSION: HAS GLOBALISATION GONE TOO FAR?

The question is often asked whether globalisation has gone too far. In recent years some criticism has gone beyond calling for just a breathing space, as globalisation by some has been accused of threatening the 'social cohesion' of countries. The WTO, however, is a member-driven organisation and every WTO member exercises ultimate control over its own decisions. Thus the further pursuance of liberalisation programmes depends on the capacity of a country's leaders to understand that such programmes are part of the public and make this clear to the public at large. In order to further the process of liberalisation, it is essential to proceed within the proper framework, that is, in a rule-based system that has the institutional capacity to ensure a balanced outcome, taking into account the diversity of interests that are at stake in any such negotiations. The WTO provides this framework and is a member-driven organisation that will do whatever is in its powers to ensure respect of rights and obligations that are reflected in the legal texts of the multilateral trading system.

The Director General of the WTO, in his opening remarks at the Fiftieth Anniversary Symposium held at the WTO on 30 April 1998, made clear that the multilateral trading system will be more important than ever to the international architecture of the new century, as an important element in bridging the gap between the national concerns of governments and the global issues they face. The system must be dynamic. The system must keep pace with technological and economic change. The WTO must favour the creation of the resources needed to build a much more equitable world inside a strategy of sustainable development. The WTO must respect cultural differences and values. The WTO has to take advantage of the equalising potential of the new borderless technologies to permit least-developed countries to accelerate dramatically their human and economic development. Policymakers are not magicians in the trading system and cannot solve every problem that comes along – nor should they be expected to. They cannot, however, afford to ignore the political reality of the interdependent world or the widening circle of issues that must be addressed in a multilateral context. Trade agreements after all are not ends in themselves – they are a valuable means to important ends such as alleviating poverty and malnutrition, widening the circles of development, sharing technological progress, sustaining the health of the planet and advancing the cause of peace. Over the next 50 years the multilateral trading system has an invaluable and indispensable contribution to make towards all of these goals – but only if we move forward with balance, coherence and imagination.

NOTE

* Counsellor at the World Trade Organisation. The views expressed in this chapter are those of the author and should not be attributed to the WTO Secretariat.

REFERENCES

Adamantopoulos, K. and D.M. Price (1995), 'Towards a multilateral investment regime: results in the Uruguay Round and prospects in the OECD', *International Banking and Financial Law Supplement: Trade and Investment,* March.

Bergsten, C.F and E.M. Graham (1992), 'Needed, new rules for foreign direct investment', *International Trade Journal,* **7** (1), Fall, 15–44.

Blackhurst, R. (1997), 'The WTO and the global economy', *World Economy,* **20** (5), August, 527–44.

Brewer, T.L. and S. Young (1995), 'The multilateral agenda for foreign direct investment: problems, principles and priorities for negotiations at the OECD and WTO', *World Competition,* **18** (4), 67–84.

Brittan, L. (1995), 'Investment liberalization: the next great boost to the world economy', *Transnational Corporations,* **4** (1), 1–10.

Buckley, P.J. and M. Casson (1976), *The Future of the Multinational Enterprise,* London: Macmillan.

Cantwell, J. (1989), *Technological Innovation and Multinational Corporations,* Oxford: Basil Blackwell.

Casson, M. (1979), *Alternatives to the Multinational Enterprise,* London: Macmillan.

Casson, M. (1982), *'Transaction costs and the theory of the multinational enterprise',* in A.M. Rugman (ed.), *New Theories of the Multinational Enterprise,* New York: St. Martin's Press.

Coase, R.H. (1937), 'The nature of the firm', *Economica,* **4,** 386–405.

DeAnne, J. (1990), *Global Companies and Public Policy: The Growing Challenge of Foreign Direct Investment,* Royal Institute for International Affairs, London: Pinter Publishers.

DeAnne, J. (1991), *Foreign Direct Investment: The Neglected Twin of Trade,* Washington, DC: Group of Thirty.

Dunning, J.H. (1988), *Explaining International Production,* London: Hyman.

Dunning, J.H. (1992), 'The competitive advantage of countries and the activities of transnational corporations', Review Article in *Transnational Corporations,* **1** (1), February, 135–68.

EC Commission (1993), *International Economic Interdependence,* discussion paper, May, Brussels: Commission of the European Communities.

Graham, E.M. and P.R. Krugman (1991), *Foreign Direct Investment in the US,* Washington, DC: Institute for International Economics.

Greenaway, D. and C. Milner (1986), *The Economics of Intra-firm Trade,* Oxford: Basil Blackwell.

Hymer, S.T. (1976), *The International Operations of National Firms: A Study of Foreign Direct Investment,* Cambridge, Mass.: MIT Press.

Kline, J.M. (1993), 'International regulation of transnational business: providing the missing leg of global investment standards', *Transnational Corporations,* **2** (1), February, 153–64.

Krugman, P.R. (1990), *Strategic Trade Policy and the New International Economics,* Cambridge, Mass.: MIT Press.

OECD (1991), *Strategic Industries in a Global Economy,* Paris: OECD.

OECD (1992a), *Technology and the Economy: The Key Relationships,* Paris: OECD.

OECD (1992b), *International Direct Investment: Policies and Trends in the 1980s,* Paris: OECD.

OECD (1992c), *Globalization of Industrial Activities,* Paris: OECD.

OECD (1993), *TheImpact of Foreign Direct Investment on Domestic Economies of OECD Countries*, Paris: OECD.

OECD (1995*), Instruments for Promoting the Liberalization of Foreign Direct Investment*, Paris: OECD.

OECD (1997), *The World in 2020: Towards a New Global Age*, Paris: OECD.

OECD (1998), *Open Markets Matter: The Benefits of Trade and Investment*, Paris: OECD.

Ostry, S. (1990), *Governments and Corporations in a Shrinking World*, New York, London: Council on Foreign Economic Relations.

Pearce, R. (1989), *The Internationalisation of R&D by Multilateral Enterprises*, London: Macmillan.

Porter, M. (1986), *Competition in Global Industries*, Boston, Mass.: Harvard Business School Press.

Porter, M. (1990), *The Competitive Advantage of Nations*, London: The Free Press.

Reich, R. (1990), 'Who is us?', *Harvard Business Review*, **90** (1), January–February, 53–63.

Rodrik, D. (1997), *Has Globalization Gone Too Far?*, Washington, DC: Institute for International Economics.

Rugman, A.M. (ed.) (1982), *New Theories of the Multinational Enterprise*, New York: St. Martin's Press.

Rugman, A.M. and A. Verbeke (1990), *Global Corporate Strategy and Trade Policy*, London: Routledge.

Sauvé, P. (1994), 'A first look at investment in the final act of the Uruguay round', *Journal of World Trade*, **28** (5), October, 5–16.

Smeets, M. (1990), 'Globalisation and the trade policy response', *Journal of World Trade*, **24** (5), October, 57–73.

Smeets, M. (1996), 'Aspects of multinational corporations', in C. Jepma and A. Rhoen (eds), *International Trade: A Business Guide Perspective*, London: Longman.

Spero, J. (1990), *The Politics of International Economic Relations*, New York: St. Martin's Press.

UNCTAD (1994), 'Globalization, integrated international production and the world economy', in *World Investment Report 1994: Transnational Corporations, Employment and the Workplace*, Geneva: UN.

UNCTC (1992), *The Determinants of Foreign Direct Investment: A Survey of Evidence*, New York: United Nations.

United Nations (1998), *World Investment Report 1998: Trends and Determinants*, New York and Geneva: UN.

Vernon, R. (1966), 'International investment and international trade in the product cycle', *Quarterly Journal of Economics*, **80** (2), May, 190–207.

Witherell, W.H. (1995), 'The OECD multilateral agreement on investment', *Transnational Corporations*, **4** (2), August, 1–14.

WTO (1998), *Annual Report 1998: Special Topic Globalization and Trade*, Geneva: WTO.

2 Globalisation of Financial Markets

Jan Annaert[*]

INTRODUCTION

The internationalisation of financial markets is remarkable. In nearly all markets the globalisation has increased dramatically over the years. This does not only show up in the growing proportion of international transactions, but also in the increased diversity of market participants. The international growth of financial markets is contrasted with the growth in some 'real' markets in Figure 2.1. It shows the growth rates over the 1979–96 period (starting in 1980 for financial market activity). Although the rates for world output and international trade in goods and services are measured on the basis of volume figures, whereas figures for international financial market activity are on a nominal basis, the differences remain spectacular. The average annual increase in world trade was 5.2 per cent, nearly 2 per cent higher than world output growth (3.3 per cent), illustrating the globalisation of the world economy.[1] In contrast, international financial market activity, as measured by the OECD and including international bond issues as well as international bank loans and issuance facilities, has grown by more than 14.9 per cent![2]

Such growth rates are also seen in other financial market segments, most obviously on the foreign exchange market, where currencies are traded both in spot and forward contracts. Comparisons of the results over time indicate that international transactions have grown exponentially. Table 2.1 shows that average daily turnover of spot, outright forward and foreign exchange swaps increased from US$188 billion in April 1986 to $1190 billion in April 1995, or an average annual increase of 22.8 per cent.[3] Even relative to world export of goods and services or total reserves excluding gold, foreign exchange turnover has more than doubled. The second biggest financial market, the market for US government securities, looks puny compared to the foreign exchange market: average daily turnover in the former market during April 1995 was only US$175 billion (IMF, 1996).

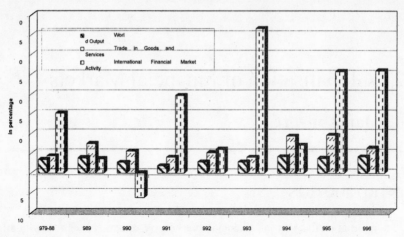

Note: Figures for 1979–88 are annual averages (period 1980–8 for financial market activity).

Sources: IMF (1997b) and OECD, *Financial Market Trends*, various issues.

Figure 2.1 Growth in world output, international trade and international financial market activity

In addition, cross-border transactions in bonds and equity are also gaining importance (Table 2.2). In relation to GDP, these transactions were puny during the 1970s, but since then they have out-grown GDP in most industrialised countries.

Table 2.1 Foreign exchange trading

	1986	1989	1992	1995
Global estimated turnover (daily average, in US$ billion	188	590	820	1190
As a ratio of world export of goods and services (%)	7.4	15.8	17.4	19.1
As a ratio of total reserves minus gold (all countries) (%)	36.7	75.9	86.0	84.3

Note: Adjusted for local and cross-border double counting.

Sources: BIS (1996) and IMF (1997a).

As a last illustration, very recently the international market in equity has developed. Over the period 1992–7, the market has increased almost fourfold

Table 2.2 Cross-border transactions in bonds and equity: gross purchases and sales of securities between residents and non-residents as a % of GDP

	1970	1975	1980	1985	1990	1995	1997
Canada	6	3	9	27	65	189	358
France	...	...	5	21	54	187	313
Germany	3	5	7	33	57	172	253
Italy	...	1	1	4	27	253	672
Japan	...	2	8	62	119	65	96
United States	3	4	9	35	89	135	213

Source: BIS (1998a). Similar data for the UK are not available.

(Table 2.3). This is to a large extent due to the increased privatisation in many countries. Also cross-border mergers and acquisitions (M&A) have boomed in recent years: in 1996, 51 cross-border M&A operations with a value of at least US$1 billion were set up, amounting to an aggregate value of US$133 billion, in 1997 the figures increased to 72 issues and US$200 billion, respectively (Shearlock, 1998).

Table 2.3 International equity issues, in US$ billion

	1992	1993	1994	1995	1996	1997
Euro equities	10.7	30.6	37.0	26.7	34.8	42.2
Other international equity issues	12.8	10.1	8.0	14.3	22.9	42.9
Total	23.5	40.7	45.0	41.0	57.7	85.1
Of which: privatisations	*1.2*	*9.3*	*13.6*	*15.2*	*17.4*	*25.0*

Source: OECD, *Financial Market Trends*, various issues

This process is not without precedent. Internationalisation of financial markets was also very strong during the late nineteenth century, a period ending at the start of the First World War. Indeed, by some measures integration of financial markets was even higher than today (see Obstfeld and Taylor, 1997). However, the present situation differs qualitatively from the one a century ago, in the sense that a larger part of the world and more independent countries are involved. Indeed, integration and globalisation is not only a characteristic of developed markets but also of emerging markets. Moreover, the speed with which capital flows can roam freely across the globe has increased spectacularly. Both observations have been illustrated during the recent turmoil in the South-East Asian markets, which was, at least in part, triggered by swift international capital movements.

The remaining parts of this survey will analyse these observations. In the following section we will discuss the processes that lead to the internationalisation of financial markets. The third section will then survey the literature on financial integration. This literature tries to establish empirically whether financial markets are integrated. We will review the main methodologies as well as the preliminary results. This is important as the costs and benefits of internationalisation, which are discussed in the fourth section, often rely on the assumption that markets are integrated. In the penultimate section, policy guidelines are given, taking into account the potential disadvantages as well as the benefits of global financial markets. Finally, we conclude.

THE INTERNATIONALISATION PROCESS

From the figures above, it is clear that the growth of international 'financial' flows has overshadowed the growth of 'real' international transactions. The combined action of at least three forces explains this surge of international capital flows: the technological evolution which made the internationalisation possible at low costs; the global tendency to proceed with market-oriented reform in a large number of countries made the process possible from a legal point of view; and finally, the increased institutionalisation of savings increased the supply of funding and overcame many practical difficulties of international investments. Below, we elaborate these issues, which – it should be stressed – are not independent from each other.

Technology

One of the most important reasons which made the huge increase in cross-border financial transactions feasible is surely the technological evolution of the last decades. Not only have telecommunication costs come down, also computer power has drastically increased over the last decade (see Table 2.4 for an illustration). Both evolutions have made it possible for financial markets world-wide always to be in contact with each other, and enable quick (or even quasi-simultaneous) position-taking in different markets, which is of course necessary if arbitrage strategies are to work.

Moreover, advanced communication and information systems are of utmost importance for sophisticated investors and market makers or dealers with highly evolved risk management and investment strategies. As an illustration, the huge volume on the foreign exchange market is to a large extent due to the hedging activity by dealers (IMF, 1997c). Also, without well-developed technology and information systems, complex derivative

Table 2.4 Evolution of telecommunication and computation costs

Year	Cost of a three-minute call, New York to London, in 1990 US dollars	US Department of Commerce computer price deflator (1990=1000)
1930	244.65	...
1940	188.54	...
1950	53.20	...
1960	45.86	125,000
1970	31.58	19,474
1980	4.80	3,620
1990	3.32	1,000

Sources: Herring and Litan (1995), as reported in IMF (1997a)

instruments would not have flourished as they did over the last decade. For these instruments adequate real-time pricing is very important for trading them and managing financial risks. In addition, the surge in the theoretical knowledge on the pricing of such derivatives, spurred by the seminal paper of Black and Scholes (1973), has been crucial to the developments of these markets.

Also from a macro-prudential point of view financial markets can only cope with huge capital flows if they can fall back on efficient and reliable clearing and settlement systems. Trading of complex financial instruments has increased the linkages between different market segments and participants, without regard to national boundaries. Disruptions in one key market are therefore likely to be transmitted quickly to other markets, threatening the stability of the world financial system. Therefore, technological advances are used to enhance settlement, clearing and payment systems, where the focus is on settlement in real-time on a gross basis (see BIS, 1997b).

Liberalisation

Of course, the technological revolution in itself is not sufficient to explain the internationalisation of financial markets. The latter was made possible by a world-wide deregulation process in which governments attached more importance to market factors for financial markets. In the period starting in the 1960s and ending in the late 1980s, many industrialised countries restored current account and capital account convertibility and lifted controls on cross-border flows, including capital outflows.[4]

Besides this external liberalisation, domestic financial markets were also deregulated. Financial innovation had totally changed business in the offshore markets by blurring the distinctions between banks and other financial institutions as well as between different market segments. In order to remain competitive, domestic markets also had to be deregulated (Blommestein and Biltoft, 1995). This is only one example where financial innovation, enabled by technological advances, quickly spreads to other markets and reduces or eliminates differences between financial markets and systems. It demonstrates that the deregulation process and the improved technology are not independent from each other, but interlinked. More sophisticated technology reduces transactions costs, thereby initiating some financial institutions to start competing with other financial institutions beyond their own traditional markets. As technology and/or financial developments make it more difficult for governments to impose effective control and regulation inconsistent with market forces, the choice is to deregulate the domestic markets or to disappear (Edey and Hviding, 1995).[5]

The processes described above are not limited to the developed countries. During recent years, capital markets in developing countries have also been deregulated. The same widespread movement towards market-oriented economic reform, cross-border flows, especially inflows, have been deregulated in many developing countries (World Bank, 1997). They also removed restrictions on payments for current account transactions to a large extent: the proportion of trade carried out by developing countries under current account convertibility has increased from 30 per cent in 1985 to nearly 70 per cent in 1997 (IMF, 1997a, p. 73). Also their domestic markets have been both widened and deepened, giving more way to market forces (World Bank, 1997).

Institutionalisation

Although necessary, the mere fact that international capital movements are possible is not sufficient to explain the surge in them. There should also be ample demand for international investments. The large cross-border portfolio investments documented in the introduction could also emerge from merely passive investment strategies. Such strategies do not require exceptional knowledge about the different markets, nor extensive infrastructure to follow up positions, nor considerable investment funds to save on transaction costs. While such passive investment strategies could explain the cross-border *stocks* of investments, they can hardly explain the much larger cross-border capital *flows*. It is clear that these flows are to a large extent due to professionals who are involved with active investment strategies, taking arbitrage positions or following sophisticated hedging strategies.

These advanced investors are to a growing extent present on the markets. In recent decades the institutionalisation of savings has grown tremendously. An ever-larger part of households' savings is entrusted to so-called institutional investors, including life insurance companies, pension funds and mutual funds. Within the OECD area, the assets of institutional investors have increased by an annual rate of 11 per cent on average over the 1990–95 period (OECD, 1997b). Over a longer horizon, the increase is even more spectacular: managed assets increased from US$3.2 trillion or 38 per cent of GDP in 1981 to US$16.3 trillion (90 per cent of GDP) in 1991 and to more than US$24.3 trillion (106.5 per cent of GDP) in 1995 (Blommestein, 1997); see also Table 2.5.

Table 2.5 Financial assets of institutional investors (% of GDP)

		1990	1991	1992	1993	1994	1995
Canada	All	58.6	64.2	66.9	76.9	80.9	87.9
	Pension funds	29.0	30.8	31.5	34.3	36.3	39.5
France	All	52.9	60.1	58.3	69.7	72.5	75.3
	Pension funds	...	...	...	...	...	...
Germany	All	36.5	38.3	33.8	38.3	44.2	46.1
	Pension funds	3.1	3.3	2.9	2.5	2.7	2.7
Italy	All	13.3	15.3	12.5	17.7	19.6	20.6
	Pension funds	3.5	4.3	3.1	3.4	3.6	4.0
Japan	All	81.7	79.3	78.1	81.4	84.9	77.4
	Pension funds	...	...	...	...	...	...
UK	All	114.5	126.2	115.3	163.8	149.6	162.3
	Pension funds	55.0	59.3	52.7	72.4	64.9	68.8
US	All	127.4	139.6	145.7	155.2	153.5	170.8
	Pension funds	46.1	50.4	53.1	54.8	53.6	59.8

Source: OECD (1997c)

This growing degree of institutionalised savings goes hand in hand with increased international diversification, especially for pension funds, as institutional investors, being more aware of international investment opportunities, being more acquainted with foreign markets and being better able to manage such portfolios than individual investors, invest an increasing proportion of their portfolios abroad (Table 2.6).

Table 2.6 Proportion of foreign assets held by institutional investors

	1970	1980	1985	1990
Germany				
Investment companies	...	11	30	41
Pension funds	0	0	1	1
Japan				
Life assurance companies	...	9	26	30
Non-life insurance companies	...	7	19	29
Trust accounts of banks	...	2	14	19
Postal life insurance	...	0	7	12
Pension funds	0	1	5	7
United Kingdom				
Insurance companies	...	8	16	18
Pension funds	2	9	15	18
United States				
Collective investment funds	...	1	1	5
Pension funds	0	1	2	4

Sources: Turner (1991, table 25); Takeda and Turner (1992, table 3); Davis (1995, table 6.12)

Of course, this evolution is to a large extent driven by the deregulation in both industrialised and developing countries. The trend towards more market-oriented reform has not only opened new markets, but has also lifted previous, sometimes severe, investment restrictions for institutional investors (Davis, 1988,1995; Blommestein, 1998). Indeed, in some cases regulators have even started to urge investors to diversify abroad (Chester, 1991; see also Blommestein, 1998). This is another demonstration of the interrelated nature of the three processes.

Moreover, the figures in Table 2.7 suggest that the internationalisation of institutional portfolios has not yet reached its peak: the proportion of international assets is still quite low. Moreover, the ageing of the population and the need to reform the pension system in several industrialised countries are likely to reinforce the trend towards institutionalisation of savings,[6] and thus also toward more international investments.

Table 2.7 International diversification of institutional portfolios: foreign equities and bonds as a % of total equities and bonds, 1996

	Pension funds	Insurance companies	Investment companies	PM market Capitalisation
Canada	17	26[a]	37	2
France	...	1[b]	...	4
Germany	5[c]	...	45[c]	6
Italy	...	15	16	4
Japan	23	13	...	18
United Kingdom	28	18	15	6
United States	11	7	7	45

Notes:
a   1991
b   1994
c   1993 and in percentage of total assets.

Sources: BIS (1998a, table V.7), and Lewis (1998, table 4) Market capitalisation is an aggregate estimate of both the debt market and the stock market. The debt market figures are amounts outstanding in December 1996 as reported by BIS, *International Banking and Financial Market Developments*, February 1998. They include domestic debt securities (Table 15) and international bonds and notes issued in the respective currencies (Table 11B). The stock market capitalisation figures are taken from MSCI, *EAFE and World Perspective*, First Quarter 1997. The figures reported are weighted averages.

INTERNATIONALISATION AND CAPITAL MARKET INTEGRATION

In view of the internationalisation documented in the introduction and the many links between the markets, it is obvious that financial markets are not totally segmented. However, the question can be asked whether financial markets are completely integrated or whether they are still segmented to some extent. This is important to fully gauge the extent to which the theoretical costs and benefits listed in the fourth section actually apply. In this section we will summarise the research undertaken to answer these questions.

Of course, to do so, one must have a clear definition of integration as well as the empirical settings to measure the extent of integration. In the literature several general approaches are found. They all basically start from the hypothesis that markets are fully integrated – sometimes supplemented by some other 'ideal' market characteristics, such as completeness – and then empirically test some of the consequences derived from these assumptions. The first approach starts with the 'Law of One Price' and argues that if markets are totally integrated, then assets with similar characteristics should have the same price regardless of where they are traded. Instead of focusing on asset prices, the second approach looks at investment portfolios: if markets are integrated these portfolios should be well diversified, implying that a substantial proportion of wealth should be invested abroad. A third approach considers the implication of diversification. In a perfectly integrated capital market investors diversify their portfolios in order to smooth their consumption path. Under certain additional assumptions, this implies that the consumption pattern across different countries (and within countries) should be perfectly correlated. An empirical measure of integration can then be found by looking at correlations between per capita consumption growth in different countries. Finally, the savings–investment approach observes international capital flows and argues that in an integrated financial world there is no national financing constraint. This implies that there should be no significant correlation between domestic savings and domestic investments. In this section, we will give an overview of the main pitfalls and difficulties that these methodologies face, as well as a summary of the literature's main results.

Price equalisation

The idea behind this approach draws on the fact that in integrated markets assets should be priced consistently. In terms of an asset pricing model this means that the prices for the different systematic risk sources should be the same regardless of the market in which the assets are traded. Following this reasoning, a large strand of literature has studied international asset pricing models, testing whether domestic excess asset returns are related to the world market portfolio excess return, as would be predicted when markets are integrated, or rather to domestic factors as would follow in totally segmented capital markets. An overview of this literature is given in Lewis (1998). The general conclusion is that although an international factor helps explain excess returns, it is not sufficient. Multiple beta models, incorporating domestic risk factors and exchange rate risk add significantly to explanatory power (De Santis and Gérard, 1997 and 1998).

Before jumping to conclusions, it should be noticed that unless very restrictive assumptions are made, the world market portfolio is not necessarily an efficient portfolio, on which most empirical tests rely. Indeed, when deviations from relative PPP exist, investors in distinct countries will look differently at real returns and will therefore hold in addition to the world market portfolio an inflation hedge portfolio, which is generally unique from each country's perspective (Adler and Dumas, 1983). The inherent difficulty, which this approach faces, is thus made clear: a test of the integration of capital markets is a joint test of both an asset pricing model and the equality of the characteristics of the assets studied. Given that traditional asset pricing models such as the Capital Asset Pricing Model (CAPM) and the Arbitrage Pricing Theory (APT) seem to be incapable of explaining systematic anomalies[7], this kind of testing is precarious.

To reduce the risk of an inadequate pricing model being used, many empirical papers have focused on simple assets which it is obvious should be priced similarly. Most straightforward is to focus on (nearly) exactly identical assets that are traded on different markets. Much attention has been given to price differences between onshore and offshore markets. Obstfeld and Taylor (1997) find that these differences narrowed over recent decades, whereas they where quite substantial between the 1950s and the 1970s, and even in the 1980s for some currencies. The narrowing of the spreads after the dismantling of controls is most visible in Table 2.8, taken from Marston (1995).[8] Still, in periods of turbulence, for example the attacks on the EMS in 1992 and 1993, divergence becomes wider again as political risk increases and liquidity and policy credibility decreases (Obstfeld, 1995). Also on the bond markets the differences disappear between eurobonds and domestic government bonds (BIS, 1997a). Of course, these comparisons are more difficult to make since the instruments differ in one or more dimensions: credit risk, coupon effects, and so on. Although returns may differ because of these elements, correlations between monthly returns of domestic government bonds, foreign bonds and eurobonds in the same currency are extremely high (Benzie, 1992).

Tests of the covered interest rate parity theorem (CIP) also fit in this framework. These tests usually focus on the return on short-term money market instruments in different currencies. Often eurocurrency deposits are compared. This has the advantage that the credit risk is similar for these assets, as the deposits are held at the same banks. To correct for the different exchange rate risk, these instruments are hedged by simultaneously selling the currency forward. In this setting no asset pricing model has to be relied on as returns in domestic currency for all instruments are known *ex ante*. In integrated markets the arbitrage process should ensure that hedged returns are equal. Long-lasting deviations from CIP thus clearly indicate market segmentation.

Generally, for the most important currencies deviations from CIP have decreased over recent decades to a level too small to allow for arbitrage profits – at least when transaction costs are taken into account. In some cases deviations are larger than normal transaction costs, but in most cases these are linked to formal capital controls or to expectations that such controls will

Table 2.8 Average interest differentials between eurodeposits and domestic instruments, monthly averages in % per annum

	With capital controls		Without capital controls
France	1973(1)–1981(4)	1981(5)–1986(3)[a]	1986(4)–1991(3)
	1.46	2.75	0.07
Germany	Tight controls	Limited controls	1981(3)–1991(3)
	1972(3)–1974(1)	1974(2)–1981(2)	–0.16
	–4.62	–0.30	
Japan	1973(1)–1974(12)[b]	1975(1)–1980(12)	1981(1)–1991(11)
	2.50	–1.18	0.25
UK	1961(4)–1971(4)[c]	1973(1)–1979(6)	1979(7)–1991(3)
	0.78	1.50	–0.03
US	1966(1)–1973(12)		1974(1)–1991(3)
	1.35		0.48

Notes:
a   Socialist government period with many capital controls
b   Period with speculative pressure against yen
c   Bretton-Woods period

Source: Marston (1995, tables 3.2, 3.3, 3.5, 3.7, and 3.8)

be set up in the near future (Marston, 1995). This indicates that CIP deviations can persist due to risk premia to cover for default or political risk. Also for developing markets, deviations are significantly higher than in mature markets (Frankel, 1991). Of course, this is not necessarily a sign of segmentation as these premia would also exist in integrated markets. This again stresses the joint hypothesis nature of this kind of test for integration.

Besides tests of the CIP using money market instruments, Popper (1993) and Fletcher and Taylor (1994) have also tested equality of hedged returns using long-term interest rates and find similar results: in periods in which no substantial capital controls are in effect, there are few arbitrage opportunities available, at least when transaction costs are taken into account. Moreover, these opportunities diminish over time.

Where CIP assumes that hedged returns on similar assets are equalised, uncovered interest rate parity (UIP) assumes that unhedged returns should also be equal. This implies that differences in nominal interest rates are neutralised by expected exchange rate changes. Empirical results nearly unanimously reject UIP,[9] but again this does not necessarily point to segmented markets. Indeed, by leaving international investments exposed to unexpected exchange rate changes, additional risk is incurred for which investors will require a risk premium. Such premia may drive a wedge between unhedged returns in different countries causing the UIP to be rejected. Also systematic biases in market participants' expectations may cause UIP violations.[10]

Even more assumptions are required to imply a convergence of *real* interest rates. In addition to UIP it also requires that relative purchasing power parity (PPP) holds: expected changes in exchange rates are due to differences in expected inflation. The crucial assumption here is integration of product markets rather than financial markets. Indeed, PPP requires that price arbitrage takes place on the real markets for deviations to disappear. As prices are sticky and real markets are more hindered by barriers than financial ones, the usually reported breakdown of PPP in the short run is therefore not necessarily evidence for segmented *financial* markets.[11]

Portfolio home bias

Instead of focusing on prices in financial markets, other tests for integration have looked at the portfolio composition of investors. Portfolio theory teaches that portfolio risk can be strongly reduced by investing in assets with low return correlations. As assets tend to have lower correlation across borders than within borders (Heston and Rouwenhorst, 1994), non-domestic assets should be abundantly present in portfolios. However, most portfolios – both private and institutional – are heavily biased towards domestic assets. Indeed, Tables 2.6 and 2.7 showed that, although the proportion of international assets in institutional portfolios is rising, it is still relatively low compared to the market capitalisation of these foreign markets.

Of course, it is difficult to describe what, from a theoretical point of view, would constitute an optimal portfolio. In the presence of deviations from relative PPP and stochastic inflation rates, the world market portfolio is generally *not* an efficient portfolio (see also above mentioned section on price equalisation). However, the home bias predicted by the country-specific inflation hedge portfolio is too small to explain empirically the observed home bias (Cooper and Kaplanis, 1994). Moreover, given plausible estimates of expected return, risk and correlation, investors should hold portfolios that are more diversified than they are in reality.[12] This indicates that either formal and/or informal barriers to foreign investments still exist. Indeed, empirical research points out that government-imposed barriers to international investment can be important sources of market segmentation (Bonser-Neal *et al.*, 1990; Hardouvelis *et al.*, 1994). However, these studies focus on emerging markets and do not explain why the home bias is also strongly present in developed, deregulated markets.

In any case, the upward trend in the international diversification of institutional investors shown in Table 2.6 is an indication that the benefits of international diversification are being acknowledged and/or that remaining barriers to international investment are being lifted.

Cross-country consumption correlations

In an integrated complete market, that is, a market in which all possible state contingent claims are traded, representative agents will tend to smooth their consumption pattern by pooling risks among each other. The first-order conditions for consumers maximising their life-time consumption utility imply that the marginal rates of substitution between current and future (random) consumption is equal across countries. If in addition one assumes a power utility function, consumption growth rates will be equalised as well (Obstfeld and Rogoff, 1996, ch. 5).

Empirical tests of this form of market integration have focused on the cross-country correlation between per capita consumption growth rates. If markets are perfectly integrated, correlation should be very high, viz. one. This will lead to consumption plans that are perfectly correlated across countries. However, usually these correlations are very low (see Lewis, 1998 for an illustration and an overview of the literature) and mostly lower than correlation between per capita output growth rates. It is thus not surprising that the hypothesis of integrated markets has been rejected statistically.

Of course, other explanations for the low correlations have been put forward, for example, the existence of non-tradables may reduce the cross-country consumption rates, even when markets are complete. However, the variability in non-tradables is too low to explain the observed weak correlations (Lewis, 1996). Moreover, Lewis (1996 and 1997) found that in countries with more capital market restrictions the country-specific consumption is more related to country-specific output than in more deregulated countries. This again points to at least weakly segmented capital markets being (partly) responsible for the weak cross-country consumption correlations.

Perhaps the most telling evidence does not follow from static evaluations, but from comparisons over time, as was also the case in the previous section. Such a comparison in Table 2.9 indeed points toward *less* segmentation over time, with Germany being an exception.[13] Here changes in current consumption are regressed on changes in transitory income. If consumption risk is perfectly shared, the latter should not have an impact on consumption spending. The slope coefficient, which is reported in Table 2.9, should thus be zero.

Table 2.9 Sensitivity of consumption to current transitory income

	1960s	1970s	1980s
Australia	0.37[a]	0.24	0.20[b]
Canada	0.30[b]	0.24	0.16
France	0.48	0.12	0.31
Germany	0.37[a]	0.67[a]	0.98[a]
Italy	0.47[a]	0.54[a]	−0.01
Japan	0.42[a]	0.31[a]	0.13
United Kingdom	0.08	0.12	0.14
United States	0.50[a]	0.47[a]	0.25

Notes:
Table entries are estimated β coefficients from $\Delta c_t = \alpha + \beta\, \Delta y_t + \varepsilon_t$, where c_t and y_t are current consumption and income respectively, and ε_t is an error term. Under the null of integrated capital markets, β equals 0.
a   Coefficient statistically different from zero at the 5% level.
b   Coefficient statistically different from zero at the 10% level.

Source: Blundell-Wignall *et al.* (1991, table 1)

The savings–investment relationship

When international financial markets are integrated, domestic investments are not restricted by the pool of domestic savings. If more financing is needed, funds are found abroad. Conversely, if more money is available, it can be invested in other countries. Therefore, in such a world there should be no reason to expect a high correlation between savings and investments, neither over time nor cross-sectionally.[14] Nevertheless, this is what is usually found in the literature (Obstfeld and Rogoff, 1996, ch. 3). Moreover, the relationship between savings and investments is weaker for developing countries than for developed countries, contradicting the intuition that the latter are more integrated than the former.[15]

To explain this puzzle, a large literature has emerged. This literature focuses on several alternative explanations: (1) imperfect goods market integration; (2) current account targeting; (3) common missing variables; (4) country size; and (5) imperfect substitutability between financial and real capital (Mussa and Goldstein, 1993). At this point, the conclusion of this subliterature is still quite indeterminate (Obstfeld, 1995). Again, like Taylor (1996), a pragmatic approach may be taken by comparing the relative strength of the relationship between savings and investments, where the comparison can be between countries or over time. Using data since 1850 for 12 countries, Taylor (1996) finds that after a major disruption from the 1930s until the 1970s, the link between savings and investments in the 1980s and early 1990s is comparable to the situation in the 1880s and early nineteenth century, a period which is often cited as an era of free capital flows.

COSTS AND BENEFITS OF GLOBAL FINANCIAL MARKETS

Although the literature reviewed in the previous section is quite diverse, the general conclusion is rather clear: financial markets are not as integrated as theoretical models imply, but for the recent years nearly all empirical tests point towards an increased integration of financial markets. Nevertheless, the literature also shows that capital integration is a difficult property to measure. Given this caveat, we summarise in this section the benefits and costs of the increased integration of international financial markets.

Benefits

Traditional advantages of financial markets
Of course, the advantages of the internationalisation of financial markets are to a large extent analogous to the advantages of the existence of financial markets in a closed economy. Without financial markets, the economic agents in a closed economy are more constrained because of the self-financing need. Applied to international finance, the economy *as a whole* is more constrained when no international capital flows are possible/allowed. In this case, the domestic financial surpluses have to match the domestic financial deficits by definition. Large investments, such as for infrastructure, or the financing of large government deficits are then only possible when the savings ratio is equally high or when other investments are postponed, thereby potentially frustrating the other economic agents' consumption and investment plans. The well-known phenomenon of *crowding-out* is an example of what can happen if insufficient capital is available and the demand for capital by a large agent is relatively little interest-elastic.

Opening up to international capital eliminates the constraint or dampens the impact on the domestic market of large financing needs as a larger pool of financial savings can be tapped. Globalisation may lead to a more efficient allocation of means and thus open the road to higher potential economic growth as more investments can be financed without having a detrimental effect on financing conditions.[16] It may also bring about additional flexibility to governments: by easing financial constraints the time necessary to adjust a situation may be extended.

Just as an excessive demand for financing can severely impact the domestic financial market, so can excessive supply. Therefore another reason to allow domestic investors to diversify their portfolios abroad is to avoid a build-up of speculative bubbles in the domestic asset market (for example, stock or real estate market). These bubbles tend to lead in the end to financial instability, usually through a banking crisis (Goldstein and Turner, 1996). Indeed, market observers point to such experiences in Asia recently to illustrate this point (for example, IMF, 1997a).

Another reason why globalisation of financial markets can be beneficial for capital exporting countries, that is, for investors, is risk reduction. Traditional portfolio theory teaches that portfolio risk can be reduced by holding assets which are less than perfectly correlated. Many empirical papers have demonstrated that asset returns are less correlated across than within national boundaries, thereby demonstrating the potential advantage of international portfolio diversification.[17] Risk reduction is also the main reason UK portfolio managers of life insurance companies and pension funds cite when they are asked about the benefits of international diversification (Davis, 1991, 1995).

Besides risk reduction, return improvement is often given as the reason to diversify internationally. Higher expected returns are to an extent due to more risk, for example, market risk, default risk and political risk, but may also be due to better investment opportunities. Most, if not all, empirical papers indeed indicate that international diversification can both yield higher return and lower risk *ex post* (see the references in note 17).[18] The search for higher return can expected to be intensive when returns in the 'home' markets are historically low. It has been observed that it is no coincidence that the recent surge of capital flows into emerging markets coincided with historically low interest rates in many major industrialised countries (IMF, 1997c).

Indirect benefits

Besides these 'traditional' advantages of financial markets, indirect advantages may also be important to defend the internationalisation process. Indeed, the World Bank cites some of these as the more important ones for the emerging markets (World Bank, 1997). As mentioned above (pp, 45–52), financial innovation in some advanced markets quickly spread towards other markets, simply because the latter have to compete with the former. This makes domestic markets broader and deeper: broader because a greater variety of assets are traded (the market becomes more complete). This does not only result in higher returns on savings and lower borrowing costs. It also implies that more flexible instruments are available such that companies (financial and non-financial alike) can better manage their financial risk and can therefore concentrate on their core business. Moreover, in the process risks are transferred to those agents who are willing and/or more able to carry them.

Internationalisation also deepens markets as more competition means more participants, sharper prices and more liquidity. As such, domestic markets become more operationally efficient and domestic institutions' productivity is enhanced. Not only have average brokering commissions decreased on most, if not all, stock markets, but also bid–ask spreads on the euromoney market have plummeted, certainly for the currencies which were deregulated most (see Table 2.10). Also productivity in the banking sector has increased tremendously, which shows up in more volume per employee and the decreasing ratio of staff costs to total income (Edey and Hviding, 1995).

Table 2.10 Bid–ask spreads on three-month eurocurrency deposits, in basis points

	1980–2	1987–9
US dollar	12.6	12.6
Pound sterling	66.7	12.0
French franc	49.0	13.4
German mark	12.8	12.9
Japanese yen	17.0	11.8

Source: DRI and IMF, as reported in Edey and Hviding (1995, table 17)

In turn, more efficiency in financial markets is likely to lead to higher standards of living. Household spending and business investments alike are less sensitive to temporary fluctuations in their income, which may boost economic welfare (OECD, 1997a). Empirical studies are consistent with this conjecture: positive associations have been demonstrated between several proxies for financial development and subsequent long-run economic growth.[19]

Finally, dismantling capital controls may also serve as a disciplining device on policymakers. Unstable policies can be limited by the threat of capital flight. It therefore becomes even more important that authorities build up credibility, which can only be achieved by implementing time-consistent policies (Obstfeld and Taylor, 1997).

Of course, this does not mean that these advantages can be taken for granted. They have to be assured: the deregulation and integration process has to be accompanied by measures to prepare the domestic financial institutions for increased competition and by steps to ensure that investor confidence is maintained in the markets. We return these issues in the next sub–section.

Costs

As already mentioned in the previous sub–section, some of the benevolent evolutions may eventually become disadvantageous. Too much capital inflow may lead to insufficient domestic savings, thereby leading to an overheated domestic economy and/or asset bubbles in the domestic markets. Moreover, an overheated economy may give rise to current account deficits, which, to the extent that they are recognised as unsustainable, may lead to a systemic breakdown, as (almost) happened in Thailand, Malaysia and Indonesia in 1997. These breakdowns were intensified – or at least not stopped – by an insufficiently developed financial system and inadequate supervision. Other fears which are sometimes raised include the possibility that globalisation would erode the autonomy of the nation-state and that internationalisation of capital markets would entail harsh consequences for employment in developed (rich and often high-cost) countries.

Social consequences for developed economies
In developed countries the fear exists, mostly in popular writings, that the globalisation of the economy is to some extent a zero-sum game, in which the winners include the countries with capital inflows[20] and investors. The losers are the capital exporting countries, and more precisely their workers. The idea is that as capital is more flexible than labour, the tax burden falls increasingly on to the latter. This will lead to unemployment if the higher costs are not compensated elsewhere. By lowering social benefits and making labour more flexible, the tendency towards higher unemployment may be stopped. More international capital flows thus lead to more unemployment and/or to a degradation of the social welfare system.[21]

However, the empirical evidence, although scarce, does not support this thesis. Increased FDI does not seem to lead to 'job-exporting'. The contrary may even hold: foreign workers seem to be complementary to rather than a substitute for domestic workers. Also, FDI does not coincide with a decrease in 'domestic' investment, but rather seems to complement it. Yet, capital mobility may potentially amplify external shocks to unemployment, as the return on capital is increasingly set in the global market. This means that the burden of adjustment to shocks is shifted to wages, which, to the extent that the latter are insufficiently flexible, may increase unemployment (IMF, 1997a). It is however possible that especially lower-skilled labour would increasingly come under pressure in the industrialised countries.

Loss of autonomy

Another fear often uttered is that the surge in international capital flows deprives national authorities of the autonomy to follow a desired policy. The fact that most countries choose to deregulate international capital flows implicitly implies that either exchange rate stability or a domestically oriented monetary policy is renounced. Indeed, given the so-called *policy trilemma* (Obstfeld and Taylor, 1997) at most two of the following three principles are mutually consistent: (1) cross-border capital mobility, (2) exchange rate stability, and (3) a monetary policy geared towards domestic goals. Given that governments choose capital mobility, they either have to sacrifice exchange rate stability or an autonomous monetary policy.

Moreover, in the previous section mention has already been made that the speed with which capital flows may enter or leave countries puts strains on the equitable distribution of taxes on capital and labour. The former is much harder to tax, as it can shift to locations where taxes are lower or quasi-non–existent. Taxing capital becomes increasingly an international matter, which is handled carefully so as not to chase off its tax base.[22]

More generally, policy is judged carefully by international investors. Good policy (and good luck?) is rewarded with low borrowing costs and ample resources, but policy deemed disastrous by the financial markets is punished severely by withdrawing funding and raising borrowing costs for future funding. The idea gathers pace that financial markets rather than governments decide what is best for an economy.

Investors and international institutions like the IMF and the World Bank retort that usually the reaction of the financial markets enforces a discipline on countries such that policies which are unsustainable in the long run are renounced at a much earlier stage, thereby minimising the costs of restructuring. The World Bank puts it as follows: 'International capital flows can act as a magnifying glass on the domestic economy, multiplying the benefits of well-structured reform programs but also increasing the cost of poor economic fundamentals and policies that are unsound' (World Bank, 1997, p. 25).

However, the problem appears that even small changes in the economic and/or political situation of a country or region can lead to dramatic changes in investor sentiment and a quick withdrawal of funds. Although such an observation is not inconsistent with rational market behaviour,[23] many commentators argue that this is evidence for inefficient financial markets. In this reasoning, financial markets tend to overreact because of speculation. Moreover, panics are swiftly transmitted to other markets which are fundamentally sound.

Overreaction and spill-overs

Many of the advantages of globalisation boil down to the more efficient allocation of capital which is made possible. Of course, this crucially depends on the efficient working of financial markets. The latter especially has received many comments in the literature. Instead of processing information efficiently, financial markets tend to overreact. Investors react to soaring prices by buying and, when markets crumble, every investor looks for the exit. Of course, these waves of optimism and pessimism lead to misalignments on the financial markets. These are eventually followed by severe corrections which may disrupt financial stability.

These kinds of overreaction are of course linked to the idea that financial markets are excessively volatile and that they have recently become even more volatile. The excess volatility debate is still going on (see, for example, Cuthbertson, 1996) with the argument focusing on how to define and measure 'normal' and 'excess' volatility. However, no sound empirical evidence exists that markets have become more volatile; see Table 2.11 for an illustration. Deregulation does not seem to have increased stock or bond

Table 2.11 Volatility of financial markets: average standard deviation of monthly changes of the G7 countries (%)

	Bond yields	Share prices	Effective exchange rates
1960–9	0.2	4.5	0.5
1970–9	0.3	4.9	1.4
1980–5	0.4	4.6	1.4
1986–9	0.4	5.8	1.4
19904	0.3	4.5	1.5

Note: Averages are unweighted.

Sources: Edey and Hviding (1995, tables 22, 23 and 24)

market volatility as volatilities peeked in the 1980s and decreased back in the first half of the 1990s. Also exchange rate volatility did not increase since the first part of the 1980s (Borio and McCauley, 1996; Edey and Hviding, 1995).

The idea exists, however, that the growing deregulation and the concomitant internationalisation have made financial markets more prone to unstable behaviour which does not necessarily show up in higher short-term volatility, but rather in infrequent discrete disruptions. First of all, the deregulation has blurred the distinction between banks and non-banks. The latter challenge the former in their traditional markets. The increased competition for market share leads to sharper pricing, which may spur financial markets and lead to a misallocation of capital. Moreover, the margins are in many cases lowered too much to cope with new or higher risks such that insufficient buffers are available to cushion eventual corrections.

Secondly, the feedback among the different markets may increase the strength of the movements. IMF (1997c) cites the interaction between emerging and mature capital markets as an example of overreaction. The capital inflows in the emerging markets lead to a building up of exchange rate reserves which the monetary authorities invest in safe instruments in the mature markets. This in turn leads to lower interest rates, which reinforces the search for higher returns, and thus to more investments in the emerging markets. When a speculative attack occurs, foreign capital flows are withdrawn, this is counteracted by the monetary authorities by liquidating their foreign exchange reserves. This in turn intensifies the crisis. Free capital flows thus exacerbate overreaction.

Thirdly, the institutionalisation can also have such an effect. Blommestein (1997) argues that institutionalisation of savings leads to a quicker transmission of short-term price movements due to herd behaviour and the growing importance of institutional investors. Indeed, the BIS estimates that although a hypothetical shift of 1 per cent of equity holdings by institutional investors in the G-7 countries only represented about 1 per cent of total stock market capitalisation in 1995, the same funds represent more than 27 per cent of stock market capitalisation in emerging Asian economies and more than 66 per cent in Latin America (BIS, 1998a, p. 90). Herd-like behaviour, spurred by the fact that portfolio managers tend to be evaluated relative to their peers and also by the increased tendency to follow similar portfolio strategies like index-tracking, can thus have devastating effects on emerging markets.

In this respect, the so-called hedge funds are often held responsible for igniting speculative crises.[24] Mr Soros, heading Quantum Fund – a hedge fund, was criticised in 1992 for speculating against several European currencies, which eventually drove the pound sterling and the Italian lira out of the European Exchange Rate Mechanism. More recently, hedge fund operators were suspected of starting off the Asian crisis. The fact that these funds, which actively use all kinds of leverage mechanisms, are able to build up important market positions explains to a large extent why they are suspected of leading the pack of speculation-prone investors. However, the (scarce) empirical evidence does not support this allegation: Brown *et al.* (1998) for instance do *not* find any evidence that the ten largest hedge funds were responsible for the crash in the Asian currencies in late 1997; see also

BIS (1998a, p. 93). Of course, the limited disclosure by such funds hampers very detailed analysis.

Finally, the increased integration of financial markets may also lead to a swifter transmission of shocks across markets (see pp. 45–52). However, no evidence exists that this also leads to more volatility. Even from an *a priori* point of view, it is equally possible that more integration leads to *less* volatility as the deeper and broader markets offer more diversification possibilities which may lead to a smoother absorption of shocks. In an extensive study on the volatility of emerging stock markets Bekaert and Harvey (1997) find more evidence in favour of the latter possibility. They report that in many countries volatility decreases after liberalisation takes effect. Also, the more open an economy is, the lower the volatility on its stock market. Demirgüç-Kunt and Levine (1996) also find that internationally integrated markets tend to be less volatile.

POLICY GUIDELINES

The previous section points out that the balance between advantages and disadvantages of global capital markets is still indeterminate. Some authors (for example, Rodrik, 1998) do not find sufficient empirical evidence on the advantages to counter the obvious disadvantages. For instance, the conclusions on the long-run impact of capital flows on investments, economic growth and inflation are very simple and methodology dependent. Among the disadvantages the endemic bubbles and crashes of financial markets stand out. Basically, these booms and crashes are due to insufficient information and speculative behaviour by important investors, including institutional investors and banks. In this section, we discuss the policy guidelines which have been proposed to alleviate the disadvantages which are ascribed to financial markets. These include capital market taxes to discourage speculation, measures to accompany the financial deregulation process, and international co-ordination between regulators.

Tobin tax and sustainable policy

The disciplining effect of financial markets is a disadvantage rather than an advantage, at least when financial markets are not functioning efficiently. In such a case even sound policies may be frustrated by speculative attacks. These attacks are usually ascribed to 'hot money' (see above), that is, short term investments. Given the fact that it is highly unlikely that a country would isolate itself from international capital flows, even if no advantages were present, a second possibility would be to erect a barrier to speculative money, while maintaining free flow of fundamental, long-term capital flows. To this end, Tobin (1978) proposed to levy a tax on all international capital flows. Even small taxes would discourage short-run speculative movements, but would not bother longer-term investments, such as FDI or long-term portfolio investments.

From a theoretical point of view, the advantages of such a tax are not clear and depend on the model used to explain the financial crisis.[25] Macroeconomic models focus on inconsistent policies (such as conflicts between fiscal and exchange rate policy) which ultimately lead to a financial crash or to shifting, self-fulfilling expectations of market participants (see Obstfeld and Rogoff, 1996, chs. 8 and 9 respectively). Although a transaction tax or capital controls may postpone crises, they will not prevent them as the causes of the crisis are not eliminated (Dooley, 1997). However, microeconomic models focusing on the mechanism of financial intermediation and the government's role therein provide some rationale for the Tobin tax. In such models, which Dooley (1997) calls *insurance models*, the seeds of an attack are found in an inconsistency between the government's desire to hold reserve assets to smooth consumption over time and its explicit or implicit commitment to insure the liabilities of residents, including resident financial institutions. This insurance leads to massive capital inflows as yields on domestic assets compare favourably to those on foreign assets. These inflows increase the government's (contingent) liabilities and as soon as these liabilities match the government's assets there is an incentive for foreign investors to withdraw their funds. From that moment onwards the possibility exists that the government's assets are insufficient to cover the insurance, thus lowering expected returns. This incentive leads to an insurance attack. To the extent that the assets of foreign investors exploiting the insurance commitment have a shorter maturity than those of stable investments, a Tobin tax would prevent these types of attacks, since the tax would eliminate the insurance benefit.

However, some empirical evidence indicates that international capital flows which are traditionally labelled 'long-term' are as volatile as flows which are usually called 'short-term' (Claessens *et al.*, 1995).[26] In any case, it is not only the difficulty of defining how and on which capital flows the tax should be levied and the need to include all major financial centres in the system that makes this proposal difficult to implement. Also the present technology and sophistication of financial markets would quickly permit loopholes to escape the tax.

Perhaps a better solution to avoid speculative and insurance attacks is to ensure that macroeconomic policies are consistent and sustainable in the long run. If in addition external debt is well managed, no reasons are left to start attacks in the first place.[27] Since external debt includes the implicit or explicit insurance of private sector liabilities, prudential supervision of financial institutions should be included in these measures.

Financial regulation and information dissemination

Indeed, to avoid financial disruptions, while maintaining the advantages of a more liberalised financial environment, it is crucial that the financial system has the means to cope with the new environment. Typically, domestic and international liberalisation go hand in hand. As described in the previous section, opening up domestic markets to foreign investors, coupled with the perception that the government will bail out domestic institutions, will massively attract foreign capital and competition. While the former provides the funding, the latter leads to more aggressive and usually more risky investments and lending by domestic banks. However, their risk management procedures are unlikely to have evolved in tandem with financial liberalisation, leading to excessive risk-taking.[28] Also prudential regulation may not have sufficient resources to cope with the additional opportunities. This situation can quickly set the right conditions for an insurance attack.

Therefore, it is of the utmost importance that financial liberalisation is not implemented too brusquely, giving both the private sector and the prudential authorities the chance to adapt to new instruments, new lending techniques and risk management. It is in this light that pleas for *temporary* capital controls in developing markets have to be interpreted (Dooley, 1997; World Bank, 1997). In any case the necessary regulatory and supervisory mechanisms should be in place as the deregulation process proceeds (OECD, 1997a).

Of course, a necessary condition for good financial intermediation and risk management is the existence of reliable and timely information. This does not only refer to microeconomic information disclosure, such as information on market positions, which is harder to compile because of the increased use of complex derivative instruments, it also implies that macroeconomic information is made available timely and according to international statistical standards. Both steps reduce uncertainty and therefore decrease the possibility of overreaction.

International co-ordination

Given the globalisation of financial markets, there is a stronger need to organise and co-ordinate financial regulation and information dissemination on an international scale. Indeed, as financial institutions are increasingly active in different countries, it is important that supervision can effectively overview the entire organisation. Also, because globalisation entails that institutions of distinct nationalities compete with each other, competitive (dis)advantages due to different regulation can be minimised when prudential regulation is co-ordinated. The fact that financial conglomerates blur the distinctions between traditional and non-traditional financial activities, together with financial innovation which may change risk distribution in a very complicated way, add complexity.

However, prudential authorities are clearly aware of these challenges. They increasingly join efforts both across borders and across traditional activities. The Basle Committee on Banking and Supervision (BCBS), hosted by the BIS, is the oldest and best-known exponent of these efforts. The 1988 Capital Accord and more recently the Market Risk Amendment are two of its achievements. The former established minimum capital requirements to cover credit risk losses, while the latter added market risk to the picture. Concerning initiatives on securities markets, there exists active co-operation between the BCBS and the International Organisation of Securities Commissions (IOSCO), where securities regulators meet. For an overview of these and other joint initiatives, see BIS (1997b) and IMF (1996, Annex IV). Lately, these have included proposals to improve information on international financial markets through the regular publication of foreign exchange market surveys and derivatives market statistics.

Another way to cope with the increasing complexity of financial activities which they have to monitor is to build in regulatory incentives for private firms to assess and manage their risks adequately. Again the Market Risk Amendment provides an example of this new philosophy. Market participants may choose either to use a standard model or their own internal risk model to compute capital requirements. This provides them with incentives to develop a model which measures risks as accurately as possible because by doing so they can save on capital. Of course, all internal models are thoroughly inspected by the prudential authorities before they can be used for these purposes.

CONCLUDING REMARKS

Because of widespread deregulation, technological improvements and insti-tutionalisation of savings, financial markets have witnessed over the last decade an internationalisation process, matched before only in the late nineteenth and early twentieth centuries. As the driving forces have not lost their strength yet, it is likely that financial markets world-wide will behave increasingly as an integrated market. Although this undoubtedly entails some quite significant advantages to the real economy, it also potentially embodies serious dangers. A global systemic breakdown and all the concomitant real output losses is the ultimate doomsday scenario. To alleviate these perils, it is important that governments take the right accompanying measures. The most important actions seem to include the avoidance of inconsistent macroeconomic and financial policies, the requirement of adequate internal risk management systems for financial institutions and high-quality supervision to foster a strong financial sector. Moreover, given the blurring of national boundaries and traditional lines of activity, regulatory bodies should co-operate very closely.

NOTES

* Comments by Frans Buelens, Marc De Ceuster, Geert Van Campenhout and Jef Van Gerwen (who discussed a previous version of this paper) are greatly acknowledged. The usual disclaimer applies.

1 See the other chapters in this volume.

2 Average annual inflation in the 'advanced economies', as measured by the GDP deflator, was 5.1 per cent over the period considered (IMF, 1997b, table A8).

3 This figure is to some extent overestimated because of the depreciation of the US$ *vis-à-vis* most other major currencies. After correcting for exchange rate developments, the increase is still buoyant; see IMF (1996). Preliminary figures indicate that average daily volume on the foreign exchange markets in April 1998 increased to US$1490 billion (BIS, 1998b).

4 For an overview of the measures taken in the most important countries, see Edey and Hviding (1995), Mussa and Goldstein (1993), and Obstfeld and Taylor (1997).

5 Of course, this leads some market observers to conclude that the deregulation process coupled with the urge to remain competitive will tend to erode supervision of financial markets, thereby enhancing system risk. To avoid this possibility, market regulators increasingly co-ordinate their supervision; see pp. 59-62.

6 For a thorough overview of the potential of pension funds, see Davis (1995).

7 Examples include the book-to-market effect, short-term momentum and the size effect; see Hawawini and Keim (1995) for an overview and more references.

8 The relative large spread for the US in the 'without controls' period is due to the reserve requirements which apply to domestic instruments only. Correcting for this, the spreads become negligible (Marston, 1995).

9 Of course, in case of credible (near-)fixed exchange rate systems nominal interest rates do tend to converge. A prominent example is the convergence of European interest rates in the preamble to EMU.

10 See Hodrick (1987) for an overview of the empirical literature and possible theoretical explanations for the rejection of UIP.

11 In the long run PPP tends to hold; see Rogoff (1996) for an overview of the empirical evidence. Rogoff argues that the short-term deviations from PPP are most likely due to less than perfectly integrated international goods markets.

12 If human capital is also considered, Baxter and Jermann (1997) show that investors should even short the domestic stock portfolio.

13 As a potential explanation, Blundell-Wignall *et al.* (1991) point to less formal regulations which were still present in Germany in the 1980s. Examples include the cartel-like behaviour of banks in their price-setting and regulation concerning the authorisation of financial activities.

14 The seminal paper in this field is Feldstein and Horioka (1980).

15 However, over a longer time period and using panel data, Vamvakidis and Wacziarg (1998) reverse this conclusion.

16   See Levine (1997) for a review of the theoretical and empirical links between financial development and economic growth.

17   The seminal papers in this area are Grubel (1968) and Levy and Sarnat (1970) for stock markets. Recent evidence is in Heston and Rouwenhorst (1994). Levy and Lerman (1988) and Annaert (1993) provide evidence for bond markets. For an overview of the literature, see Isimbabi (1992). Divecha *et al.* (1992) showed that for US investors, investments in emerging stock markets both reduce risk and increase return.

18   For the pitfalls of an *ex post* analysis in stead of an *ex ante* analysis, see Jorion (1985) and Annaert (1995).

19   Levine and Zervos (1996) show that liberalisation of capital controls spurs stock market development. The latter is positively linked with long-term economic growth, even after correcting for other determinants. See World Bank (1997, ch. 3) for an overview of the main findings of this empirical literature.

20   Although, given the recent Asian experience and the Mexican crisis, the same authors point out that for these countries the benefits are not clear either; cf. infra.

21   Eichengreen (1997) notes that this mechanism does not necessarily hold, as better social systems may lead to more productive workers, and thus more profitable investments.

22   See, for example,. the sluggish progress within the European Commission to tax non residents from other EU member states on their capital income because of the fear that large investors will deposit their investments in non-EU countries to escape the tax.

23   See, for example, Kennedy et al. (1998) who indicate, by using a simple dividend discount model, that even small changes in expected returns or growth rates can lead to dramatic changes in the price level of major stock markets.

24   See 'Mahatir, Soros and the currency markets', *The Economist*, 27 September 1997, p. 91. Hedge funds have a more speculative nature than the usual mutual funds. They have a greater risk tolerance and by operating as onshore investment partnerships or offshore investment funds, they are not subject to the same stringent disclosure requirements.

25   See ul Haq *et al.* (1996) for an overview of the advantages and disadvantages of the so-called Tobin tax.

26   These results are debated by Chuhan et al. (1996), who argue that when the composition of capital flows is studied multivariately, short-term investments respond more dramatically to disturbances in other capital flows and other countries than foreign direct investment. This would indicate that short-term investments do carry some aspects of hot money with spill-over effects.

27   This is consistent with Dornbusch (1998) who notes that a Tobin tax not only lengthens the investment horizon and thus reduces 'noise' in the capital flows, but does not solve the initial problems.

28   The situation depicted here is not typical for the internationalisation process, but rather for the concomitant deregulation process. Indeed, in the wake of domestic deregulation, households in the United Kingdom, the United States and several Scandinavian countries strongly increased their financial leverage to finance real estate investments. Their financial position was too vulnerable to cope with changing macroeconomic conditions such as increasing interest rates. Arguably, this is also a case of inadequate risk management.

REFERENCES

Adler, M. and B. Dumas (1983), 'International portfolio choice and corporation finance: a synthesis', *Journal of Finance*, **38** (3), June, 925–84.

Annaert, J. (1993), *The International Diversification of Bond Portfolios: An Analysis of the Foreign Exchange Risk and the Effectiveness of Various Hedging Strategies*, unpublished Ph.D. thesis, University of Antwerp, University Centre of Antwerp.

Annaert, J. (1995), 'Estimation risk and international bond portfolio selection', *Journal of Multinational Financial Management*, **5** (2/3), 47–71.

Baxter, M. and U.J. Jermann (1997), 'The international diversification puzzle is worse than you think', *American Economic Review*, **87** (1), March, 170–80.

Bekaert, G. and C.R. Harvey (1997), 'Emerging equity market volatility', *Journal of Financial Economics*, **43** (1), January, 29–77.

Benzie, R. (1992), *The Development of the International Bond Market*, BIS Economic Papers No. 32, Basle: Bank for International Settlements.

BIS (1996), *Central Bank Survey of Foreign Exchange and Derivatives Market Activity*, Basle: Bank for International Settlements.

BIS (1997a), 'What is left of the traditional distinction between eurobonds, foreign bonds and domestic bonds?', *International Banking and Financial Market Developments*, February, 21–5.

BIS (1997b), *Real-Time Gross Settlement Systems. Report Prepared by the Committee on Payment and Settlement Systems*, Basle: Bank for International Settlements.

BIS (1998a), *68th Annual Report*, Basle: Bank for International Settlements .

BIS (1998b), *Press Release. Central Bank Survey of Foreign Exchange and Derivatives Market Activity in April 1998: Preliminary Global Data*, Basle: Bank for International Settlements.

Black, F. and M.S. Scholes (1973), 'The pricing of options and corporate liabilities', *Journal of Political Economy*, **81** (3), May–June, 637–54.

Blommestein, H. (1997), 'The impact of institutional investors on OECD financial markets', *Financial Market Trends*, 68, November, 15-54.

Blommestein, H. (1998), *Institutional Investors in the New Financial Landscape*, Paris: OECD.

Blommestein, H. and K. Biltoft (1995), 'Trends, structural changes and prospects in OECD capital markets', in OECD, *The New Financial Landscape. Forces Shaping the Revolution in Banking, Risk Management and Capital Markets*, Paris: OECD, 287–319.

Blundell-Wignall, A., F. Browne, and S. Cavaglia (1991), *Financial Liberalisation and Consumption Behaviour*, OECD Department of Economics and Statistics Working Paper No. 81, Paris: OECD.

Bonser-Neal, C., G. Bauer, R. Neal and S. Wheatley (1990), 'International investment restrictions and closed-end country fund prices', *Journal of Finance,* **45** (2), 523–48.

Borio, C. and R. McCauley (1996), *The Economics of Recent Bond Market Volatility*, BIS Economics Paper No. 45, Basle: Bank for International Settlements.

Brown, S.J., W.N. Goetzmann, and J. Park (1998), *Hedge Funds and the Asian Currency Crisis of 1997*, NBER Working Paper No. 6427, Washington, DC: National Bureau for Economic Research.

Chester, A.C. (1991), 'The international bond market', *Bank of England Quarterly Bulletin,* **31** (4), 521–28.

Chuhan, P., G. Perez-Quiros, and H. Popper (1996), *International Capital Flows: Do Short-term Investment and Direct Investment Differ?*, Policy Research Working Paper 1669, Washington, DC: World Bank.

Claessens, S., M.P. Dooley, and A. Warner (1995), 'Portfolio capital flows: hot or cold?', *World Bank Economic Review*, **9** (1), January, 153–74.

Cooper I. and E. Kaplanis (1994), 'Home bias in equity portfolios, inflation hedging, and international capital market equilibrium', *Review of Financial Studies*, **7** (1), Spring, 45–60.

Cuthbertson, K. (1996), *Quantitative Financial Economics: Stocks, Bonds and Foreign Exchange*, Chichester: John Wiley.

Davis, E.P. (1988), *Financial Market Activity of Life Insurance Companies and Pension Funds*, BIS Economic Papers No. 21, Basle: Bank for International Settlements.

Davis, E.P. (1991), *International Diversification of Institutional Investors*, Bank of England Discussion Papers, Technical Series No. 44, London: Bank of England.

Davis, E.P. (1995), *Pension Funds: Retirement-Income Security and Capital Markets: An International Perspective*, Oxford: Clarendon Press.

Demirgüç-Kunt, A. and R. Levine (1996), 'Stock market development and financial intermediaries: stylized facts', *World Bank Economic Review*, **10** (2), May, 291–321.

De Santis, G. and B. Gérard (1997), 'International asset pricing and portfolio diversification with time-varying risk', *Journal of Finance*, **52** (5), December, 1881–912.

De Santis, G. and B. Gérard (1998), 'How big is the premium for currency risk?', *Journal of Financial Economics*, **49** (3), September, 375–412.

Divecha, A.B., J. Drach, and D. Stefek (1992), 'Emerging markets: a quantitative perspective', *Journal of Portfolio Management*, **19** (1), Fall, 41–50.

Dooley, M.P. (1997), *Financial Liberalization and Policy Challenges*, Working Paper No. 363, Washington: Inter-American Development Bank.

Dornbusch, R. (1998), 'Capital controls: an idea whose time is past', in S. Fischer *et al.*, *Should the IMF Pursue Capital-Account Convertibility?*, Essays in International Finance, Princeton, New Jersey, No. 207, 20–7.

Edey, M. and K. Hviding (1995), *An Assessment of Financial Reform in OECD Countries*, OECD Economics Department Working Paper No. 154, Paris: OECD.

Eichengreen, B. (1997), 'The tyranny of the financial markets', *Current History*, 377–82.

Feldstein, M. and C. Horioka (1980), 'Domestic savings and international capital flows', *Economic Journal*, **90** (358), 314–29.

Fletcher, D.J. and L.W. Taylor (1994), 'A non-parametric analysis of covered interest parity in long-date capital markets', *Journal of International Money and Finance*, **13** (4), August, 459–75.

Frankel, J. (1991), 'Quantifying international capital mobility in the 1980s', in D. Bernheim and J. Shoven (eds), *National Saving and Economic Performance*, Chicago: University of Chicago Press, pp. 227–60.

Goldstein, M. and P. Turner (1996), *Banking Crises in Emerging Economies: Origins and Policy Options*, BIS Economic Papers, No. 46, Basle: Bank for International Settlements.

Grubel, H.G. (1968), 'Internationally diversified portfolios: welfare gains and capital flows', *American Economic Review*, **58** (5), 1299–314.

Hardouvelis, G.A., R. La Porta, and T.A. Wizman (1994), 'What moves the discount on country equity funds?', in J.A. Frankel (ed.), *The Internationalization of Equity Markets*, Chicago: University of Chicago Press, pp. 345–97.

Hawawini, G. and D.B. Keim (1995), 'On the predictability of common stock returns: world-wide evidence', in R.A. Jarrow, V. Maksimovic, and W.T. Ziemba (eds), *Finance*, Handbooks in Operations Research and Management Science, Vol. 9, Amsterdam: Elsevier Science, pp. 497–544.

Herring, R.J. and R.E. Litan (1995), *Financial Regulation in the Global Economy*, Washington, DC: Brookings Institution.

Heston, S.L. and K.G. Rouwenhorst (1994), 'Does industrial structure explain the benefits of international diversification?', *Journal of Financial Economics*, **36** (1), August, 3–27.

Hodrick, R.J. (1987), *The Empirical Evidence on the Efficiency of Forward and Futures Foreign Exchange Markets*, Fundamentals of Pure and Applied Economics, Chur: Harwood Academic Publishers.

IMF (1996), *International Capital Markets. Developments, Prospects, and Key Policy Issues*, Washington, DC: International Monetary Fund, September.

IMF (1997a), *World Economic Outlook. Globalization. Opportunities and Challenges*, Washington, DC: International Monetary Fund, May.

IMF (1997b), *World Economic Outlook*, Washington, DC: International Monetary Fund, October.

IMF (1997c), *International Capital Markets. Developments, Prospects, and Key Policy Issues*, Washington, DC: International Monetary Fund, November.

Isimbabi, M.J. (1992), 'Comovements of world securities markets, international portfolio diversification, and asset returns: a survey of empirical evidence', in S.J. Khoury (ed.), *Recent Developments in International Banking and Finance*. Blackwell Publishers, Oxford, UK, Volume 6, pp. 115–46.

Jorion, P. (1985), 'International portfolio diversification with estimation risk', *Journal of Business*, **58** (3), July, 259–78.

Kennedy, M., A. Palerm, C. Pigott, and F. Terribile (1998), *Asset Prices and Monetary Policy*, OECD Economics Department Working Paper No. 188, Paris: OECD.

Levine, R. (1997), 'Financial development and economic growth', *Journal of Economic Literature*, **35** (2), June, 688–726.

Levine, R. and S. Zervos (1996), 'Stock market developments and long-run growth', *World Bank Economic Review*, **10** (2), May, 323–39.

Levy, H. and Z. Lerman (1988), 'The benefits of international diversification in bonds', *Financial Analysts Journal*, **44** (5), September–October, 56–64.

Levy, H. and M. Sarnat (1970), 'International diversification of investment portfolios', *American Economic Review*, **60** (4), September, 668–75.

Lewis, K.K. (1996), 'What can explain the apparent lack of international consumption risk-sharing?', *Journal of Political Economy*, **104** (2), April, 267-97.

Lewis, K.K. (1997), 'Are countries with official international restrictions liquidity constrained?', *European Economic Review*, **41** (6), 1079–109.

Lewis, K.K. (1998), *International Home Bias in International Finance and Business Cycles*, NBER Working Paper No. 6351, Washington, DC: National Bureau for Economic Research.

Marston, R.C. (1995), *International Financial Integration: A Study of Interest Differentials Between the Major Industrial Countries*, Cambridge: Cambridge University Press.

Mussa, M. and M. Goldstein (1993), 'The integration of world capital markets', in *Changing Capital Markets: Implications for Monetary Policy*, Kansas City: Federal Reserve of Kansas City.

Obstfeld, M. (1995), 'International capital mobility in the 1990s', in P.B. Kenen (ed.), *Understanding Interdependence: The Macroeconomics of the Open Economy*, Princeton, NJ: Princeton University Press, pp. 201–61.

Obstfeld, M. and K. Rogoff (1996), *Foundations of International Macroeconomics*, Cambridge, MA: MIT Press.

Obstfeld, M. and A.M. Taylor (1997), *The Great Depression as a Watershed: International Capital Mobility over the Long Run*, NBER Working Paper No. 5960, Washington, DC: National Bureau for Economic Research.

OECD (1997a), 'Regulatory reform in the financial services industry: where have we been? Where are we going?, *Financial Market Trends*, **67**, June, 31–96.

OECD (1997b), 'New financial statistics', *Financial Market Trends*, **67**, June, 97–105.

OECD (1997c), *Institutional Investors: Statistical Yearbook 1997*, Paris: OECD.

Popper, H. (1993), 'Long-term covered interest parity: evidence from currency swaps', *Journal of International Money and Finance*, **12** (4), August, 439–48.

Rodrik, D. (1998), *Who Needs Capital-Account Convertibility?*, Essay in International Finance No. 207, Princeton University Press.

Rogoff, K. (1996), 'The purchasing power parity puzzle', *Journal of Economic Literature*, **34** (2), June, 647–68.

Shearlock, P. (1998), '1997 yields a bumper crop', *The Banker*, February, 20–3.

Takeda, M. and P. Turner (1992), *The Liberalisation of Japan's Financial Markets: Some Major Themes*, BIS Economic Papers No. 34, Basle: Bank for International Settlements.

Taylor, A.M. (1996), *International Capital Mobility in History: the Savings–Investment Relationship*, NBER Working Paper No. 5743, Washington, DC: National Bureau for Economic Research.

Tobin, J. (1978), 'A proposal for international monetary reform', *Eastern Economic Journal*, **4** (1), 153–9.

Turner, P. (1991), *Capital Flows in the 1980s: A Survey of Major Trends*, BIS Economic Papers No. 30, Basle: Bank for International Settlements.

ul Haq, M., I. Kaul, and I. Grunberg (eds) (1996), *The Tobin Tax: Coping with Financial Volatility*, New York: Oxford University Press.

Vamvakidis A. and R. Wacziarg (1998), *Developing Countries and the Feldstein-Horioka Puzzle*, IMF Working Paper No. 98/2, Washington, DC: International Monetary Fund.

World Bank (1997), *Private Capital Flows to Developing Countries: The Road to Financial Integration*, New York: Oxford University Press.

3 Globalisation, Competitiveness, Unemployment and Social Protection Co-ordination

Glenn Rayp[*]

INTRODUCTION

In 1985, when Jacques Delors became chairman of the EC Commission and began his ambitious project of European market unification, he immediately and simultaneously took new initiatives in the field of European social policy and protection. Together with the complete liberalisation of the European market, the EC Commission wanted to provide a warranted minimal social protection at the European level and to safeguard some as basic considered social rights by extending their application to the whole Community.

What were the origins of this concept of a Community-wide harmonised set of warranted minimal provisions? Modesty is one possibility, following the experience with Community social policy in the 1970s, when too ambitious plans like the Social Action Programme inevitably ended in deception about the achievements. But the EC Commission motivated its concept of a harmonised basic social protection in a different way. In its absence one might have:

> Member-States, firms which attempt to obtain an advantage over their competitors at the expense of what must be called social decline. (Commissie van de Europese Gemeenschappen, 1985, p.12)

In other words, the Commission feared that the unification of the Common Market and the removal of the last barriers to a fully free circulation of commodities, services and production factors might result in a worsening of social labour conditions. Harmonisation of social provisions had primarily to prevent or to anticipate a levelling, if not a general downward movement, of social protection: the so-called 'social dumping'. Delors was quite specific on this point at the discussion of the Social Charter in the European Parliament:

What is it about? On the one hand to avoid social dumping, on the other hand to prevent the dismantling of fundamental rights, which are explicitly set out in the Social Charter. We have two important reasons to intervene actively in this field. Not only the aim of social progress at the level of the Community, but also, and this is for you [the Parliament] of great importance, the rejection of unfair competition by reverting to practices which must be considered as social dumping. (Commissie van de Europese Gemeenschappen, 1985, p.12)

Both passages point out that, apparently, the Commission took seriously the (increased) possibility to conduct a 'beggar-thy-neighbour' policy by means of income or social security measures in a unified market or a monetary union. These social security measures would be very appealing, as other instruments of economic policy such as trade or monetary policy, are severely restricted and the relevance of income policy is increased. Moreover, the potential benefits (at member state level) of this policy could be more important precisely because of market unification, if competition and price elasticity of demand increased. As has been repeatedly mentioned, all members of an economically unified area would have an unambiguous incentive to behave strategically by means of the appropriate income or social policy. Either one may improve its competitiveness if other countries refrain from a similar policy, or one prevents a deterioration of its relative position in case they try to improve their competitiveness. In accordance with the classical 'prisoner's dilemma', this would result in a situation where competitiveness remained more or less unchanged, but where wages and social protection would be lower than in the case of co-operative behaviour.

What's the link with the globalisation question? The consequences of increased world trade with (and investment in) low-wage emerging economies are mostly understood within a standard Heckscher–Ohlin–Samuelson (HOS) framework, along the lines of the Stolper–Samuelson theorem. If trade with low-skilled labour-abundant countries is made easier, then this would cause a fall in the relative price of low-skilled labour-intensive products and, because of the (Jones) magnification effect, a more than proportional decline in the relative reward of unskilled labour. Krugman (1995) spells out the consequences in employment terms for unskilled workers in an economy where wages are rigid, which is more in line with European labour market characteristics than the perfect competitive HOS–framework. However, at present, the evidence supporting a substantial effect of globalisation through international trade with unskilled-labour abundant countries is, at least, not overwhelming.[1] Hence, either globalisation, as understood here, has had no influence on increased inequality and shifts in employment opportunities according to skill level (giving way to the skill biased technological change hypothesis) or the (adverse) effects of globalisation on wages and employment work in another way, not necessarily connected with increased trade possibilities with low-skilled labour abundant emerging economies. It is the latter that we want to stress here, by showing how and in what conditions social protection levels may be suboptimally low in an economic and monetary union, purely because of competition between member states, that is, even without shifts in the bargaining power of trade unions and employers.

Was the EC Commission right when it feared these kinds of negative consequences from the completion of the European construction? In this chapter, we try to deal with this question taking account of imperfect competition in the commodity and the factor markets (more especially the labour market) as reported by Driffill and Van der Ploeg (1995) and Huizinga (1993). However, we will not consider employment or wage effects from the transition to an economic union or the trade policy consequences of labour market imperfections, as shown by, for example, Brander and Spencer (1988) and Mezzetti and Dinopoulos (1991). Instead, we will concentrate on the equilibrium outcomes of the economic (and monetary) union as such (Abraham, 1993,1994, Lejour, 1995 and Lejour and Verbon, 1996). Our approach to the social security policy is close to Alesina and Perotti (1994), but here social benefits are considered as a government strategic variable. This allows us to analyse the dynamics of social security policy at home and abroad as fiscal policy (see Andersen and Sørensen, 1995, Andersen *et al.*, 1996, and Sørensen, 1996).

However, this might not be sufficient to spell out the whole issue. Even if the concerns of the Commission were legitimate, then it still remains to be established if its policy option, that is, the imposition of a uniform basic social protection to the whole Community, was indeed the right one. Most observers agree that initiatives like the 'European Social Space', the Social Charter and the 'Social Addendum' to the Maastricht Treaty did not quite meet the same success as their economic and monetary counterparts. To a certain extent, this is readily explained by the attitude of the United Kingdom regarding social policy (at least until 1997), but not entirely. After all, the EC (EU) Commission anticipated in many cases British resistance to social policy and circumvented it by submitting propositions which only required a qualified majority to be approved. Though this still doesn't exhaust the obstruction possibilities of a single country, it yet implies that the sluggish approval of often merely symbolic measures could reckon on the discrete co-operation of other member states. Support for the British attitude from Ireland or Southern Europe would indeed seem logical when social policy is conceived as the safeguarding of some fundamental social rights and labour condition regulations. Precisely those countries would be obliged to *unilaterally* adjust of their social laws (provided that Community measures have an influence in practice) and would face a deterioration of their competitiveness with respect to the richer member states of the Community. In this perspective the absence of noteworthy institutional progress on social policy after the unilateral acceptance of the 'Social Addendum' to the Maastricht Treaty is not really a surprise.

Should this be explained as resistance due to short-sighted, narrow national interests against what is sound for the Community? Or is there perhaps something wrong with the concept of a uniform social protection level for the whole Union, in the sense that it is not the right answer for the social dumping problem? And if the latter is true, what should Delors have done instead? This question will be answered in the third section of the chapter, after presenting the elements of our argument in the second section. The fourth and final section concludes.

INTERNATIONAL TRADE WITH IMPERFECT COMMODITY AND FACTOR MARKETS

In this chapter, our purpose is not to elaborate the formal model on which our claims rest. We will confine ourselves to the spelling out of the assumptions made and the conclusions they allow us.[2] We would like to concentrate on the argument about how a failure of public policy co-ordination might explain a deterioration of social protection, as an alternative way along which economic integration or globalisation might (negatively) influence social security. Alleged negative consequences of market globalisation refer mainly to the Stolper–Samuelson theorem, or to the factor-price equalisation theorem in a Heckscher–Ohlin framework of perfect competition and constant returns to scale, as for example in Wood (1994). One may doubt to what extent this model is fully adequate to describe the economy of the highly developed industrial countries, or the overwhelming part of their international transactions. Hence, scepticism concerning the impact of globalisation along these lines is not uncommon (see, for example, Bhagwati and Dehejia, 1994, or Freeman, 1995), though the matter is at present not definitely empirically settled. Anyhow, this does not exclude other and perhaps more important ways for globalisation to exert a downward pressure on social and labour conditions. Our argument is precisely that policy responses to European integration, that is, economic and institutional developments within the Union, may in this respect not be lost from sight. These may have nothing to do with member states losing power or control over their economy, that is, with the inability of the states to carry out a certain policy,[3] but simply with conflicting national interests and rationality.

The commodity markets

We follow standard international trade theory in assuming a world consisting of just two countries with consumers having identical preferences, characterised by a 'love of variety'. The mere number of different goods of which consumers may dispose is assumed to be also important to them, besides the quantity of each product which they may consume. Hence, as difference counts, goods are only to a limited extent substitutable but not completely, that is, the fixed[4] n (home) + n* (foreign) goods that contribute to their utility are imperfect substitutes. These preferences may for instance be described by a Dixit–Stiglitz CES utility function:

$$u = \left[\sum_{i=1}^{n+n^*} c_i^{(\sigma-1)/\sigma} \right]^{\sigma/(\sigma-1)}$$

The substitution elasticity σ is identical for all goods, trade of which we assume to be unrestricted in a monetary union or under a system of fixed exchange rates. A price index P is associated with u:

$$P = \left[\sum_{i=1}^{n+n^*} p_i^{1-\sigma} \right]^{1/(1-\sigma)}$$

From the first-order conditions of utility maximisation, we obtain an expression of the demand for a commodity i of the individual consumer. Total demand for commodity x_i is then determined by aggregating over all consumers at home and abroad. Choosing a numeraire, like Grossman and Helpman (1991), that is, setting total nominal world expenditures equal to 1, total demand may be expressed as a (negative) function of its relative price and a (positive) function of total real world demand:

$$x_i\left[\frac{p_i}{P}, \frac{1}{P} \right]; \quad x_{i1} = \frac{\partial x_i}{\partial \frac{p_i}{P}} < 0; \quad x_{i2} > 0$$

Following , for example, Sørensen (1994), the supply side of the economy is kept as simple as possible. We assume the n (n*) commodities to be a same linear function of labour l (l*), which is the only input we consider. International differences in technology are allowed for by including a (fixed) sectoral identical but internationally distinct labour productivity (a, a*). Hence, we obtain as an expression for the production of the commodities:

$$x_i = a l_i \quad i = 1,...,n; \quad x_j^* = a^* l_j^* \quad j = n+1,...,n^*$$

Despite the constant returns to scale production function, we do assume increasing returns in production, as a consequence of some fixed cost f (f* abroad) for all commodities (for instance, a lump sum contribution from the firms to the redistribution policy of the government). Under Bertrand competition, one firm will monopolise the whole market for each individual commodity. If there are two firms in the market and marginal cost pricing is adopted, then no firm would be able to cover its fixed cost and they both would incur losses. This would force one of the firms to abandon the market, allowing the other firm to gain net profits. Because fixed costs cannot be recovered, market entry is not a credible threat.

Profit maximising prices will then be set at a fixed mark-up of unit labour costs, as a function of the 'perceived' elasticity of demand[5] (which is equal to σ):

$$p_i = \left(\frac{\sigma}{\sigma - 1} \right) \frac{w_i}{a}, \quad i = 1,...,n$$

An analogous expression applies for the commodities $j = n + 1,...,n^*$. In the presence of free and immediate diversification as long as the number of existing varieties is less than n (n*), we may exclude the possibility of firms attempting to take over a market for an individual commodity from a foreign supplier. As diversification is free, each firm can make more profits by supplying a new variety than from engaging in a price war and trying to take over the market for an existing variety. Or, when confronted with a new competitor, the supplier of an existing variety can decide to switch to the supply of a new variety, which will allow the same level of net profits as before. As long as the number of existing varieties is less than n (n*), it's not to the advantage of any firm to compete for the market in existing products. Hence, in addition to the absence of (permanent) entry of competitors of the same nationality, a firm has neither to fear entry from foreign competitors.

Next, the expression for the profit-maximising price of each individual variety is substituted in the price index, in the individual variety demand and in production. This allows us to write the quantity produced, the labour input it requires and the profits of the firm, as functions of the wages in the n + n* production sectors (equal to the number of commodity varieties because of sector monopoly). Hence, employment, production and profits just depend on home and foreign labour costs, negatively on the former and positively on the latter (at least in this specification). In this way, competitiveness (admittedly restricted to its traditional labour–cost dimension) may matter for national income and welfare. But before considering this, we have to specify how wages are determined.

The labour market

For given values of the technological and other parameters, the model is determined if we know the wage in each sector. Here we assume that workers organise in a trade union powerful enough to influence the outcome of the labour market and that wage and/or employment are settled by negotiation between firms and trade unions. Once agreement on this is reached, firms determine the profit-maximising price, from which the other variables follow.

The result obtained depends however on what one assumes to be the object of the negotiations and what one supposes the power or attitude of the parties to be. We opted for the commonly used 'monopoly trade union' approach, where the trade union unilaterally decides on the workers' wage and lets employment depend on employers' profit maximisation, which gives an inefficient, though plausible, outcome.[6]

We assume that all workers join one sectoral trade union, which gets the monopoly on labour supply and can prevent entry of workers from other sectors. In this way, we can exclude a too powerful central union, which would unite all workers and would fully interiorise the consequences of its attitude. Each sector is characterised by L_i workers, who either are employed and earn a wage w_i or are unemployed and get a social security allowance b. The social security system is, besides the mentioned lump sum contribution of the firms, financed with a wage contribution τ, which implies that each wage earner disposes of a net income $(1 - \tau)w_i$. Yet, the social security allowance is determined by the government and as such given for the trade union. τ follows for a given allowance from the balanced budget requirement of the social security system.

The sector trade union has as an objective the maximisation of its members' utility, given by:

$$l_i\, u_e + (L_i - l_i)\, u_u$$

that is, the number of employed members times their individual utility added to the equivalent for the unemployed members. After substituting the indirect utility function (with the price index and income as its arguments) for u, we may write the trade union's objective as:

$$\underset{w_i(1-\tau)}{\text{Max}}\ V_i = \underset{w_i(1-\tau)}{\text{Max}}\ l_i\, \frac{w_i(1-\tau)}{P} + (L_i - l_i)\frac{b}{P}$$

in view of the income obtained when employed or unemployed.

The trade union does not take into account the consequences of its behaviour on the general price index P, just as the monopoly firm did not when it set the profit-maximising price. This allows us, together with the exogenous kept number of commodity varieties produced with the same technology (which implies that the labour demand function in all sectors is identical), to neglect potential complications related to the degree of centralisation of the wage negotiations (Moene *et al.*, 1993, pp.75–6). Hence, from the union's objective we obtain as wage:

$$w_i = \frac{\sigma}{(\sigma - 1)} \frac{b}{(1 - \tau)}$$

The workers net wage is a fixed mark-up of the social security allowance (and alternative income source) b and does not vary with the level of the social security contribution, as in Holmlund *et al.* (1989). Social security taxation is entirely passed on to the gross wage and employment adjusts correspondingly. One may notice that the wages in all sectors are equal and, consequently, also the price of the (nationally produced) commodities, sector demand and production, and employment. In this way, sectors may be considered as perfectly symmetrical. The determination of the gross wage or labour cost requires in addition a value for the social security contribution rate τ, which is, as already mentioned, derived from the budget balance of the social security system. This is denoted as τ_b (respectively, $\tau^*{}_{b*}$), from which we assume on intuitive grounds:

$$\frac{\partial \tau_b}{\partial b} > 0; \qquad \frac{\partial \tau_b}{\partial b^*} \leq 0$$

An increase in the home social security allowance implies an increase in the contribution rate in order to keep the budget balanced. An increase in the social security allowance abroad (b*) implies a lower contribution rate, because of an increase in home competitiveness, and hence, a higher demand for home products and lower unemployment (as long as full employment has not been reached) for a given allowance.

THE ROLE OF THE GOVERNMENT AND THE SOCIAL SECURITY SYSTEM

The previous section showed that all the variables in our model are determined once the worker's wage is known. The latter is, in its turn, a function of the social security allowance, which belongs in the competence of the government. Hence, prices and commodities and labour demand ultimately depend upon the income and transfer policy of the government.

Yet, the government does not exert a sovereign influence on the economy, because the position of the country with respect to the rest of the world, that is, its *competitiveness*, has to be taken into account. This is represented by the relative price of the commodities: all (national) variables are influenced by the price level of the foreign commodities through P, the price index of all supplied commodities. As the price of the foreign goods depends, for a given technology, (in part) on the foreign wage, then all variables will be determined, after the necessary substitutions, by the social security allowances b and b* and, hence, by the government income policy at home and abroad.

The outcome of the government's policy is thus conditioned by the strength of foreign policy. Competitiveness requirements create a mutual cross-border dependency, which may constitute a potential motive for international policy co-ordination. If governments exploit national competitiveness in optimising their objective and use incomes policy in an attempt to take a strategic position with respect to the rest of the world, then the unco-ordinated result will not necessarily be optimal, especially in terms of social protection. Because of the country's competitiveness, each government has an interest in as high as possible a foreign social security allowance in terms of the home allowance and this could induce a general downward movement of social protection, to lower levels than otherwise preferred.

To show how this may be possible, let's start from benevolent governments, which intend to attain the highest possible utility for national economic subjects. Using the indirect utility function, we can write utility as a function of income and the price level. Aggregating over all individuals, assumed to be L + n in number, of which (n * l) are employed as workers, n run a firm and L − (n * l) are unemployed, gives us the following expression for total national utility:

$$\frac{\left[n l w (1 - \tau_b) + n \pi + (L - n l) b \right]}{P}$$

Inserting the budgetary equilibrium constraint of the social security system:

$$\left(L - n l \right) b = n f + \tau_b n l w$$

and the previously derived expressions for wages and profits, written in terms of the social security allowances b and b*, total national utility may be simplified as:

$$\gamma\!\Big/\!P$$

with

$$\gamma = \frac{n\left(\dfrac{b}{a}(1-\tau_b)\right)^{(1-\sigma)}}{\left[n\left(\dfrac{b}{a}(1-\tau_b)\right)^{(1-\sigma)} + n*\left(\dfrac{b*}{a*}(1-\tau_{b*}^{*})\right)^{(1-\sigma)}\right]} \qquad 7.$$

However, together with the national utility level, we assign to the governments an explicit income distribution objective. Either they take *sufficiently* into account the consequences of their policy on income distribution (in which case we define the country and its government as 'socially oriented') or they do not, for example, by disregarding all income distribution consequences when attempting to reach the highest possible utility (and income) level. Hence, we include the variance of income, scaled by total population (that is, the sum of squared differences from mean income) in the social welfare function with a weight α, which indicates the relative importance of income dispersion to the income level. In the first case, α must be in absolute terms (sufficiently) greater than 0, in the latter case α is 0 or close to it. We will only consider situations in which governments are either socially oriented or indifferent with respect to income distribution consequences. Situations where governments attach positive value to increased income inequality seem rather difficult to reconcile with the concept of a benevolent government and are not taken into consideration. Hence, we impose $\alpha \leq 0$.

Finally, we have to take account of the government's anticipations of foreign policy reactions. We start with unco-ordinated government policies, where governments determine independently their policy from a 'nationalistic' point of view, that is, considering the foreign consequences of its policy fully as externalities. Foreign policy is taken as fixed and given and no revision of it in the function of its own policy (the determination of the social security allowance) is anticipated.

The government's objective may subsequently be written as:

$$\text{Max}_{b}\ SW\ =\ \text{Max}_{b}\ \big((n+L)\big(\mu + \alpha\sigma_\mu^2\big)\big),\ \ \alpha \leq 0$$

with

$$\mu = \gamma\!\Big/\!(n+L)P$$

and

$$\sigma_\mu^2 = \frac{1}{(n+L)}\left[n\,l\left(\frac{w(1-\tau_b)}{P}\right)^2 + n\left(\frac{\pi}{P}\right)^2 + (L-n\,l)\left(\frac{b}{P}\right)^2 - \frac{1}{(n+L)}\left(\frac{y}{P}\right)^2 \right]$$

Labour and profits are in this specification monotonously declining functions of the social security allowance, that is: $\partial l/\partial b < 0$; $\partial \pi/\partial b < 0$.

This implies that a lower and an upper bound for b can be determined for which the social welfare function is defined. The lowest possible social security allowance is b_{FE}, at which full employment is reached. The value of the social security benefit at which profits become negative constitutes the upper limit. If b falls below the level compatible with full employment, then production capacity is exhausted and the demand for labour exceeds supply. The model specification is too parsimonious to consider the consequences of the latter in this context. On the other hand, if b rises to a level at which the required contribution rate turns profits into negative values, then the incentive for production vanishes, the total population becomes unemployed and national income falls to 0.

In any case a high employment level requires a low social security allowance and consequently weak protection of the unemployed. However, the allowance which maximises employment is not necessarily equal to the one which satisfies the first-order condition of the social welfare function. This is given by:

$$\partial SW/\partial b = 0 \quad \Leftrightarrow \quad \left[\frac{\partial(n+L)\mu}{\partial b} + \alpha\left(\frac{\partial(n+L)\sigma_\mu^2}{\partial b}\right) \right] = 0$$

where we can show that :

$$\frac{\partial(n+L)\mu}{\partial b} < 0 ; \qquad \frac{\partial(n+L)\sigma_\mu^2}{\partial b} < 0$$

Governments face a trade-off between income level and distribution: an increase in average (and total) income is obtained at the price of a higher income inequality. This may be considered as intuitively appealing or at least acceptable. Moreover, it can also be shown that:

$$\frac{\partial(n+L)\mu}{\partial b^*} > 0 ; \qquad \frac{\partial(n+L)\sigma_\mu^2}{\partial b^*} > 0$$

From the latter condition, we impose a lower limit on α, in addition to its upper bound of 0 already mentioned, that is: $\partial SW/\partial b^* < 0$.

Higher foreign social protection will exert a positive influence on the home (average) income level through the improvement in competitiveness and the increase of profits. On the other hand income inequality increases, which has a countervailing influence on social welfare. For the global effect of an increase in b* on home social welfare to be positive, the first partial effect must dominate the latter. This implies that the relative weight of income distribution concerns may not be so high that countries prefer a worsening of their competitiveness in order to increase their national welfare.

We could have let the exact value of α and, more generally, the question of whether it matters if a country is sensitive to income distribution, depend on a political decision process, by making it, for example, a function of the properties of the median voter, as in Gabscewicz and van Ypersele (1995). However, for our purposes here, it seems sufficient to assume without any further specification that α merely belongs to the specified range, as in Alesina and Rodrik (1991) (but in a dynamic and national context). Hence, we discuss the first-order condition of social welfare from the point of view of the 'qualitatively different' values α can take.

If α is equal or 'sufficiently' close to 0 and the government is (more or less) indifferent to income distribution concerns, then the first-order condition reduces to:

$$\partial SW \Big/ \partial b = \partial (n+L)\mu \Big/ \partial b < 0 \,.$$

An interior solution for the maximisation problem does not exist in this situation. If the government is indifferent to the income distribution consequences of its policy, it will opt for an allowance as low as possible, corresponding to the full employment social security allowance b_{FE}. This choice does not depend on the policy of the foreign government, as the first derivative is negative for all possible values of b*. Consequently, the reaction curve of the government may be represented by a vertical straight line through b_{FE}. Whatever the foreign government does, when only the maximisation of national social welfare counts and income distribution does not matter 'enough', then the lowest home allowance will be chosen. This does not mean that the government would be insensitive to social policy abroad. In fact, the higher the foreign social security allowance, the higher is national social welfare (as can be seen from the sign of the first derivative of national social welfare to the allowance abroad). Figure 3.1 illustrates this. SW is depicted as a function of b for different values of b* and is seen to be monotonically declining in b, in accordance with the negative first derivative for the whole (valid) range of b. An increase in b* however causes SW to shift upwards, just as a lowering of b* results in the opposite. Hence, SW reaches its maximum in b_{FE} for all values of b*.

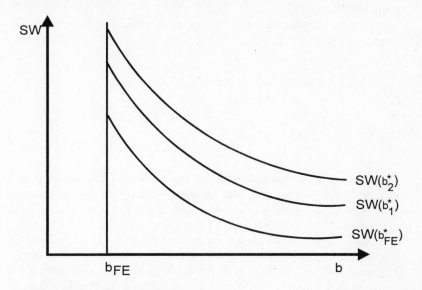

Figure 3.1 Social welfare when $\alpha = 0$

If the same policy is followed abroad, because economic subjects (or at least their government) are equally indifferent to income distribution when optimising the social security allowance, then the international equilibrium will be (b_{FE}, b*$_{FE}$). Maximal social welfare at home and abroad will coincide with a global minimum social protection but also full employment. In this case, we get for employment nl = L (n*l* = L*), from which we derive, inserting the expression for l (l*):

$$\frac{w}{w^*} = \left(\frac{L^* n}{Ln^*}\right)^{\frac{1}{\sigma}} \left(\frac{a}{a^*}\right)^{\frac{(\sigma-1)}{\sigma}}.$$

Relative wages are proportional to the relative degree of diversification and relative labour productivity, but are inversely related to total labour supply.

A minimum social protection maximises in the given circumstances the utility of the economic subjects in both countries for a given foreign policy, but is this really the best governments can do? Because national social welfare is increasing with foreign social protection (which is constrained by the home social allowance through competitiveness requirements, however), would a country not gain from a policy which permits the foreign country to increase its protection?[8]   And, if this occurs, would the foreign country equally benefit from it?

Suppose the government takes a co-operative position and interiorises the consequences abroad of its policy. Its objective, with α, $\alpha^* = 0$, will then be:

$$\operatorname*{Max}_{b}\left(SW+SW^*\right)= \operatorname*{Max}_{b}\left(\frac{\gamma}{P}+\frac{\gamma^*}{P}\right)= \operatorname*{Max}_{b}\frac{1}{P}$$

$$\text{as } \gamma^* = (1-\gamma).$$

However, with all assumptions made until now, $\partial P/\partial b$ is greater than 0 and hence the first-order condition for maximisation will lead to the same corner solution as in the case of unco-ordinated social policy. The Nash strategy under these conditions is also Pareto optimal. Economic integration is then basically neutral for the income and transfer policy of the government with the given preference (or power) structure, that is, when income distribution matters are kept out of consideration when determining the optimal policy. Policy co-ordination or international agreements have no significance: governments choose anyhow for minimal social protection and full employment, and economic integration does not interfere with this. We may also provide an intuitive ground for this conclusion. Any constraint of economic integration on social protection through competitiveness will take the form of an upper bound on social allowance, which will not be effective considering the orientation of the countries and economic integration will have no consequences for government social policy.

However, this pattern changes substantially when we assume α 'sufficiently' smaller than 0. Because $\alpha = 0$ constitutes a sufficient condition for a corner solution of the first-order conditions for the maximisation of social welfare and for minimal social benefits (and full employment), $\alpha < 0$ is a necessary condition for an interior solution. Let's assume that α and α^* are sufficiently smaller than 0 (still remaining within the boundaries we imposed), such that the first-order condition for maximal social welfare at home and abroad have an interior solution, i.e. $\partial SW/\partial b = 0$. Social security benefits will then be superior to their minimal value, that is, b_{FE}, which is compatible with full employment. Equity concerns drive the government to accept a price in economic efficiency and to forsake realising full employment at any (distribution) cost. We can associate this position for instance with the present policy in the majority of EU countries, who keep their distance from the 'American' or 'Anglo-Saxon' option of letting wages fluctuate freely in order to achieve full employment, even if the latter implies severe reductions of social protection. This seems closer to behaviour represented by $\alpha = 0$.

From an interior solution of the maximisation problem it will also follow that the optimal social security benefit under independent government policies will be lower than the allowance under policy co-ordination. In the latter situation the government internalises all the consequences of its policy and considers the maximisation of common or global welfare (SW + SW*) as its objective. If we look at the orientation of this function in the Nash equilibrium point (that is, the unco-ordinated equilibrium) indicated by (b_{NA}, b^*_{NA}), then we obtain:

$$\left(\frac{\partial SW(b_{NA}, b^*_{NA})}{\partial b} + \frac{\partial SW^*(b_{NA}, b^*_{NA})}{\partial b} \right) = 0 + \left(\frac{\partial SW^*(b_{NA}, b^*_{NA})}{\partial b} \right) \geq 0$$

as social welfare increases in the social security allowance abroad. A similar result applies for b* along the same lines. In other words, the global welfare function is increasing at (b_{NA}, b^*_{NA}). Hence, the optimum social policy under co-operation lies to right of that point and corresponds with higher allowances in all countries. An interior solution for the income and transfer policy of the government in a situation of independent policy determination is sufficient for the countries to choose higher social protection under co-operation.

One may also explain intuitively how the constraints of economic integration on income and transfer policy become binding when concerns for income distribution are important enough. Social security will be subject to downward pressure as each country tries to increase its welfare by improving its relative position and competitiveness with respect to foreign countries. Each country hopes to gain by keeping its wages and social benefits low for a given technological position. This results, however, in a situation where social protection and global welfare are lower in comparison with the situation where countries co-operate and refrain from attempts to improve their position at the expense of others. Yet, each country individually gets an incentive to the contrary, because a solitary 'stand still' on competitiveness would precisely allow other countries to improve their position and to increase their welfare. When countries are (sufficiently) concerned with the income distribution consequences of their policies, then economic integration may have the properties of a prisoners' dilemma.

The adequate policy of a group of countries in this situation would be to increase the social protection level collectively and in a co-ordinated way in *all* countries. This would improve global welfare yet lower employment, which might then be a consequence of economic integration when income policies are co-ordinated. We follow Abraham's (1993, 1994) reservations with respect to an international social policy, focusing on social minimum

improving its competitiveness at the expense of other countries, are in this situation inadequate or superfluous to most (to the extent that they are not effective).

In a strong asymmetric, if not antagonistic, situation, where preferences concerning equity and efficiency differ to the point that one country chooses minimal protection but the other does not, social minimum clauses may be appropriate. In this situation, the country which takes exclusively economic efficiency into consideration, benefits from a positive externality because of unilateral abstention from a minimal protection level in the other country and hence the lower competitiveness it accepts. Policy co-ordination is unable to modify the relative position of the countries to the benefit of the socially oriented country which does care about equity. To achieve this aim, social minimum clauses might well be suited.

NOTES

*   University of Ghent
1   See amongst others Freeman (1995), Burtless (1995), Deardorff and Hakura (1994), and Collins (1998).
2   Formal proofs are available from the author upon request.
3   Where one should be at least able to explain why, in the occurring situation, governments aren't able to form a coalition.
4   The assumption of an exogenous number of commodities is somewhat restrictive, not so much in regard of the persistence of an economic equilibrium with positive profits but more because of the static framework to which we are confined. Technological differences are taken account of, but not technological dynamics, nor economic growth. This shortcoming will have to be dealt with in a subsequent version of this chapter.
5   As explained in Helpman and Krugman (1985, p. 119) this is justified when n is considered as 'sufficiently' large.
6   The outcome is inefficient because unions and employers could bargain for higher employment and lower wages, which would increase profits and utility of the trade union members. However, employment would exceed the level determined by the labour demand schedule and employers would have a unilateral incentive to cheat (because it would allow them to make more profits). Hence, Pareto optimal bargains seem difficult to enforce.

The assumption of a trade union which unilaterally determines the wage is as such too strong. In reality, trade unions have to negotiate on wages with employers. Hence, the closest to observed practices is the so-called 'right to manage' approach (for example, Oswald, 1985 and Holmlund *et al.*, 1989) where it is indeed assumed that the employer unilaterally decides on employment, but bargains with the trade union over the wage. However, the results and implications of a 'monopolistic union' approach are qualitatively similar, so 'Ockhams razor' may be invoked to prefer the latter (see Oswald, 1985). Some care remains necessary though. The results of the two approaches correspond provided that, on the one hand, the distribution between the profits of the firm and the monopoly rent of the union, and employment on the other, depend only on the wage (Holmlund *et al.*, 1989, p. 20). Yet :

the Occam's razor argument for using monopoly union models, rather than Nash bargaining solutions, is valid when focusing on variables that influence wages via the union's outside income opportunities. (Holmlund *et al.*, 1989, p. 21).

This is precisely at stake here, as we consider the 'strategic use' of the social security allowance (in view of a nation's competitiveness), which constitutes for the trade union members the alternative, i.e. external, income opportunity for labour reward.
7   γ^* is defined in a similar way. Hence $\gamma + \gamma^* = 1$
8   This is easily seen in Figure 3.1.

REFERENCES

Abraham, F. (1993), 'The social dimension of an integrated Nordic economic area', in J. Fagerberg and L. Lundberg (eds), *European Integration: A Nordic Perspective*, Aldershot, Hants: Ashgate, pp. 313–31.

Abraham, F. (1994), 'Social protection and regional convergence in a European monetary union', *Open Economies Review*, **5** (1), 89–119.

Alesina, A. and R. Perotti (1994), *The Welfare State and Competitiveness*, NBER Working Paper Series 4810, Cambridge, Mass.: National Bureau for Economic Research.

Alesina, A. and D. Rodrik (1991), *Distributive Politics and Economic Growth*, NBER Working Paper Series 3668, Cambridge, Mass.: National Bureau for Economic Research.

Andersen, T. M. and J. R. Sørensen (1995), 'Unemployment and fiscal policy in an economic and monetary union', *European Journal of Political Economy*, **11** (1), March, 27–43.

Andersen, T. M., B. S. Rasmussen and J. R. Sørensen (1996), 'Optimal fiscal policy in open economies with labour market distortions', *Journal of Public Economics*, **63** (1), December, 103–17.

Bhagwati, J. and V. Dehejia (1994), 'Freer trade and wages of the unskilled – is Marx striking again?', in J. Bhagwati and M.H. Kosters, *Trade and Wages: Levelling Wages Down?*, Washington, D.C.: AEI Press, pp. 36–75.

Brander, J. and B.J. Spencer (1988), 'Unionized oligopoly and international trade policy', *Journal of International Economics*, **24** (3/4), May, 217–34.

Burtless, G. (1995), 'International trade and the rise in earnings inequality', *Journal of Economic Literature*, **33** (2), June, 800–16.

Collins, S. (ed.) (1998), *Imports, Exports and the American Worker*, Washington, DC: Brookings Institution Press.

Commissie van de Europese Gemeenschappen (1985), 'Verklaring over de beleidlijnen van de Commissie van de Europese Gemeenschappen', *Bulletin van de Europese Gemeenschappen*, Supplement 1/85, Luxemburg: Bureau voor de officiële publicaties der Europese Gemeenschappen.

Commissie van de Europese Gemeenschappen (1990), 'Werkprogramma van de Commissie voor 1990', *Bulletin van de Europese Gemeenschappen*, Supplement 1/1990, Luxemburg: Bureau voor de officiële publicaties der Europese Gemeenschappen.

Deardorff, A. and D. Hakura (1994), 'Trade and wages – what are the questions?', in J. Bhagwati and M.H. Kosters, *Trade and Wages: Levelling Wages Down?*, Washington, D.C.: AEI Press, pp. 76–96.

Driffill, J. and F. Van der Ploeg (1995), 'Trade liberalization with imperfect competition in goods and labour markets', *Scandinavian Journal of Economics*, **97** (2), June, 223–43.

Freeman, R. (1995), 'Are your wages set in Beijing?', *Journal of Economic Perspectives*, **9** (3), Summer, 15–32.

Gabscewicz, J. and T. van Ypersele (1995), 'Social protection and political competition', in GREQAM and ADRES, *Recent Developments in International Economics*, Conference Proceedings, International Greqam/Leqam Conference, Aix-en-Provence, 14–16 June.

Grossman, G. and E. Helpman (1991), *Innovation and Growth in the Global Economy*, Cambridge, Mass.: MIT–Press.

Helpman, E. and P.R. Krugman (1985), *Market Structure and Foreign Trade*, Brighton: Harvester Wheatsheaf.

Holmlund, B., K. Løfgren and L. Engstrøm (1989), *Trade Unions, Employment and Unemployment Duration*, Oxford: Clarendon Press.

Huizinga, H. (1993), 'International market integration and union wage bargaining', *Scandinavian Journal of Economics*, **95** (2), 249–55.

Krugman, P.R. (1995), 'Growing world trade: causes and consequences', *Brookings Papers on Economic Activity Microeconomics*, **1**, 327–62.

Lejour, A.M. (1995), *Social Insurance and the Completion of the Internal Market*, Center Paper 9561, Tilburg: Center for Economic Research.

Lejour, A.M. and H.A.A. Verbon (1996), 'Capital mobility, wage bargaining and social insurance policies in an economic union', *International Tax and Public Finance*, **3** (4), October, 495–514.

Mezzetti, C. and E. Dinopoulos (1991), 'Domestic unionization and import competition', *Journal of International Economics*, **31** (1), August, 79–100.

Moene, K.O., M. Wallerstein and M. Hoel (1993), 'Bargaining structure and economic performance', in R.J. Flanagan, K.O. Moene and M. Wallerstein (eds), *Trade Union Behaviour, Pay-Bargaining and Economic Performance*, Oxford: Clarendon Press, 65–154.

Oswald, A. (1985), 'The economic theory of trade unions', *Scandinavian Journal of Economics*, **87** (2), 160–93.

Pencavel, J. (1985), 'Wages and employment under trade unions: microeconomic models and macroeconomic applications', *Scandinavian Journal of Economics*, **87** (2), 197–225.

Sinn, H.W. (1994), *A Theory of the Welfare State*, NBER Working Paper Series 4856, Cambridge, Mass.: National Bureau for Economic Research.

Sørensen, J. R. (1994), 'Market integration and imperfect competition in labor and product markets', *Open Economies Review*, **5** (1), 115–30.

Sørensen, J. R. (1996), 'Coordination of fiscal policy among a subset of countries', *Scandinavian Journal of Economics*, **98** (1), March, 111–18.

Wood, A. (1994), *North–South Trade, Employment and Inequality: Changing Fortunes in a Skill-Driven World*, Oxford: Clarendon Press.

4 Reconstructing the Political in a Globalising World: States, Institutions, Actors and Governance

Philip G. Cerny[*]

Globalisation is usually presented as a primarily socio-economic phenomenon manifested in structural changes in the scope and scale of cultural change, global capital flows and the like. In this light, political variables are seen as dependent rather than independent. In contrast, this chapter surveys a range of political aspects of globalisation and argues that they involve independent factors promoting, accelerating and shaping globalisation in ways exogenous social and economic variables cannot. In effect, political variables are the key independent variable generating globalisation at the turn of the century. In other words, the range of multiple equilibria or alternative potential outcomes presented by those complex processes of internationalisation and transnationalisation which constitute globalisation[1] are very wide. How these processes will interact in path-dependent fashion is uncertain. In these conditions, political structuration is the primary independent and intervening variable driving and shaping the overall process. In particular, the capacity of political actors to act as *political and institutional entrepreneurs* is crucial to the way complex structures of governance, weaving together the new and the old, will be generated in the twenty-first century.

In the next section, globalisation is situated in the wider context of historical political change. The following section looks at a range of changes taking place in the underlying structure of the public/private goods equation and at how these changes are impacting on the patterns of constraints and opportunities faced by agents in the globalisation process. The fourth section evaluates processes of change occurring within the single most important institutionalised structure of the modern era – the transformation of the state from the national industrial welfare state to the competition state. The fifth section focuses on strategically situated actors who may have the potential to become institutional entrepreneurs in the political globalisation process – a stylised survey of the universe of

and through national states (Cerny, 1999c). And when political philosophers
have defined normative social and political values such as justice, civic virtue
and the public good, they have expected these to be embodied in better, fairer,
or more just states – a situation which is only just beginning to change on the
eve of the new millennium.

Externally, states have not been mere mutual antagonists in an unorganised
world. In the first place, relations between states took on a systematic character
because powerful forces within each state, starting in Europe, recognised their
potential mutual vulnerability in a hostile world. Through expanding diplomatic
relations and standards of behaviour, through a desire to be free from outside
interference and yet have access to the benefits of cosmopolitan culture and
foreign material goods, and through a competitive interdependence which
fostered both interstate rivalry and a common Western hegemony over the rest
of the world, European and later other elites secured their power as much
through international (interstate) relations as through domestic consolidation
(Kennedy, 1988, ch. 3). And they drew middle-class and later working-class
groups into these 'national culture societies' (Znaniecki, [1952] 1973) by
imposing national languages, taxation, military conscription, the development
of national markets and ultimately liberal democracy based in national political
institutions, all of which reinforced the capabilities of these evolving units to act
more effectively in their foreign relations too. Occasional wars, revolutions, and
the changing balance of power further entrenched the interstate character of the
international system, while at the same time allowing it to adjust to a fluctuating
and evolving range of social, political and economic pressures and structural
changes, both old and new.

Despite its long gestation and organisational durability, however, the modern
nation-state as we have known it represents only one particular kind of
governance structure among many possibilities. In the broad sweep of history,
of course, many kinds of societies and forms of political organisation have
existed in the world, from isolated village societies and more outward-looking
city-states, to traditional empires and looser leagues and confederations, as well
as to the more hierarchically structured states of the modern world.[2]
Furthermore, although most modern political philosophers since Machiavelli
have seen the future of the 'good society' to lie in national consolidation and
state institutionalisation, others such as Grotius and Kant have suggested that a
more internationalist, cosmopolitan world order might be possible. And finally
– like the cross-cutting and overlapping social bonds and authority relations of
the Middle Ages – a range of factors including ethnic and religious ties,
multiculturalism, transnational communities and the internationalisation of
production, consumption and finance have fostered the emergence of a vast
range of alternative sources of economic advantage, political influence and
social identity. Only in the Second Industrial Revolution did the modern nation-

state develop the range of socio-economic functions we are accustomed to seeing today, when mass production and modern industrial enterprises (Rupert, 1995; Chandler, 1990), the Weberian bureaucratic revolution in both public and private sectors, and mass politics brought together a range of structural elements conducive to the development of the industrial welfare state of the mid-twentieth century (Cerny, 1995).

Whereas these alternative orders have long been debated in theory and practice – after all, medieval Christendom itself represented a cosmopolitan order, and nationalist revolutions from below have often been about many things other than the nation-state *per se* – it is only when the state itself can no longer effectively carry out its dual institutional role as arena of collective action and source of credible commitments that such possibilities have any chance of being realised in practice. Of course, it is unlikely that states will become entirely redundant or disappear; after all, the nobility and the Church did not disappear when feudalism declined (Mayer, 1981). At worst they will be caught up in webs of power that limit or transform their activities by altering the context within which they exist and operate. Nevertheless, the prospect of significant transformation has been opened up in the second half of the twentieth century by 'globalisation'. Globalisation, I have argued, is not an end state. It is a process (or a complex set of processes) made up of the addition or cumulative results of denser relations among states ('internationalisation'), denser relations cutting across states ('transnationa-lisation'), and the interaction effects of the two with each other.

This transformation, I suggest, has three main interlocking dimensions. The first and most obvious dimension involves a change in the character of the state's domestic tasks, roles and activities. This basically involves the way so-called 'public goods' are perceived, pursued and provided (Cerny, 1999b). The notion of the 'public interest' as it was understood in the period of the 'high' modern nation-state, especially since the advent what Karl Polanyi (1944) called 'The Great Transformation', is undergoing dramatic changes. In particular, the aim of social justice through redistribution has been challenged and profoundly undermined by the marketisation of the state's economic activities (and of the state itself) and by a new embedded financial orthodoxy (Cerny, 1990, epilogue; Cerny, 1994a). These changes not only constrain the state in its economic policies (Cerny, 1996), but also alter people's understanding of what politics is for (Cerny, 1999a) and challenge the political effectiveness of the national liberal democratic political systems which are supposed to represent what the people want (Cerny, 1999c).

The second dimension involves a fundamental reorientation of how states interact economically with each other. Rather than perceiving the international tasks, roles and activities of the state as stemming from traditional 'inside/outside' concerns, state actors (politicians and bureaucrats) are increasingly concerned with promoting the competitive advantages of particular production and service sectors in a more open and integrated world economy (Cerny, 1999d). They do this not only in order to produce collective economic gains, but also to build new coalitions and expand the scope and reach of their power and influence. In pursuing international competitiveness, states – or, more to the point, a range of state agencies closely linked with those economic sectors most closely plugged into the world economy (Cerny, 1995) – accept and indeed embrace those complex interdependencies and transnational linkages thought to be the most promising sources of profitability and economic prosperity in a rapidly globalising world.

The final dimension concerns the relationship between structure and agency – in other words, people, the individuals and groups who actually bring these changes about, directly or indirectly, intentionally or unintentionally. This does not merely concern those global ideologists in business studies, important as they are, who declare that we live in a 'borderless world', nor just the rapid growth of transnational pressure and interest groups like Greenpeace who focus on the problems of 'the planet'. It also involves *strategic action* across both public and private domains not only for more concrete competitive advantages in the world market place but also for *reshaping social and political institutions* to reflect new distributions of power and resources ('distributional changes') and new ways of looking at the world ('social epistemologies').[3] In this process, for example, the focus of the economic mission of the state has shifted considerably from its traditional concern with production and producer groups to one involving market structures and consumer groups, and from its understanding of the state as a 'decommodifying agent' to one as a 'commodifying agent' (Cerny, 1990). Later in this chapter, I will focus on three alternative types of potential 'institutional entrepreneurs' – economic, political and social – and suggest the strengths and weaknesses of each given the current structural context in which they are acting.

These three dimensions, I suggest, add up to a profound challenge to the traditional structures both of the domestic nation-state and of the interstate system, undermining key aspects of the previously symbiotic relationship between the two. Thus we should not expect the nation-state to wither away; indeed, in some ways it will continue to expand and develop its tasks, roles and activities. The crucial point, however, is that those tasks, roles and activities will not just be different, but will lose much of the overarching, macro-political and philosophical character traditionally ascribed to the effective state, the good state or the just state, all of which concepts have assumed a level and quality of internal coherence and of difference from the external 'other' that the state's most essential – and most ideologically and culturally legitimate – task has been to protect. Future structural developments will be the product of an increasingly transnational, cross-cutting structure of micro- and meso-interdependencies, partially mediated through the state but with their own autonomous dynamics too. The state can attempt to manipulate and influence these but cannot fundamentally change them. In the long run, state actors must adapt their own strategies to *perceived* global realities, while other kinds of actors, economic and social, will play key roles too in restructuring the political arena (Cerny, 1999a).

PROBLEMATISING THE STATE: THE SHIFTING STRUCTURE OF PUBLIC GOODS

The power structure of a globalising world inevitably becomes increasingly complex and diffuse, diffracted through a prismatic structure of socio-economic forces and levels of governance[4] – from the global interaction of transnational social movements and interest/pressure groupings, multinational corporations, financial markets, and the like, on the one hand, to the re-emergence of subnational and cross-national ethnic, religious and policy-oriented coalitions and conflicts of the type familiar in domestic-level political sociology, on the other. World politics – that is, both domestic politics and international relations, taken together – is being transformed into a 'polycentric' or 'multinucleated' global political system operating within the same geographical space (and/or overlapping spaces) analogous to the emergence of coexisting and overlapping functional authorities in metropolitan areas (Ostrom *et al.*, 1961).

The underlying governance problematic in such multilayered and asymmetrical political systems is at least twofold: in the first place, it becomes harder to maintain the boundaries which are necessary for the efficient 'packaging' of public or collective goods; and in the second place, it becomes harder to determine what collective goods are demanded or required in the first place – that is, even to measure what is the 'preferred state of affairs' (ibid., pp. 832–5). State actors themselves – although they continue to have a range of significant economic, financial, political and bureaucratic resources at their disposal and are still crucial actors in regulating particular economic and social activities – paradoxically act in routine fashion to undermine the holistic and hierarchical character of traditional state sovereignty, authority or *potestas* (Cerny, 1999d) – a 'hollowing out of the state' (Jessop, 1997). The result is a growing 'privatisation of the public sphere', not only by selling off or contracting out public services and functions, but in the deeper sense of reducing society itself to competing 'associations of consumers' in which administrators are little more than buyers in competing corporations (Ostrom *et al.*, 1961, p. 839). The state shifts from being essentially a 'civil association' to an 'enterprise association' (Oakeshott, 1976; Auspitz, 1976; Cerny, 1995).

Now such privatisation, marketisation or commodification of the state is not something exclusive to globalisation; indeed, globalisation is often seen as just one of a number of wider 'exogenous factors' at work in transforming the nature of governance today, also including decentralisation, fiscal constraint, distrust of government, increasing participation (functional representation) by special interests, and the like (Peters, 1997). Yet the rediscovery of the role of states historically in promoting markets, and more recently the popularisation of such notions as 'competitive governments' (McKenzie and Lee, 1991), 'entrepreneurial government' (Osborne and Gaebler, 1992), or the 'competition state' (Cerny, 1990, ch. 8 and 1999d) – along with the emergence of the 'new institutional economics' and the development of the concept of governance in the theory of the firm (Williamson, 1975 and 1985) – have changed the terms of institutional discourse. The distinction between 'state' and 'market' has not simply blurred; the goalposts have changed too.

More than that, *both* state and economic institutions have been shown to consist of mixtures of hierarchical and market-like characteristics. In an era when markets, production structures and firms increasingly operate in the context of a cross-border division of labour, can the state any longer remain a structure apart? Today, public policy and management analysis is increasingly focusing on what has been called the 'post-modernist critique' of 'the existing public sector paradigm' (Prowse, 1992). Such concerns cut across democracy and deal directly with the potential for market-like behaviour in the state apparatus itself – the 'commodification' or 'marketisation' of the state *per se*, both in its endogenous structure and behaviour *and* in its mode of economic 'intervention'. They also cut across, as does Reich (1991) in the economic literature, the concept of the state as a *territorial* unit. Similarly, literature on neo-corporatism has shifted its ground from 'peak-level' tripartism – the original focus of pioneering writers like Schmitter (1974) – to the more diffuse sectoral and local corporatist forms known as 'meso-' and 'micro-corporatism' (Cawson, 1985; Cerny, 1990, ch. 6) or even to firm-level 'entrepreneurial corporatism' (which, according to Robert Cox, 1986, is the product of the transnationalisation of social forces). Phrases like 'public–private partnership', or the promotion of 'competitive advantage' (as distinct from comparative advantage: Zysman and Tyson, eds, 1983; Porter, 1990), have moved from the world of academic analysis into the rhetoric and programmes of politicians on both right and left.

This combination of structural trends, I suggest, involves a reassessment of the conception of public or collective goods in a globalising world. Collective goods are those from the enjoyment or use of which *insiders* cannot be excluded, requiring authoritative mechanisms for identifying and excluding *outsiders* (Olson, 1965; Ostrom *et al.*, 1961; Ostrom and Ostrom, 1977) – a classic task of hierarchical governments (states). Complex systems, in contrast, are characterised by 'overlapping memberships' and 'cross-cutting affiliations'

(Cerny, 1993). In the international/transnational/global context – whether we look at states and state actors, multinational corporations, interest groups, and/or individuals – their tasks, roles and activities cut across the different levels and structures discussed earlier. Without the state and its authoritative capacity to enforce the rules of the game, transnational complexity would seem to imply instability. Thus the key to understanding the shape of new and complex governance structures in the global era lies in the way economic competition is changing in the world. Many of what were thought to constitute collective goods at the time of the Second Industrial Revolution are either no longer controllable by the state because they have become transnational in structure and/or constitute private goods in a wider world market place.

In terms of etymology, political philosophy and everyday political language, the idea of what is public is essentially normative; it denotes matters that people think *ought* to be treated as common or collective concerns, as distinct from what ought to be left to individuals or private groups to decide and/or do for themselves. Today, the heart of political debate is about choosing among competing conceptions of what should be treated as public and what should not. In contrast, the economic theory of collective goods argues that only what is most *efficiently* organised and run publicly (that is, which provides the best possible product at the lowest possible cost when organised according to the definition set out below) ought to be so organised and run. In the economic theory of collective goods (for example, Olson, 1965), the main issue is *indivisibility*, on two levels: goods are truly 'public' when both the structure of production *and* the structure of consumption lead to conditions of indivisibility.

The first condition, concerning the structure of production, is referred to as 'jointness of supply'. This concerns the extent to which technological economies of scale in production plus the structure of transactions costs mean that large factories, long production runs, and so on, make collective provision through hierarchical management structures (usually seen in *political* terms as involving an existing governmental structure, that is, municipal, regional or national) more efficient than private or free-market provision – as is said to be the case with so-called 'natural monopolies'. In a globalising world, however, such calculations become more complex. In some industries, goods that once may have been most efficiently produced on a collective basis (especially on a national scale) may nowadays be more efficiently organised along lines which imply larger, *trans*national optimal economies of scale, making traditional 'public' provision unacceptably costly and uncompetitive; whereas in other cases, technological change and/or flexible production may actually *reduce* optimal economies of scale, turning such goods effectively into private goods, which also are increasingly produced and traded in a global rather than a national market place.

With regard to consumption, economists refer to the criterion of 'excludability'. Public goods are by definition 'non-excludable', which means that collective provision has to be organised in such a way as to prevent non-paying users (so-called 'free riders') from making the provision of the good too expensive for the rest – that is, such goods must be financed through forced payments (taxes). Again, in a globalising world it has become increasingly difficult to exclude non-paying users (free riders) from outside national boundaries from benefiting from nationally provided collective goods in ways that are unacceptably costly in terms of domestic politics and public policy. Thus with regard to both production and consumption, it is becoming more and more difficult to maintain the sort of public or collective boundaries necessary for efficient state provision of public or collective goods.

Different categories of collective goods have different kinds of normative and economic characteristics. I refer to four such categories: regulatory, productive, distributive and redistributive collective goods (adapting the categories developed by Lowi, 1964). Each of these categories has been transformed by the structural changes associated with globalisation and the other economic and political trends that are inextricably intertwined with globalisation. For example, the Third Industrial Revolution has profoundly altered the conditions of supply of all types of goods – public, private and mixed (goods with mixed characteristics are referred to by various labels such as club, toll, common-pool, and so on) – through differentiation and flexibilisation within production processes, 'lean' management structures, and the segmentation of markets, while the globalisation of finance has increasingly divorced financial capital from the state. In this context, political control, stabilisation, regulation, promotion, and facilitation of economic activities have become increasingly fragmented.

The first category, regulatory collective goods, involves the establishment of a workable economic framework for the ongoing operation of the system as a whole, involving the establishment and application of rules for the operation – and interaction – of both market and non-market transactions and institutions. Typical regulatory goods include establishment and protection of private (and public) property rights, a stable currency system, abolition of internal barriers to production and exchange within the national market, standardisation of a range of facilitating structures such as a system of weights and measures, a legal system to sanction and enforce contracts and to adjudicate disputes, a regulatory system to stabilise and co-ordinate economic activities, a system of trade protection, and various facilities which can be mobilised to counteract system-threatening market failures (such as 'lender of last resort' facilities, emergency powers, and so on). Real or potential inefficiencies in the provision of regulatory collective goods can have exceptionally wide ramifications, because their provision in and of itself can be said constitute a sort of 'collective collective good' given the role of regulation as a framework within which not only other collective goods, but also *private* goods, are produced and supplied. Regulatory collective goods, therefore, are inextricably intertwined with the very foundations of the capitalist state.

In a world of relatively open trade, financial deregulation and the increasing impact of information technology, however, property rights and other basic rules are increasingly complex for states to establish and maintain. For example, cross-border industrial espionage, counterfeiting of products, copyright violations and the like made the multilateral protection of intellectual property rights a focal point of international disputes and a controversial cornerstone of the Uruguay Round negotiations. Furthermore, international capital flows, the proliferation of offshore financial centres and tax havens, and so on, have made the ownership of firms and their ability to allocate resources internally through transfer pricing and the like increasingly opaque to national tax and regulatory authorities. Traditional forms of trade protectionism are both easily bypassed and counterproductive. Currency exchange rates and interest rates are set in rapidly globalising market places, and governments attempt to manipulate them often at their peril. Legal rules are increasingly evaded, 'soft law' becomes more and more important, and attempts to extend the legal reach of the national state through the development of extraterritoriality are generally ineffective and hotly disputed. In this context, the ability of firms, market actors and competing parts of the national state apparatus itself to defend and expand their economic and political turf through activities such as transnational policy networking and regulatory arbitrage has both undermined the control span of the state from without and fragmented it from within.

The second and third categories of collective goods involve various specific directly or indirectly state-controlled or state-sponsored activities of production and distribution – *productive* collective goods on the one hand, and *distributive* collective goods on the other. Although these two categories often overlap, and I have previously treated them as a single category (Cerny, 1995), the differences between them can be quite significant, as can be seen in recent theories of public policy, the 'new public management', and 'reinventing government' (see Ostrom *et al.*, 1961, for an early example of this argument) – which are themselves closely linked with discourses of globalisation. In line with the economic definition of public goods set out above, the concept of productive collective goods refers to the production of goods and services, whereas distributive collective goods involve the delivery of those goods and services.

With regard to productive collective goods, the validity of public ownership of politically, economically or militarily 'strategic' industries, along with the establishment and maintenance of state monopolies in a range of public services, has usually been seen to derive from economies of scale and transactions cost savings in their production (although normative considerations have also played a major political role for both nationalists and socialists). However, the interaction of the advent of flexible manufacturing systems and competing low-cost sources of supply – especially from firms operating multinationally – has been particularly important in undermining state-owned and parapublic firms, for example in the crisis of public ownership and the wave of privatisation of the 1980s and 1990s. Competitiveness counts for far more than maintaining an autonomous, self-sufficient national economy. Third World countries too have increasingly rejected import substitution industrialisation and embraced export promotion industrialisation – thereby imbricating their economies even more closely into the global economic order (Harris, 1986; Haggard, 1990). The same can be said for more traditional forms of industrial policy, such as state subsidies to industry, public procurement of nationally produced goods and services, or trade protectionism. Even social liberal[5] economists nowadays regard the battle to retain the idea of the 'national economy' as lost, and see states as condemned to tinkering around the edges (Reich, 1991).

With regard to distributive collective goods, we are talking about the supply or provision of products and services to the public (or to different publics) on a collective basis, whether produced in the private sector or in the public sector. In contrast to productive collective goods, distributive collective goods are characterised less by their technical indivisibility – economies of scale and transactions cost economies deriving from 'hard' production systems – and more by potential 'soft' scale and transactions cost economies deriving from their management structures, on the one hand, and from the collective characteristics of their consumers rather than their producers, on the other. In recent years, policy-oriented economists have come to consider a much larger range of such goods as being appropriate for market or quasi-market provision. This changing perspective has resulted both from a revaluation, on the one hand, of the nature of demand – the belief that 'publics' are essentially collections of self-regarding consumers rather than embedded in like-minded or homogeneous social collectivities such as 'workers' – and, on the other, from a belief that public sector hierarchies are inherently costly and cumbersome superstructures. In this sense, many of those basic public services and functions such as the provision of public health, education, garbage collection, police protection, certain kinds of transport or energy infrastructure, and so on, which have been at the bureaucratic heart of the modern industrial welfare state, are being disaggregated and commodified in a range of experimental ways (Dunleavy, 1994; Osborne and Gaebler, 1992).

In this sense, distributive collective goods increasingly overlap with the fourth category, redistributive collective goods – the nature of which has always been seen to be even more fundamentally political, with their public and collective character deriving typically from political decisions about justice and fairness rather than from the economic efficiency (or inefficiency) of those public allocation mechanisms which they engender. Many of these goods are 'collective' or 'public' goods only because political decisions have been made (whether or not in response to public demand) to *treat them* as public for reasons of justice, equity or other normative considerations. Redistributive goods have included health and welfare services, education, employment policies, unemployment insurance and other benefits, systems for corporatist bargaining, environmental protection, and the like – indeed, the main apparatus of the national industrial/welfare state. Today, the provision of redistributive collective goods is changing dramatically. Corporatist bargaining and employment policies are under challenge everywhere in the face of international pressures for wage restraint and flexible working practices. Although developed states have generally not found it possible to reduce the overall weight of the welfare state significantly as a proportion of GDP, long-term structural growth in such expenditures has been checked and there has been a significant transformation in the balance of how welfare funds are spent – from the maintenance of free-standing social and public services to the provision of unemployment compensation and other 'entitlement' programmes, and from maintaining public bureaucracies to devolving and privatising their delivery (Clayton and Pontusson, 1998). And the most salient new sector of redistributive public goods, environmental protection, is particularly transnational in character; pollution and the rape of natural resources do not respect borders.

The outer limits of effective action by the state in the changing collective goods context are usually seen in its relative capacity to promote a favourable investment climate for transnational capital by providing a circumscribed range of public goods or specific assets, described as 'immobile factors of capital'.[6] These include: 'human capital' (the skills, experience, education and training of the work force); infrastructure (from public transportation to high-tech 'information highways'); support for new technology; provision of the basic public services necessary for a good 'quality of life' for new elites and middle managers; and the maintenance of a public policy environment favourable to investment and profit-making by potentially 'footloose' companies (whether domestic or foreign-owned) (Reich, 1991). Particularly central to this transformation, of course, has been the changing technological and institutional context in which *all* goods are increasingly being produced and exchanged – especially the rise of 'post-Fordism', characterised by a wider process of industrial 'flexibilisation' (see Amin, ed., 1994). At the heart of flexibilisation in both production processes and the structures of firms themselves has been the explosive development of information technology. This expanded monitoring capability leaps national borders and brings firms, markets and consumers into a single, global production process in an increasing number of sectors. In addition, as the trade and production structures of the Third Industrial

Revolution evolve, they will be increasingly co-ordinated through the application of complex financial controls, rapidly evolving accounting techniques, financial performance indicators and the like in both public and private sectors.

But these aspects of the Third Industrial Revolution – flexibilisation of production, firm structure, and monitoring – only represent the supply side of the equation. The demand side involves the development of ever more complex consumer societies and the resulting *segmentation of markets*. The technological capacity to produce flexibly – the ability of business to produce at the appropriate scale – has combined with an increasing differentiation of the class system in advanced capitalist societies. Much of the Long Boom grew out of burgeoning first-time markets for such products as cars, so-called 'white goods' (refrigerators, washing machines, and so on), or television sets. Customers coming back a subsequent time looking to buy new models, however, have demanded higher specifications and greater choice. Differentiating demand and flexible supply, then, converged on market segmentation – producing a wider range of variations on a particular product or set of product, with each variation targeted on a particular sub-set of consumers. This process has also created consumer demand for foreign-produced goods and has forced firms to internationalise. These pressures now apply to the provision of public goods by governments as well, with 'choice' replacing standardised collective provision – and with consumers increasingly replacing producers as the key interest groups.

Thus the overarching, inclusive, multitasking, 'civil association' character of politics and governance – the core of the modern nation-state – is under increasing pressure from both above and below, from new transnational economies of scale and from the disaggregation of national culture societies and political 'publics' at home and abroad. Governance in the future will no longer look so much like 'government'. Structures and processes of governance must adjust to this multilayered and asymmetric reality, although the precise form it will take will only emerge historically, in path-dependent fashion. In this context, the discourse of globalisation – still torn between the simplistic jargon of business management, on the one hand, and the limited political terrain of the competition state and fragmented international regimes, on the other – is still in the process of evolution and very much up for grabs.

THE STATE IN THE INTERNATIONAL ARENA: ERODING THE 'INSIDE/OUTSIDE' DISTINCTION

The crisis of the national industrial welfare state lay in its decreasing capacity to insulate national economies from the global economy – and from the combination of stagnation and inflation which resulted when they did try to do so. Today, rather than attempt to take certain economic activities *out* of the market – to 'decommodify' them as the welfare state was organised to do – the competition state has pursued *increased* marketisation in order to make economic activities located within the national territory, or which otherwise contribute to national wealth, more competitive in international and transnational terms. Despite the vulnerability of the welfare state model, however, national policymakers have a range of potential responses, old and new, with which to work. The challenge of today's 'competition state' is one of getting the state to do both *more* and *less* at the same time. Getting more for less has been the core concept, for example, of the 'reinventing government' movement which is a major manifestation and dimension of the competition state approach (Osborne and Gaebler, 1992). The competition state involves both a transformation of the policy roles of the state and a multiplication of specific responses to change. In terms of policy transformation, several levels of government activity are affected.

The essence of these changes lies in the differential capacity of the state to promote distinct types of economic development, usually called 'extensive' and 'intensive' development. On the one hand, strong state intervention in the past – whether Soviet-style planning, import-substitution industrialisation (ISI) in the post-independence Third World (that is, creating domestic industries which would replace imports in internal markets behind protectionist barriers), or the fashion in the mid-to-late twentieth century for the so-called 'developmental state' based on export promotion industrialisation (EPI), especially in Asia (Harris, 1986; Haggard, 1990) – has actually been extremely effective at times at promoting extensive development. Extensive development means finding and bringing in new *exogenous* resources and factors of capital (land, labour, physical capital like factories and infrastructure, and financial capital) to undeveloped economies. Governments can help undermine feudal and peasant structures and use taxes, spending, regulation – and physical force – to channel investment, raw materials, labour, and so on, away from non- or pre-industrial uses into capitalist industry and finance. That's how Germany developed at the end of the nineteenth century – what Barrington Moore (1991) called the 'modernisation revolution from above'. But the potential drawbacks are obviously similar to those usually associated with ISI, in Latin America in particular – an emphasis on producing costly and increasingly technologically outdated goods which are already produced more cheaply elsewhere, featherbedding of labour and management, corruption and overbureaucratisation, leading to a vicious circle of inefficiency, hyperinflation, and often state authoritarianism to keep the system going (Kemp, 1983).

On the other hand, state intervention is notably poor at promoting intensive development. Intensive development occurs mainly after extensive development (although they can occur simultaneously) and means improving the *endogenous* efficiency of production, investment and market structures and processes. As Adam Smith wrote, 'to improve land, like all other commercial projects, requires exact attention to small savings and small gains'. This involves continually improving the microeconomic efficiency, competitiveness and profitability of industry – even to the extent of regularly engaging in what Joseph Schumpeter (1939) called 'creative destruction' of old capital and technology to make way for the latest cutting-edge production, financing and marketing methods. It means giving individual owners, managers and workers market-based incentives to involve themselves in a day-to-day process of improvement of the competitiveness of the firm, rather than acting parasitically or free-riding (as in the Soviet Union, for example). The developmental state, then, like Stalinist Russia and the authoritarian bureaucracies of ISI, worked for a while, but could not adjust to the requirements of intensive development, as demonstrated in the Asian financial crisis of 1997–98.

In today's world of the competition state, there have been fundamental changes in the ways in which states and economies interact.[7] The interaction of transnationalisation, internationalisation and domestic restructuring has forced four specific types of policy change to the top of the political agenda: (1) a shift from macroeconomic to microeconomic interventionism, as reflected in both deregulation and industrial policy; (2) a shift in the focus of that interventionism from the development and maintenance of a range of 'strategic' or 'basic' economic activities (in order to retain minimal economic self-sufficiency in key sectors) to one of flexible response to competitive conditions in a range of diversified and rapidly evolving international marketplaces, that is, the pursuit of dynamic 'competitive advantage' as distinct from the more static 'comparative advantage'; (3) an emphasis on control of inflation and neoliberal monetarism – supposedly translating into non-inflationary growth – as the touchstone of state economic management and interventionism; and (4) a shift in the focal point of party and governmental politics away from general maximisation of welfare within a nation (full employment, redistributive transfer payments and social service provision) to the promotion of enterprise, innovation and profitability in *both* private and public sectors. In this context, there have been some striking similarities as well as major differences between leading capitalist countries.

Among more traditional measures is, of course, trade policy, including a wider range of non-tariff barriers and targeted strategic trade policies. The core issue in the trade issue-area is to avoid reinforcing through protection the existing rigidity of the industrial sector or sectors in question, while at the same time fostering or even imposing adaptation to global competitive conditions in return for *temporary* protection. Transnational constraints are growing rapidly in trade policy, however, as can be seen in the establishment of the North

Atlantic Free Trade Area (NAFTA), the Asia-Pacific Economic Co-operation group (APEC), and the World Trade Organisation (WTO). Two other traditional categories, monetary and fiscal policy, are perhaps even more crucial today, but here the key change is that relative *priorities* between the two have been reversed – tighter monetary policy alongside looser fiscal policy (mainly through tax cuts rather than expenditure) with more emphasis on balanced budgets. And exchange rate policy, difficult to manage in the era of floating exchange rates and massive international capital flows, is none the less still essential however; it is increasingly intertwined with monetary and fiscal policy (Frieden, 1991).

Potentially more innovative, combining old and new measures, is the area of industrial policy (and related strategic trade policy). By targeting particular sectors, by supporting the development of both more flexible manufacturing systems and transnationally viable economies of scale, and by assuming certain costs of adjustment, governments can alter some of the conditions which determine competitive advantage: encouraging mergers and restructuring; promoting research and development; encouraging private investment and venture capital while providing or guaranteeing credit-based investment where capital markets fail, often through joint public/private ventures; developing new forms of infrastructure; pursuing a more active labour market policy while removing barriers to mobility; and the like. The examples of Japanese, Swedish and Austrian industrial policy have been widely analysed in this context.

A third category of measures, and potentially the most explosive, is, of course, deregulation. The deregulation approach is based partly on the assumption that national regulations, especially the traditional sort of regulations designed to protect national market actors from market failure, are insufficiently flexible to take into account the rapid shifts in transnational competitive conditions characteristic of the interpenetrated world economy of the late twentieth century. However, deregulation must not be seen just as the lifting of old regulations, but also as the formulation of new regulatory structures which are designed to cope with, and even to anticipate, shifts in competitive advantage. In essence, deregulation is rarely a true *reduction* in regulation, but a form of *re*-regulation in which market-friendly regulations are substituted for market-controlling regulations (Cerny, 1991; Vogel, 1996). Furthermore, these new regulatory structures are often designed to *enforce* global market-rational economic and political behaviour on rigid and inflexible private sector actors – to break up cosy cartels and expose sheltered, non-competitive sectors – as well as to make state actors and agencies more market-minded in their decisions and structures. The institutions and practices of the state itself are thus increasingly marketised or 'commodified', and the state becomes the spearhead of structural transformation to market norms both at home and abroad.

Although each of these processes can be observed across a wide range of states, however, there are significant variations in how different competition states cope with the pressures of adaptation and transformation. There is a dialectic of divergence and convergence at work, rather than a single road to competitiveness. The original model of the competition state was the strategic or developmental state discussed above, which writers like John Zysman and Chalmers Johnson associated with France and Japan (Zysman, 1983; Johnson, 1982). This perspective identifies the competition state with strong-state technocratic *dirigisme* and lives on in the analysis of newly industrialising countries (NICs) in Asia and other parts of the Third World.

However, the difficulty with this approach has been that the scope of control which the technocratic patron-state and its client firms can exercise over market outcomes diminishes as the integration of these economies into global markets and the complexities of cross-national games proceeds, as the recent Asian 'financial meltdown' demonstrates. Beyond a certain threshold, even the most tightly bound firms and sectors will be forced to act in a more autonomous fashion in order to keep up with international competitive pressures. And as more firms and sectors become linked into new patterns of production, financing and market access, often moving operations offshore, their willingness to follow the script declines. However, there are distinctions even here. Within this category, for example, the Japanese bureaucracy's 'administrative guidance' and the ties of the *keiretsu* system, which groups industrial and financial firms through interlocking shareholdings, have remained relatively strong despite a certain amount of liberalisation, deregulation and privatisation (Vogel, 1996), whereas in France the forces of neoliberalism have penetrated a range of significant bastions from the main political parties to major sectors of the bureaucracy itself (Schmidt, 1996).

In contrast, the *orthodox* model of the competition state today is not the developmental state but the 'neoliberal state' (in the European sense). Thatcherism and Reaganism in the 1980s provided both a political rationale and a power base for the renascence of free-market ideology generally – not just in the United Kingdom and the United States but throughout the world. The flexibility and openness of Anglo-Saxon capital markets, the experience of Anglo-American elites with international and transnational business and their willingness to go multinational, the corporate structure of American and British firms and their greater concern with profitability and shareholder returns rather than traditional relationships and market share, the enthusiasm with which American managers have embraced lean management and downsizing, and the relative flexibility of the US and UK labour forces, combined with an 'arm's-length' state tradition in both countries (Zysman, 1983), are widely thought to have fought off the strategic state challenge and to have eventually emerged more competitive today. Nevertheless, liberalisation, deregulation and privatisation have not reduced the role of state intervention overall, just shifted it from decommodifying bureaucracies to marketising ones and from redistributive functions to enforcement ones.

Throughout the ongoing debate about the merits of the Japanese model versus the Anglo-American model, however, a European model, rooted in the post-war settlement and given another (if problematic) dimension through the consolidation of the European Community (now the European Union), has been presented by many commentators as a middle way. In bringing labour into institutionalised settings not only for wage bargaining but also for other aspects of the social market, in doggedly pursuing conservative monetary policies, in promoting extensive training programmes, and in possessing a universal banking system which nurtured and stabilised industry without full-blown strategic state interventionism, the European neocorporatist or 'co-ordinated economy' approach (as practised in varying ways in Germany, Austria and Sweden in particular) has seemed to its proponents to embody the best aspects of both the others. However, despite the completion of the Single European Market and the signing of the Maastricht Treaty, the signs of what in the early 1980s was called 'Eurosclerosis' have reappeared; the European Monetary Union project is widely regarded as deflationary in a context where costs are unevenly spread; and the liberalising, deregulatory option is increasingly on the political cards again (as it was, for a while, in the mid-to-late1980s), especially in the context of high and intractable German unemployment.

On one level, then, 'national developments' – that is, differences in models of state/economy relations or state/societal arrangements – have, then, driven changes in the global economy' (Zysman, 1996). At another level, of course, states and state actors seek to convince, or pressure, other states and actors such as multinational corporations or international institutions to adopt measures which shift the balance of competitive advantage in their favour. The search for competitive advantage thus adds further layers and cross-cutting cleavages to the world economy which increase the complexity and density of networks of interdependence and interpenetration. Finally, genuinely transnational, cross-cutting pressures can develop – whether from multinational corporations or from nationally or locally based firms and other interests (such as trade unions) caught in the crossfire of the search for international competitiveness – for the establishment or expansion of transnational regimes, transnational neocorporatist structures of policy bargaining, transgovernmental linkages between bureaucrats, policymakers and policy communities, and the like.

In all of these settings, then, the state is less and less able to act as a decommodifying hierarchy, taking economic activities out of the market. It must act more and more as a collective commodifying agent – putting activities *into* the market – and even as *a market actor itself*. It is financier, middleman, advocate and even entrepreneur, in a complex economic web not only where the frontiers between state and market become blurred, but also where their cross-cutting structures become closely intertwined and their behavioural modes become less and less easy to distinguish. Emerging political and economic structures are closely intertwined but not yet very clear, and the possibilities for multiple equilibria – for alternative pathways in the future – still quite fluid. Of course, states and markets have always been intertwined and mutually supporting. Indeed, the state still remains the central focus for consensus, loyalty, and social discipline – the 'collective capitalist' (Holloway and Picciotto, 1978). But this role nowadays puts the state into an increasingly contradictory location. Not only is it more complicated for the state to act as a genuine 'collective capitalist' within the traditional territorial confines of national society, but states are also increasingly quasi-market actors and commodifying agents themselves. In such complex conditions, the state is sometimes structurally fragmented, sometimes capable of strategic action – but increasingly caught up in and constrained by cross-cutting global/transnational/ domestic structural and conjunctural conditions.

Under pressure from recessionary conditions in a relatively open world economy, first in the 1970s and then in the early 1990s, then, the problems faced by all capitalist industrial states have given rise to certain similarities of response – in particular, the shift from the welfare state model, nurtured by the long boom from the 1950s to the oil crisis of 1973–74, to a more differentiated repertoire of state responses to the imperatives of growth and competitiveness. However, despite these elements of convergence, significant divergences remain, for different states have different sets of advantages and disadvantages in the search for international competitiveness. They differ in endogenous structural capacity for strategic action both domestically and internationally. They differ in the extent to which their existing economic structures, with or without government intervention, can easily adapt to international conditions. And they differ in their vulnerability to international and transnational trends and pressures.

In this context, states are less and less able to act as 'strategic' or 'developmental' states, and are more and more 'splintered states' (Machin and Wright, 1985). State actors and their different agencies are increasingly intertwined with 'transgovernmental networks' – systematic linkages between state actors and agencies overseeing particular jurisdictions and sectors, but cutting across different countries and including a heterogeneous collection of private actors and groups in interlocking policy communities. Furthermore, some of these linkages specifically involve the exchange of ideas rather than authoritative decision-making or power-broking – what have been called 'epistemic communities' (Haas, 1992; Stone, 1996). In international terms, states in pursuing the goal of competitiveness are increasingly involved in what John Stopford and Susan Strange (1991) called 'triangular diplomacy' – complex interactions and negotiations at state-to-state, state-to-firm and firm-to-firm levels. But this concept must be widened further. Interdependence analysis has focused too exclusively on two-level games and on the state as a Janus-faced institutional structure. Although this is an oversimplification, complex globalisation has to be seen as a structure involving (at least) *three*-level games, with third-level – transnational – games including not only 'firm–firm diplomacy' but also transgovernmental networks, transnational policy communities, internationalised market structures, transnational pressure and interest groups (of both the 'sectional' and 'cause' varieties) and many other linked and interpenetrated markets, hierarchies and networks.

As states and state actors get drawn more and more into the minutiae of cross-cutting and transnational economic relations, their activities become further constrained by the less manageable complexities of complex situations. Thus the amount of government imbrication in social life can actually *increase* while at the same time the power of the state to control specific activities and market outcomes continues to diminish. One example is the way financial globalisation and deregulation have intensified pressures for governments to increase monitoring of financial markets, criminalisation of insider trading, tracking of money laundering activities and the like (Helleiner, 1998). The growth of competing authorities with overlapping jurisdictions does not reduce interventionism; it merely expands the range of possibilities for splintered governments and special interests to carve out new fiefdoms, both domestically and transnationally, while undermining their home states' overall strategic and developmental capacity. The attempt to make the state more 'flexible' has moved a long way over the past decade, not only in the United States and Britain – where deregulation, privatisation, and liberalisation have evolved furthest – but also in a wide range of other countries in the First and Third Worlds (and more recently in the Second World too). In a globalising world, the competition state is more likely to be involved in a process of competitive *de*regulation (and marketising *re*-regulation) and thus of 'creeping liberalisation'. In this way complex globalisation not only undermines but also transforms the state's structural capacity to constitute an effective arena of endogenous collective action and make credible exogenous commitments.

CONSTRUCTING A NEW WORLD ORDER? STRUCTURE AND AGENCY IN THE TRANSFORMATION PROCESS

The focus of this chapter so far has been on structural changes in the way the state and the international system interact, rather than on the agents conceiving and implementing that transformation. The second half will therefore focus on the potential for agency to make further change happen within the structural context outlined above. As Marx observed, people do not make history in circumstances of their own choosing. Agents do not act on a *tabula rasa*; they develop perceptions of what they are doing (and what they are supposed to be doing) within the context of real existing (and often deeply embedded) structures with particular, 'locked-in' payoff matrices or distributional patterns, cultural frameworks and the like – that is, within complex 'structured fields of action' (Crozier and Friedberg, 1977) characterised by pre-existing (but continually evolving) sets of multilayered opportunities and constraints. Nevertheless, within this context, agents possess what has been called 'bounded rationality' (Simon, 1997). Not only do they search to maximise their utilities within existing structural constraints, but they also search for 'wiggle room' and try to 'test the edges of the envelope'. Most importantly, of course, when structured fields of action are flawed or fluid – that is, when structural opportunities outweigh structural constraints – agents can and occasionally do reshape those very fields themselves in specific real-time historical contexts, engaging in a process of 'structuration' which is essentially 'path-dependent' (Cerny, 1990, ch. 1; Giddens, 1979; Granovetter, 1985 and 1992). Both incrementally modified and more radically altered structures might then be further 'locked in' and 'embedded' over time, often in an uneven process of 'punctuated equilibrium'.

In order for actors to impact upon and effect change in the system itself, they must overcome two kinds of structural constraints: those based on endurance over time, and those based on the particular shape or pattern formed by the structured action field. The first involves the *embeddedness* of whatever structures and/or institutions already exist to shape the system and keep it together; the second kind involves the fact that differently *configured* structures shape and channel human behaviour in distinct ways. Structures themselves,[8] because of their very complexity, will tend to cohere and persist so long as the cumulative pattern of agents' actions maintains and reinforces the rules of game and the distributions of resources which make up those structures.[9] However, those actions can also have a potentially significant cumulative transformative impact on the form of a structure itself. This can be especially true where they effectively exploit – whether as a consequence of conscious, strategic action, on the one hand, or because of the incidental or accidental impact of unwitting or merely tactical choices, on the other – existing contradictions, tensions and/or gaps in a structure. The actual form which a structure takes – the particular rules of the game in question, and the specific distribution of resources which characterises the system – can either constrain the actions of particular agents or provide structured *opportunities* which reinforce and multiply the impact of the actions of those agents.[10] However, most agents, most of the time, are heavily constrained by structures; it is usually easier to keep things the way they are and to manoeuvre within the interstices of the system than to counteract that inertia.

Traditional 'structuralist' analysis, of course, places greatest emphasis on the constraining effects of structure upon agents. However, the shape of particular structures themselves – the 'structure of the structure', so to speak – can potentially not only reinforce but even generate pressures for change from specific agents or groups of agents, and structurationist approaches put much greater emphasis on this aspect. For example, it is easy to see that there can be two kinds of potential crises within a system: (1) crises of embeddedness, when a particular structural equilibrium no longer reflects the effective balance of forces underpinning it because of wider, exogenous historical changes, and the settlement which 'locks in' that equilibrium is weakened; and (2) crises of structural *form*, when built-in contradictions or tensions in the system itself actually *generate* changes in the balance of forces.[11] Indeed, broad structural change usually involves a complex feedback process between the two levels. At one level, then, structures can be characterised by *permissive conditions* for action that can be exploited by actors. At another level, however, structures can also, in a quasi-mechanical sense, *generate* seminal or *causative conditions* which may induce or even necessitate system-challenging or system-changing actions. This is especially true, in the latter case, as the consequence of the existence of fundamental or pivotal in-built structural tensions and opportunities, the transformative effects of which may be triggered by, for example, changing exogenous conditions (from climate to technology) and/or the uneven or problematic operation of the system itself (for example, a tendency to gridlock or the perpetuation of centralised control) – or, usually, both. A range of ideal-type scenarios can be envisaged of circumstances in which actors can initiate and/or precipitate broad structural change.[12]

Debates on issues like globalisation and internationalisation are essentially debates about the nature of ongoing structuration in the international system. They address three fundamental questions. First, to what extent is the pre-existing structure of the international system characterised by tensions, anomalies, uncertainties, structural gaps or flaws which constitute or generate incentives to engage in system-challenging behaviour – that is, how *vulnerable* is the existing system in structural terms? Secondly, do the various exogenous processes of social, economic and political change which have been identified in the international system in recent decades add up to a wider, cumulative process of structural change, often called 'globalisation'? And finally, what kind of choices *might* agents be able to make – or have they *already* been able to make – which potentially could shape those processes of change cumulatively in the future – whether to slow them down or speed them up, whether to consciously resist or promote the emergence of new structural patterns, whether to pursue different kinds of values or goals in the process of change, and so on?

In this context, the main hypothesis of this chapter is that the international system is currently in the early stages of a process of 'institutional selection'

(Spruyt, 1994) in which the structure of that system is no longer viable in its pre-existing form. In particular, it will be argued that the development of a range of 'transnational opportunity structures' provide vital structural space for key agents to act in potentially transformative ways, in turn increasing the vulnerability of the system in feedback fashion. At the same time, however, such changes also give rise to adaptive as well as transformative modes of behaviour. Therefore the particular *shape* a transformed international system is likely to take will be determined primarily by which sets of actors – in particular, which competing 'institutional entrepreneurs' or 'change masters' (Kanter, 1993) – are best able (whether strategically or accidentally) to exploit most effectively the manifest and latent structural resources or political opportunity structures available to them in a period of flux. A key variable in explaining actor-led change is thus the presence of *strategically situated actors* in a flawed and/or fluid structural context. Their presence constitutes a necessary but not a sufficient condition of structural change.

Of course, where what is *perceived* to be a highly constraining organisational pattern has been deeply embedded over a long period of time, most actors, even strategically situated ones, will take that pattern for granted and work within it rather than trying to change it. There is thus a strong tendency towards inertia built into most social structures most of the time. However, there are two ways in which strategically situated actors can in fact effect change. Either they *believe* that the combination of their preferences and objectives, along with a perceptive understanding of the fault lines and gaps in the existing structure, will bring about change, and therefore they systematically and consciously act in a rational fashion to pursue that outcome. Or they accidentally or incidentally interact with others in such a way that the pursuit of their ostensibly system-bound preferences puts strain on the structure itself in contingent fashion, opens up existing gaps, and creates new possibilities for forms of coalition-building and power-seeking that alter existing resource distributions and ultimately force *de facto* changes in fundamental, system-sustaining rules or resource distributions. It must be remembered, however, that the success of both of these forms of action is contingent upon the effective balance of forces between such system-challenging actors, on the one hand, and those whose actions continue to reinforce the existing structural settlement, on the other. Judging the state of that balance of forces is a risky business both intellectually and practically.

As I have argued in previous sections of this chapter, the existence of major structural fault lines in the 'modern world order' – that is, the domestic structural predominance of the nation-state form of 'political system', on the one hand, and the international predominance of the so-called 'states system', on the other – has opened the way for a significant range of strategically situated actors *potentially* to act in such a way as to open up further and/or wider gaps in that order and therefore make it vulnerable to widespread structural change.

For example, rapid technological diffusion and the cross-border expansion of a range of different economic markets are straining the links between territoriality and *political* demands for economic results. Sectoral pressure groups and economic coalitions are seeking to manipulate a range of both old and new 'access points' – multiple access points, often in different territorial jurisdictions, which they attempt to manipulate on several levels at the same time. The perceived inability of states to co-ordinate their responses to such complex pressures in a strategic fashion – and to be *seen* to do so by more transnationally aware publics – is said to have several structurally significant consequences. One of those is the fragmentation of domestic state responses to political pressures – that is, the 'splintering' of the state itself. Another is the necessity for such responses to be co-ordinated across borders, leading to an increasing process of institutional *bricolage* at the level of formal and informal transnational structures and processes. And a third, linking the first two, is the development of transgovernmental networks among significant but internally fragmented state actors, often playing *ad hoc* games of catch-up to adjust regulation and government intervention to perceived new economic realities.

Within this context, key sets of agents who in the past have been closely bound up with the territorial nation-state are increasingly experimenting with new forms of quasi-private regulation of their activities. Businesses and business pressure groups, for example, are more and more divided between those representing site-specific activities seeking old-fashioned government protection, but whose economic base is often declining, and those more active in transnational markets, seeking deregulation and liberalisation (Milner, 1988; Frieden, 1991). The latter want more scope to engage in new forms of competition such as research-and-development-based or product-by-product strategic alliances which not only cut across national economies but also undermine traditional state activities in the antitrust area (Portnoy, 1999). Furthermore, the securitisation and transnational integration of financial markets have undermined traditional state–bank–industry relationships of finance capital (Chernow, 1997). Labour movements, too, which were such a crucial element in the consolidation of the welfare state, are being eroded from both above and below, as their relationships with state actors and agencies become increasingly ineffectual in achieving their collective demands, leading to a strengthening of 'free-riding' tendencies (Olson, 1965). And state actors themselves, once said to be 'captured' by large, well-organised domestic constituencies, are increasingly captured instead by transnationally linked sectors which set state agencies against each other in the desire to 'level the playing field' for their domestic clients in the wider world.

Alongside these economic developments has come a range of social and political developments. The impact of new technologies has intensified pressures resulting from the interaction of previously compartmentalised social and cultural categories, with an emphasis on the sheer speed of that interaction (Douglas, 1999). The development of MacLuhan's 'global village' has been paralleled (or, for some, even superseded) by a postmodernist fragmentation of cultures and societies (Deibert, 1997). In political terms, the re-identification of societies as 'multicultural', emphasising shifting identities and loyalties (Dombrowski, 1998), is unravelling the consolidation of 'national cultural societies' (Znaniecki, [1952] 1973) which was at the heart of the nation-state project from Bismarck to postcolonial 'nation-building' (Bendix, 1964). Major social causes and cause groups are less concerned with negotiating benefits from the state and more focused on transnational issues such as the environment, women's issues, the international banning of landmines, opposition to the holding of political prisoners, promoting 'sustainable development', and the like. In particular, the end of the Cold War has unleashed a huge number of social and political demands which had previously been kept in ideological and political check. In this context, the notion of the 'public interest' itself is being questioned, and perhaps being transformed, releasing actors from the rigid ideological categories of the mid-twentieth century.

The growing salience of a range of fault lines in existing domestic and international political structures has therefore first of all created *permissive conditions* for broadly based, paradigmatic structural change. In a deeper sense, however, the increasing salience of those fault lines and their interaction in complex, changing exogenous circumstances, are themselves generating *causative conditions* for change. Whether such change will actually occur, however, will depend on the complex interaction of such permissive and causative conditions. This interaction involves three sets of variables. In the first place, although specific changes may take place, whether change overall is fundamental and far-reaching enough to be paradigmatic – that is, *transformative* – change will depend upon the balance of forces between sets of agents whose actions continue to reinforce existing structural forms and practices – including those who are able to channel the pressures described above in the direction of adapting existing forms to better meet new structural challenges – and those whose actions generate and reinforce new forms and practices.

Secondly, change will depend upon the way the latter agents actually act in practice; although they might be expected to act in ways which challenge the structure, they also may for various reasons – including cultural and ideological reasons as well as calculations of short-term gains – not be able, *or even not choose*, to act in such ways. *Adaptive* behaviour may in the end be the preferred course of action for many strategically situated actors. And finally, those alternative structural forms – the potential but contingent outcomes (multiple equilibria) which may in theory be possible – may prove either too ambitious, on the one hand, or too amorphous and fragmented, on the other, to form an effective foundation for those agents' strategic or tactical calculations. *Alternative equilibria may also be too flawed and/or fluid to be a ground for effective action.* At this point, then, let us look at how specific changes, at different structural levels, involving different sets of key agents, are more or less likely to shape the outcome of wider processes of transnational structuration in the context of globalisation.

The capacity of *economic* agents, for example, to become effective institutional entrepreneurs or change masters is most directly influenced by changing production processes, the multinationalisation of corporate structures, the integration of transnational financial markets, the growth of world trade, the development of new consumption patterns, and the like. *Political* agents (politicians and bureaucrats), in the world of the nation-state and the states system, are the category which has traditionally been most identified as containing both actual and potential institutional entrepreneurs; when paradigmatic system change seems to be possible, mass publics and the chattering classes alike still expect state actors to be the main ones to try to do something about it. *Social* agents have a less precise profile than either economic or political agents, because of the wide range of different types of social activity and organisation which they reflect and represent. Nevertheless, several widespread (and conflicting) types of social change, from the emergence of a cultural global village to the fragmentation of post-modernity, involve agents operating across the domestic/international divide and challenging the traditional nineteenth and twentieth century sociological identification of 'societies' (as distinct from the more amorphous 'society') with *national* societies (Robertson, 1992). In particular, transnational social movements are seen with increasing frequency to be at the cutting edge of transnational structuration, by exploiting *and creating* 'transnational opportunity structures' out of the flawed infrastructure of the states system.

Economic agents

The main assumption in most of the literature on globalisation that I have seen is that the key category of agents in terms of developing transnational linkages which have structurally transformative potential consists of economic agents, mainly because globalisation is most often seen as a primarily economic process. The story goes something like this. In the first place, the 'modern' division of the international economy into relatively or partially insulated *national economies* is widely seen to be both (1) somewhat flawed from the start and (2) breaking down again. In the mid-to-late nineteenth century, the world economy was already highly transnationalised, with relative levels of trade and international capital flows comparable at least with those of the 1980s (although it is arguable that such levels have been superseded in the 1990s). The consolidation of national economies in the advanced capitalist world from the

emphasised, throughout modern history structural developments in the financial services field have been driven at key times by industrial firms with large financial surpluses either forming alliances with banks and financial market participants or seeking to enter the financial services field themselves. Should Microsoft choose to use its large profits in this way, for example, it could quickly become a leading, if not a dominant, player, given the nature of competition among existing successful financial services firms. At another level, had Ted Turner decided to put his excess cash into entering the financial services field instead of giving it to the United Nations, he would also have had competitive advantages. The likes of George Soros are vulnerable in such circumstances. Still, the real economic 'change masters' are not likely to be the most obvious public personalities; as Kanter points out:

> The art and architecture of change, then, also involves *designing reports about the past to elicit the present actions required for the future* ...; power may need to remain less than fully visible; 'prime movers' may need to make sure others are equally credited; room at centre stage may need to be given over to those people and activities that are now necessary to go on from here – such as the marketing people instead of the product developers becoming the 'heroes' of the account.

> Change masters should understand these phenomena and work with them; they should know how to create myths and stories. But we should not confuse the results with lessons about guiding organisational change. ... We need to understand what goes on behind and beyond official accounts ... (Kanter, 1993, p. 188)

In terms of economic agents, then, despite their central and widespread interaction with the latent and manifest transnational opportunity structures existing in both political and economic terms, it is unlikely that the more powerful among them will seek to promote a paradigm shift in the broader transnational structuration process – although they may inadvertently drive *other* actors to attempt to effect more far-reaching structural change to counteract perceived negative political, economic and social consequences of economic transnationalisation. To be successful, such counter-action, blocked for the most part at domestic level, will need to be played out on the international and transnational fields. Economic agents themselves, however, are most likely to continue to adopt adaptive forms of behaviour in structurational terms, for example, promoting a dialectic of regulatory competition and co-operation in the financial market sector, supporting the continuing reduction of trade barriers and the consolidation of international regimes such as the World Trade Organisation and fora like the G-7, and so on.

The main direct influence of economic transnationalisation in terms of agent behaviour will be felt in two ways: in the first place, through the spread of an *ideology* of market globalisation through the mass media, the teaching of management in business schools, popular business literature (the 'airport bookshop' approach to globalisation), and the like;[14] and secondly, through the impact of economic transnationalisation on *other* categories of agent – that is, on political agents attempting to reconfigure forms of political authority to meet the potential challenge of transnationally rooted market failures and the demands of popular constituencies for the reassertion of political values such as the 'public interest' in the face of the economic, social and indirect political power of economic agents. In the last analysis, it will be networks which cut across the crude economic-political-social boundaries examined here that will determine the shape of change. At the end of this chapter, I will suggest what kinds of structural scenarios are likely to develop should economic agents of different kinds prove to be directly or indirectly hegemonic in the transnationalisation process.

Political agents

In this context, pressures on political agents to act as institutional entrepreneurs are likely to grow; nevertheless, their actual *capacity* to act is likely to increase in some ways and decline in others. Such patterns of opportunity and constraint are distinct in several ways from the patterns described above with regard to economic agents, however. In the first place, as mentioned earlier, politicians and bureaucrats are to a great extent *expected* to act as institutional entrepreneurs in the modern world, a role which they generally attempted to fulfil in the world of the nation-state and states system. Their *authority* and their *legitimacy* depend upon their role as upholders (and to some extent, designers) of constitutions and institutional systems, their capacity to use 'non-economic coercion' (Holloway and Picciotto, 1978) to achieve collective action (or hegemonic domination ...), their role in protecting and furthering the 'national interest' *vis-à-vis* foreigners (even to the point of expecting citizens to go to their deaths in its name), and their manipulation of symbols of elemental social bonds, belonging, loyalty, and so on. Political agents are expected to combine carrots and sticks in the pursuit of, ideally, collective goals (or at least the goals of dominant groups), to blend 'voice' and 'loyalty' (in different combinations) while minimising threats of 'exit' or 'free-riding'. At the same time, that very authority and legitimacy are inextricably intertwined with the *multifunctionality* of their authority (Cerny, 1995), and that multifunctionality is only made possible by limiting their power to the domestic arena (and/or to the international strategic/diplomatic arena).

The capacity of political agents to act as institutional entrepreneurs therefore takes on a quite different *form* in a transnationalising international system, but their role is still central. Of course, political leaders with their 'foreign policy' or 'statesmen' hats on (and traditional diplomatic bureaucrats too) will still play an important – and salient – role, especially in constructing symbolic representations of change (as in the recent visits to the United States of both the Chinese President and Prime Minister in 1998 and 1999 respectively); they can also initiate forms of international co-operation, such as the Uruguay Round of trade negotiations which led to the establishment of the World Trade Organisation or treaties on aspects of environmental regulation. In a sense, however, such agents are often condemned to play 'catch-up' with complex endogenous and exogenous trends reinforcing or generating transnational linkages and opportunity structures in such issue-areas; they are rarely change masters, but they can to some extent shape change and, most importantly, they can sometimes legitimate it. At the same time, however, they suffer from a growing disillusionment with governments, politicians and bureaucrats generally – a disillusionment which results from the increasing political *immobilisme* and poverty of public policy which transnational constraints impose on publicly visible, formal officials. This disillusionment increasingly penetrates down into the interstices of domestic policy as traditional state policy instruments – especially those of the national industrial welfare state – are seen to be less effective because of those constraints (and the combination of those transnational constraints with other internal constraints, often sharing related causes and effects).

In this context, too, traditional pressure and interest groups, especially sectoral pressure groups, are increasingly divided amongst themselves along transnationally rooted fault lines. We have already mentioned, in the context of our discussion of economic agents, the problems faced by trade unions in this environment. Pressure groups are perceived less and less as parts of a positive-sum, pluralistic process of negotiating satisfactory compromises within the national political arena, and more and more as 'special interests', acting against the public interest or free-riding on the collective actions of others. Of course, the idea of cross-cutting affiliations or overlapping groups as a positive, stabilising force in political life (Truman, 1951; Coser, 1956) has always represented a rosy scenario, open to fundamental critiques from elite and class analytical perspectives, among others. Nevertheless, with the splintering of the state and the crystallisation of more and more complex transnational opportunity structures, many domestically oriented interest and pressure groups are increasingly 'out of the loop', condemned to pursue politically problematic goals such as protectionism, and open to marginalisation as obsolete representatives of the old left or the populist right. Transnationally linked interest groups, on the other hand, are better able to use their influence at a number of different domestic and transnational levels at the same time, even playing state actors off against each other in their desire to 'level the playing field' in a politically as well as an economically competitive world.

It is at this level that political agents do play a key entrepreneurial role, by acting as intermediaries between transnational pressures and interests and domestic pressures and interests. However, no longer having the capacity to systematically privilege the latter over the former, the new political consensus which enables political agents to become change masters is a consensus which identifies international competitiveness as the main criterion for policy success. I have already mentioned the notion of the 'competition state', which is the key to understanding the impact and potential of their entrepreneurial role, the new categorical imperative of political life. Political agents, especially state actors, by identifying international competitiveness as the chief totem of political discourse, put themselves in a position where they require of themselves – and evoke expectations in others, whether businessmen or mass publics – that they must attack not only domestic protectionism but also the state-enforced decommodification of socially deleterious economic activities and practices in the name of levelling the international playing field and, indeed, that they must provide domestic economic agents with greater competitive advantages in a more open world. Political agents have been extremely successful in doing just this, despite deep-seated domestic opposition. President Clinton's patronage of the North American Free Trade Agreement in 1993, against a major campaign led by the labour unions and powerful members of his own party, is a salient example of this trend.

However, it is not at this obvious level, but in the day-to-day transformation of state intervention – and of state-business-labour relations (what Hart, 1992, calls 'state-societal arrangements' or SSAs), often challenging the very vested interests imbricated in different 'national models' of capitalism (Crouch and Streeck, 1997) – by politicians and bureaucrats in their interaction with transnationalising pressures and interests that the state itself becomes a major collective agent in the structuration process, creating through ongoing *bricolage* a complex new set of transnational opportunity structures. Paradoxically, although the state is internally divided and its traditional policy instruments less useful – or partly *because of* those very developments – political agents are potentially among the main change masters of the transnationalisation process simply because they must attempt to manage key developments in that process through participating in and attempting to manipulate transgovernmental networks and transnational policy communities.

What is called 'policy transfer' – that is, the adoption for domestic purposes of policy agendas which reflect policy experiences in other countries and in transnational regimes – puts political agents, often on the lower rungs of the political or bureaucratic ladders as well as higher up, at the core of transnational and transgovernmental policy networks and epistemic communities (Evans and Davies, 1999; Stone, 1999). They can cut across not only national boundaries but also economic-political-social boundaries to form action networks to pursue specific changes which can add up to transformative change without necessarily realising the impact of their actions. And they are often all the more effective because their actions are masked by their continued use of traditional national symbolism and state authority, and even by their ability to shape the institutional environment itself. For example, the capacity of treasuries, finance ministries and central banks, along with the closely knit transgovernmental and transnational policy communities in which they are enmeshed, to embed global imperatives in day-to-day national decisionmaking – by, for example, framing the limits not only of macroeconomic policies but also of the ability of 'spending ministries' to address the problems of their particular jurisdictions – shows how embedded, quasi-camouflaged political and institutional entrepreneurs can influence not only policy *per se* but also the structural and institutional arenas within which policies are shaped. They can restructure state institutions and activities behind a veil of democratic legitimacy, reinventing the story of politics from behind the scenes as they go along in much the way Kanter describes above.

At the same time, however, the capacity of political agents to act is still inextricably intertwined with the maintenance of state institutions and national discourses. Political agents are not about to try to deconstruct the state itself and design overtly transnational constitutional processes to replace it. Indeed, in a paradoxical fashion, the weight of state interventionism increases – often significantly – as states undertake enforcement functions on behalf of (especially) transnationally linked economic agents, functions which transnational structures are unable or unwilling to undertake. The state may be becoming the main terrain of political conflict and coalition-building between forces favouring globalisation and those seeking to resist it, but political agents will not be willing to undermine the state itself as the central institutionalised political arena – and thereby undermine the most significant single source of their own power. Thus the state may be dramatically altered through a wide range of *adaptive* behaviours on the part of political agents, but it will not itself be fundamentally left behind. The state may be transformed, but it will be neither transfigured nor transcended by political change masters alone.

Social agents

Social agents, as pointed out earlier, are in a complex position with regard to their capacity to reinforce and generate transnational structural change. The depth of politically imposed national identities in the developed world enabled nation-states and the states system during most of the twentieth century to spawn two World Wars and the Cold War as well as to dominate processes of political development in the postcolonial era. Nevertheless, especially in the last two decades of the century, increasing tensions over the distribution of economic and political goods and a proliferating set of demands by diverse social actors cutting across both global and domestic arenas throughout the world, have fuelled endemic dissatisfaction with existing institutions and processes of governance. The uncertain and destabilising processes of democratic transition, globalisation, and the rapid formation of new collective identities have created tremendous social as well as political volatility and inspired popular pressure both for new kinds of control and accountability and for specific policy remedies. As with the other two categories of agents discussed earlier, there are three aspects to consider: the population of agents; the changing structured action field in which they operate; and the potential for their action to direct or shape structural change.

In the first place, there is emerging a new range of pressures from below. The proliferation of social agents on the international and transnational levels has been widely noted. The numbers and activities of such groups have grown in range, scale and scope. Some are more like traditional pressure or interest groups (Willetts, 1982), adjusting the scale of their organisation to conform with the scale of problems facing particular categories of people in a global setting. Probably the least represented at this level have been what the traditional pressure group literature called 'sectional groups'; such groups have been much more imbricated with domestic state structures and processes because states have in the past been able to marshal far more resources to respond to demands for, especially, distributive and redistributive policies. For example, labour groups have always had international-level bureaux, but these were usually either moribund or captured by Cold War state agents, reflecting the struggle between Communists and anti-Communists in trades unions across the world from the 1920s to the 1970s. Such international bureaux now find conditions somewhat more favourable to their activities, although their members remain for the most part locked into national-level unions, and organising industrial action across borders is still highly problematic. In particular, they can now interact with an increasing range of international regimes, especially with the recent revival of the International Labour Organisation in Geneva.

However, more emphasis is placed today on the recent growth of what the traditional group literature called 'cause groups', or what at global level are now called 'transnational advocacy coalitions (or networks)' (Keck and Sikkink, 1998) in issue-areas like environmental activism, women's rights, population policy, socio-economic development, and even military policy, as in, for example, the campaign for an international treaty banning the use of landmines. The last of these, organised entirely on a private campaigning basis through the internet, resulted not only in the signing of a major international treaty in 1998 but also the award of the Nobel Peace Prize to the campaign's leaders in the same year. These advocacy groups do not merely mimic domestic cause groups, for three reasons. In the first place, they target issues which are international and/or transnational in scope. In particular, they pursue objectives which either are not being responded to or *cannot* be effectively responded to at national level because of the structural linkages among different levels and spaces (both territorial and virtual). The indivisibilities characteristic of environmental issues are well-known (global warming, and so on). But in the case of the anti-landmines campaign, it was necessary to break through the intense opposition of national military bureaucracies concerned with the constraints of the traditional security dilemma (Cerny, 2000b).

Another reason is that they can bring together a range of coalition partners who would not normally be prepared to work closely with each other in a national setting for a variety of structural and historical reasons. For example, rainforest campaigns in Latin America can bring together displaced workers and peasants, women, quasi-elite groups concerned with environmental degradation *per se*, indigenous groups and organisations concerned with Third World economic development and the like – and that is just *within* the developing state or states involved in the action. Furthermore, each of these indigenous groups will have links with external, often First World-based organisations (non-governmental organisations or NGOs) concerned with directing campaigns in the international and national media in the developed world, not to mention links with other kinds of elite and mass networks, including various scientists and experts ('epistemic communities'), in developed countries. These broad (but shifting) coalitions usually either have established relationships, through transnational policy networks and policy communities, with international (intergovernmental) regimes and with state actors in particular agencies in the richer countries too, or else they are in the process of developing those links through new activities. Finally, the internet and other new communications and information technologies give these coalitions great reach and flexibility in the ways they can target different agents in states, international institutions, academics, the media and the like. In this sense, the narrower pressure group model overlaps more and more with the NGO model, which in turn overlaps considerably with broader egalitarian New Social Movements (Murphy 1998), creating a potential virtuous circle of action – although the very diversity of such a process also can lead to overcomplexity and uncertainty.

Secondly, these groups of social agents also benefit from the changing structured field of action, or what Krieger and Murphy (1998) have called the 'Transnational Opportunity Structure' or TOS (to shadow what Tarrow, 1998, called the 'Political Opportunity Structure' or POS). The TOS (like the POS) refers to what in the traditional public policy and pressure group literature were called 'points of access', that is, structural openings in political and bureaucratic institutions where pressure groups can influence particular interlocutors within the state apparatus, whether individual state actors, specific agencies, or so-called 'iron triangles' of the policy network type. Whereas the traditional pressure group and social movement literature focuses on the more embedded institutional points of access of the state, commentators on NSMs and NGOs are increasingly pointing to opportunities at the international and transnational levels. These points of access include, of course, international regimes, particularly the United Nations, which has always been open to such groups in both formal and informal ways (Willetts, 1982); particular state agencies with jurisdictional scope in the very issue-areas focused on by these coalitions (environmental agencies, and so on); wider epistemic communities of experts, think tanks, scientists and the like (Haas, 1993; Stone, 1996); the proliferation of new fora such as UN-sponsored conferences on social development, population, human settlements, women's health, climate change and the like (Betsill, 1999; Clark *et al.*, 1999; Dodgson, 1999); and private organisations in other spheres, particularly business.

Indeed, cause groups can strategically 'whipsaw' policymakers at local, national and international levels, going back and forth between applying traditional pressure group tactics to government officials, organising local resistance and pursuing international or transnational media and other campaigns, as shown by a case study of the Clayoquot and Great Bear rainforest campaigns in Canada (Krajnc, 1999). The landmines treaty was negotiated over the opposition of the supposedly hegemonic United States, with other states (and state agencies), international organisations and pressure groups. And in the Brent Spar affair, in which Greenpeace and other transnational groups opposed the decision of the oil multinational Shell to sink a disused oil platform in the ocean, the resolution of the issue (after boycott and other campaigns against Shell around the world) came in direct negotiations between Shell and Greenpeace; indeed, the British government was strongly opposed to the settlement that was reached, but was bypassed (see *Nature*, 1996). Interestingly, there are increasing interaction effects here, as NGOs, international organisations, government agencies, the media and business interact with each other on a more and more ongoing and regularised basis; particular venues like the UN-sponsored conferences mentioned above have been said to have a particularly strong multiplier role in this sense, spawning new and expanding networks which then continue to interact outside of the venue and beyond the time frame of the conferences themselves. Even traditional pressure groups such as labour unions are being brought into this universe through trade and environmental treaties and, in particular, the virtual resurrection of the International Labour Organisation, a long-established international institution based in Geneva, but semi-moribund for decades, in a growing international, transnational *and domestic* debate over labour standards. The ILO increasingly comprises an important node of contact, networking and influence.

In this context, then, social agents involved in the processes just described are increasingly strategically situated in a changing global order. Their influence is still heavily constrained by the regularised allocation of resources and the public goods decisions faced on a routine basis by states and state actors.

Nevertheless, state actors are being increasingly drawn into this wider universe. On the one hand, the hollowing out of the state has led to the contracting out of previously central state functions to a range of different levels of governance, whether local, transnational, private or mixed (Lahav, 1999; Savitch, 1998). For example, there is a burgeoning literature attempting to address the vexed question of how to conceptualise the growing institutionalisation of the European Union in this context. At the same time, of course, many of the actors within such groups and coalitions are not only aware of this situation, but working feverishly in proactive, entrepreneurial ways to further develop and institutionalise these network linkages. As the latter become more and more utilised and embedded, the more will their mission become institutionalised – unless, of course, they become 'captured' by existing state and intergovernmental apparatuses in the process (as is often said to be the case with domestic social movements: Tarrow, 1998). Of the three sets of agents dealt with in this chapter, social agents perhaps have the most collective and individual potential to become 'change masters' in a globalising world.

Nevertheless, it can also be argued that transnational opportunity structures, unlike national ones, are not configured primarily by hierarchical state structures, but by multilayered, quasi-anarchical, overlapping and cross-cutting – transnational – structural formations, including not only states-in-flux but also transnational economic and transgovernmental linkages. In such conditions, it is at least conceivable that the standard POS wisdom may be stood on its head, and that transnational social movements may nurture the growing influence of sets of social agents which themselves will impose new structural forms on the transnational field. At one level, then, social agents, in the form of NGOs and NSMs, may be the most strategically situated agents of all and have the greatest potential leeway – ability to exploit gaps and tensions in the structure of the international system – to imagine and to construct new forms of transnational structuration. However, the embeddedness of existing state and governmental institutions continues to constitute a major constraint. Whether their diverse bases of support and complex areas of involvement and expertise would permit them to develop an overall structural impact of a kind that could transform the international system itself is somewhat more problematic. As with economic and political agents, of course, the key will not be the action of social agents taken in isolation; rather it lies in the way that social agents can alter the shape of cross-cutting networks linking all three categories of agent in a globalising world.

CONCLUSION: THE DYNAMICS OF GLOBAL STRUCTURATION

This chapter has focused on both sides of the global structuration process. In the first place, I attempted to situate globalisation in its wider historical context. In the third section, I identified a range of changes taking place in the underlying structure of the public/private goods equation and at how these changes are impacting on the patterns of constraints and opportunities faced by agents in the globalisation process. In the following section, I looked at processes of change occurring within the single most important institutionalised structure of the modern era – the transformation of the state from the national industrial welfare state to the competition state. Indeed, I even suggested that 'the state' (state and state-related agents operating collectively within those constraints and opportunities) not only was changing, but was in many ways *driving* the globalisation process by pursuing international competitiveness as a goal and internalising that and related goals in a new discourse of globalisation. In the next section, however, I turned the argument on its head and looked at the other side of the globalisation coin – a stylised survey of the universe of agents who may be more or less likely to have an impact on this process, whether proactively or inadvertently. Thus a key part of the argument here is that the sorts of outcomes that might be hypothesised with regard to any ongoing process of transnational structuration, given the increasing openness of the system to pressures for a paradigm shift, will depend on the way strategically situated agents of all kinds consciously or unwittingly shape that process.

The final question must then be: 'What sorts of outcomes can be anticipated in the case of particular groups of entrepreneurs shaping the structuration process in specific ways?' Murphy (1998), inspired by Polanyi's (1944) idea of an ongoing 'double movement' in the structuring of modern societies and their interactions, argues that each historical transition to a more encompassing industrial order has initially been marked by a period of relatively slow economic growth; during this stage, rapid marketisation takes place, the state seems to retreat, and uncompromising versions of *laissez-faire* liberalism triumph. Up to now, however, he asserts, a second phase has always followed, marked by the growing success of egalitarian social movements – movements which then take the lead in shaping new institutions and structural patterns, that is, acting directly or indirectly as institutional entrepreneurs. This second phase, or the second part of Polanyi's 'double movement', has always been associated with the consolidation of the whole range of 'governance' institutions – from the interstate level down to the shop floor. Those institutions, for a time, help maintain a period of relative peace and relative prosperity over a larger industrial market area in which a whole new generation of lead industries become dominant. In time, however, various social conflicts, including those that arise from the restraints on liberal innovation imposed by each era's governance institutions, lead to crises; in these periods of crisis, *laissez-faire* 'first movers' provide the initial, successful social response, but then new egalitarian movements arise. These new movements provide not only the social impetus but also the entrepreneurial capacity for structural *bricolage* and institution-building which lay the foundations for a new stage of development, a new phase of the double movement.

Taking our cue from Murphy, we could look at the recent era of relatively slow growth, rapid marketisation, and the relative retreat of the state (Strange, 1996) as merely a stage in the development of a wider social-liberal 'world order' or more transnationalised 'embedded liberalism'. If the earlier pattern holds, prospects for movement to the next phase might be linked to the relative success of a whole range of egalitarian social movements. Transnational social movements, in this context, might be seen to have not only the widest *scope* for potential action – in order to succeed, they must, in a sense, target the world (or at least a growing range of embryonic but crystallising international and transnational structures and processes) – but also the greatest *range* or scale of potential action – that is, they can pick and choose their issue-areas to reflect the qualitatively 'global' issues they most value and which they are best at pushing (even when those issues appear 'local' in purely territorial terms). Even if such a view is too far-reaching, it is clear that such movements will always play a vital role in creating new forms of identity in a more transnationally structured international system, and may indirectly cause new lines of conflict and coalition-building, new transformative conditions, to crystallise. But let us look at some alternative scenarios.

A first alternative scenario might suggest that the structural developments outlined above do *not* entail a paradigm shift in the international system. From this perspective, globalising pressures merely trigger a range of *adaptive* behaviours on the part of the most significant strategically situated actors in each of the categories developed above and who are still significantly constrained in their capacity to form effective transformative networks cutting across those categories. In such circumstances, it is likely that the key to understanding structural change (however limited) is most likely to rest with traditional political agents. Such agents, enmeshed in deeply embedded nation-states and the states system, would react to pressures for change and the operation of endogenous structural tensions by increasing the adaptive capacity of, for example, traditional forms of international co-operation, along with pressure on domestic actors to adapt as well (the competition state). A second alternative scenario might be based on the predominance of transnational social movements and their ability to shape the agendas of other actors both within and cutting across states. Two linked hypotheses can be raised again here: on the one hand, the development of a 'global civil society', based on common transnational norms and values; and on the other, the emergence of a cross-cutting Coserian pluralism (or 'plurilateralism': Cerny, 1993). Held (1995), for example, has suggested that some mixture of analogous developments might well lead to the emergence of a transnational 'cosmopolitan democracy'. It might especially be the case that, should transnational NSMs prove to be the predominant change masters of the transnational structuration process, then a more complex, supranational process of 'mainstreaming' might well provide the glue for some form of *de facto* democratisation-without-the-state. Nevertheless, this remains a 'rosy scenario', an idealised state of affairs which it might be unwise to expect.[15]

However, the dominant image of transnationalisation and globalisation today, as suggested earlier, is still that of economic and business globalisation. Economic agents, through the transnational expansion of both markets and hierarchical (firm) structures and institutions, increasingly shape a range of key outcomes in terms of the allocation of both resources and values. Neoliberal ideology presents such developments as inevitable; in Mrs Thatcher's famous phrase, 'There is no alternative' (TINA). Should transnational social movements prove more peripheral to the structuration process than a Polanyian 'double movement' might suggest, and should political actors and the state continue to act as promoters of globalisation and enforcement, then the 'governance' structures of the twenty-first century international system will be likely to reflect in a more direct and instrumental way the priorities of international capital. Without a world government or set of effective 'international' (co-operative-political) governance mechanisms, private economic regimes such as internationalised financial markets and associations of transnationally active firms, large and small, are likely to shape the international system through their ability to channel investment flows and set cross-border prices for both capital and physical assets as well (Cerny, 2000a). In this sense, the shape of the governance structures of such a system will merely mimic the structures of capital itself.

This raises a number of issues. In the first place, it has been suggested that capital cannot directly control society. Capitalists are concerned first and foremost with competing with each other, not with policing the system (which can eat up profits); and there is no collective mechanism, no 'ideal collective capitalist' to regulate the system in the interests of capital *as a whole*, other than the *state* (Holloway and Picciotto, 1978). Nevertheless, indirect forms of control, for example through Gramscian cultural hegemony, may be more important than the state *per se* (especially in its limited guise as a 'nation-state'). Gill (1990), for example, sees the Trilateral Commission, the World Economic Forum (Davos) and other formal and informal networks among transnationally linked businessmen and their social and political allies as bearers of such hegemony. In this sense, then, it may be possible to hypothesise that, should transnational capital take a relatively holistic hegemonic form, then the international system of the twenty-first century will represent a truly liberal (or neoliberal) capitalist society in a way that no capitalist state has ever been able to. Private sector-based mechanisms of control at a transnational level may indeed replace the state as a 'committee of the whole bourgeoisie'. However, the crystallisation of other structural forms of international capital can also be envisaged, reflecting an unequal distribution of power or representation, for example among different economic sectors. For instance, in the 1970s what essentially were cartels of multinational corporations were thought by many on both sides of the political divide to be the form that international capital would take in the future. But in the 1990s' world of dramatic international capital movements, it is more often the financial markets which might be seen as exercising a 'sectoral hegemony' over the international system (Cerny, 1994a, 1994b and 1996). In either case, however, any significant transfer of power or system control from political agents (via states) to economic agents would represent a massive paradigm shift.

A final scenario, which I have explored elsewhere (Cerny, 1998, 2000b), is that exogenous pressures on the nation-state/states system, interacting with and exacerbating the tensions within that system, will cause that system to erode and weaken in key ways, but *without providing enough in the way of structural resources to any category of agents (or combination of categories) to effectively shape the transnational structuration process*. In other words, no group or group of groups will be the steering wheel of change in the international system, and competition between different groups will in turn undermine the capacity of any one of them to exercise such control. In such circumstances, the outcome might be what has been called 'neo-medievalism' – a fluid, multilayered structure of overlapping and competing institutions, cultural flux (postmodernism?), multiple and shifting identities and loyalties, with different 'niches' at different levels (social issues, economic sectors and so on) for groups to focus their energies on. As Minc (1993) has argued, the medieval world was not a world of chaos; it was a world of 'durable disorder'. Unless some coherent group of institutional entrepreneurs or change masters emerges to control and direct the process of transnational structuration, the medieval analogy may provide a better guide to understanding the international system in the twenty-first century than previous models involving states and the states system, both domestically and internationally. There is no reason in principle, after all, why 'governance' in this broad sense has to be tidy and logically coherent. The nation-state as such, and in particular the national industrial welfare state of the Second Industrial Revolution, may well be caught up in such wider, more complex webs, leading to increased uncertainty and possible disorder. At the same time, however, crosscutting networks of economic, political and social agents will lead to an increase in the influence and power wielded by transnationally linked institutional entrepreneurs, some of whom will certainly attempt to transcend the limits of adaptive behaviour and develop new institutional strategies for transforming and reconstructing the political in this fluid, globalising world.

NOTES

* Professor of International Political Economy at the University of Leeds, UK.

1 I am grateful to Jim Mosher for informing me that this can be expressed in the equation $G = i + t + (i \times t)$ – in other words, globalisation (as a process, not an end-point or state of affairs) is the sum of (a) processes of internationalisation (the increasing range and density of interdependencies *among states*), (b) processes of transnationalisation (the increasing range and density of linkages among behind-the-border actors *cutting across states*) and (c) the *interaction effects* of (a) plus (b). In other words, globalisation is the result of (at least) *three-level games*, not two-level games. A more complex version of this definition might be developed further to include discrete changes at the *domestic* level, as I will argue later in this chapter.

2 The word 'modern' is used here as historians would use it, that is, to denote a long period lasting from around the seventeenth century to sometime in the twentieth.

3 On distributional changes and social epistemologies (a term taken from Ruggie, 1993, p. 157), see Deibert (1997, pp. 31–7).

4 The 'prismatic society' concept was first developed and applied to complex domestic political systems by Riggs (1964).

5 Traditionally, Europeans use the word 'liberalism' to mean free-market, 'nineteenth century' liberalism, that is what Americans call 'conservatism'. Americans, in contrast, generally think of 'liberalism' as centre-left, quasi-social democratic state interventionism. In order to clarify this lexical confusion, Australians use the phrase 'social liberalism' for the latter.

6 The following draws on Cerny, 1995.

7 The following draws on Cerny, 1999d.

8 The word 'structure' is here used to denote the genus, a general organisational pattern, which, among other things, includes different types ranging from informal to formal structures; thus 'institutions' are seen as a particular species, that is, of more formal structures, although, as with any scalar distinction, there are many overlaps and shadings between the two terms. 'Institutionalist' theories are therefore seen as a special type of 'structuralist' (or in this case, 'structurationist') theory (Cerny, 1990).

9 Giddens (1979) defines structures as consisting of rules and resource distributions.

10 Deibert (1997), for example, shows how changes in communications media have both empowered and disempowered particular social, economic and political groups both in the historical transition from feudalism to the nation-state and in the current age of emerging 'hypermedia'.

11 The latter process is more widely studied in the disciplines of anthropology, sociology and linguistics than in political science or economics.

12 Parsons (1964) explores the notion that system change is cumulative in nature. For a consideration of some such scenarios, see Cerny (1990, ch. 1).

13 Including the development of craft-based industrial regions (Piore and Sabel, 1984), usually with strong transnational market linkages.

14 Again, the increasing embeddedness of globalisation discourse is probably more important for global policy transmission than material power (see Sinclair, 1999).

15 Hirst and Thompson (1996) suggest that the first of these two scenarios is most likely, with the possibility that a new social democratic consensus might be forged within it.

REFERENCES

Amin, Ash (ed.) (1994), *Post-Fordism: A Reader,* Oxford: Basil Blackwell.

Auspitz, Joshua L. (1976), 'Individuality, civility, and theory: the philosophical imagination of Michael Oakeshott', *Political Theory,* **4,** (2), August, 261–352.

Bendix, Reinhard (1964), *Nation-building and Citizenship: Studies of our Changing Social Order,* New York: John Wiley.

Betsill, Michele M. (1999), 'Changing the climate: NGOs, norms and the politics of global climate change', paper delivered at the *Annual Convention of the International Studies Association,* February, Washington, DC.

Cawson, Alan (ed.) (1985), *Organized Interests and the State: Studies in Meso-Corporatism,* London and Newbury Park, CA: Sage.

Cerny, P.G. (1990), *The Changing Architecture of Politics: Structure, Agency, and the Future of the State,* London and Newbury Park, CA: Sage.

Cerny, P.G. (1991), 'The limits of deregulation: transnational interpenetration and policy change', *European Journal of Political Research,* **19** (2) (3), March, 173–96.

Cerny, P.G. (1993), 'Plurilateralism: structural differentiation and functional conflict in the post-cold war world order', *Millennium: Journal of International Studies,* **22** (1), Spring, 27–51.

Cerny, P.G. (1994a), 'The infrastructure of the infrastructure? Towards embedded financial orthodoxy in the international political economy', in Ronen P. Palan and Barry Gills (eds), *Transcending the State–Global Divide: A Neostructuralist Agenda in International Relations,* Boulder, CO: Lynne Reinner, pp. 223–49.

Cerny, P.G. (1994b), 'The dynamics of financial globalization: technology, market structure and policy response', *Policy Sciences,* **27** (4), November, 319–42.

Cerny, P.G. (1995), 'Globalization and the changing logic of collective action', *International Organization,* **49** (4), Autumn, 595–625.

Cerny, P.G. (1996), 'International finance and the erosion of state policy capacity', in Philip Gummett (ed.), *Globalization and Public Policy,* Cheltenham, UK and Brookfield, US: Edward Elgar, pp. 83–104.

Cerny, P.G. (1998), 'Neomedievalism, civil wars and the new security dilemma', *Civil Wars,* **1** (1), Spring, 36–64.

Cerny, P.G. (1999a), 'Globalizing the political and politicizing the global: concluding reflections on international political economy as a vocation', *New Political Economy,* **4** (1), January, 147–62.

Cerny, P.G. (1999b), 'Globalization, governance and complexity', in Aseem Prakash and Jeffrey A. Hart (eds), *Globalization and Governance,* forthcoming, London: Routledge.

Cerny, P.G. (1999c), 'Globalization and the erosion of democracy', *European Journal of Political Research,* **35** (5), July.

Cerny, P.G. (1999d), 'Restructuring the political arena: globalization and the paradoxes of the competition state', in Randall Germain (ed.), *Globalization and its Critics,* London: Macmillan.

Cerny, P.G. (2000a), 'Embedding global finance: markets as governance structures', in Karsten Ronit and Volker Schneider (eds), *Private Organizations, Governance and Global Politics,* London: Routledge.

Cerny, P.G. (2000b), 'The new security dilemma: divisibility, defection and disorder in the global era', *Review of International Studies,* forthcoming.

Chandler, Alfred D. Jr (1990), *Scale and Scope: The Dynamics of Industrial Capitalism,* Cambridge, MA: Harvard University Press.

Chernow, Ron (1997), *The Death of the Banker: The Decline and Fall of the Great Financial Dynasties and the Triumph of the Small Investor,* Toronto: Vintage Canada.

Clark, Anne Marie, Elisabeth J. Friedman and Kathryn Hochstetler (1999), 'Sovereignty, global civil society, and the social conferences: NGOs and states at the UN conferences on population, social development, and human settlements', paper presented at the Annual Convention of the International Studies Association, Washington, DC, 16–20 February.

Clayton, Richard and Jonas Pontusson (1998), 'Welfare state retrenchment revisited: entitlement cuts, public sector restructuring, and inegalitarian trends in advanced capitalist societies', *World Politics,* **51**(1), October, 67–98.

Coser, Lewis A. (1956), *The Functions of Social Conflict,* London: Routledge and Kegan Paul.

Cox, Robert (1986), 'Social forces, states and world orders: beyond international relations theory', in R.O. Keohane (ed.), *Neorealism and Its Critics,* New York: Columbia University Press, pp. 204–254.

Crouch, Colin and Wolfgang Streeck (eds) (1997), *The Political Economy of Modern Capitalism: Mapping Convergence and Diversity,* London: Sage.

Crozier, Michel and Erhard, Friedberg (1977), *L'Acteur et le système: les contraintes de l'action collective,* Paris: Éditions du Seuil.

Deibert, Ronald J. (1997), *Parchment, Printing, and Hypermedia: Communication in World Order Transformation,* New York: Columbia University Press.

Dodgson, Richard (1999), 'Contesting neoliberal globalization at UN global conferences: the women's health movement and the International Conference on Population and Development', paper presented at the Annual Convention of the International Studies Association, Washington, DC, 16–20 February.

Dombrowski, Peter (1998), 'Fragmenting identities, shifting loyalties: the influence of individualisation on global systems change', *Global Society,* September.

Douglas, Ian Robert (1999), 'Globalization *as* governance: toward an archaeology of contemporary political reason', in Aseem Prakash and Jeffrey A. Hart (eds), *Globalization and Governance,* London: Routledge.

Dunleavy, Patrick J. (1994), 'The globalisation of public services production: can government be "best in world"?', *Public Policy and Administration,* **9** (2), Summer, 36–64.

Evans, Mark and Jonathan Davies (1999), 'Understanding policy transfer: a multi-level, multi-disciplinary perspective', *Public Administration,* forthcoming.

Frieden, Jeffry (1991), 'Invested interests: the politics of national economic policies in a world of global finance', *International Organization,* **45** (4), Autumn, 425–52.

Giddens, Anthony (1979), *Central Problems in Social Theory: Action, Structure and Contradiction in Social Analysis,* London: Macmillan.

Gill, Stephen (1990), *American Hegemony and the Trilateral Commission,* Cambridge: Cambridge University Press.

Granovetter, Mark (1985), 'Economic action and social structure: the problem of embeddedness', *American Journal of Sociology,* **91** (4), November, 50–82.

Granovetter, Mark (1992), 'Economic institutions as social constructions: a framework for analysis', *Acta Sociologica,* (35), 3–11.

Haas, Peter M. (1992), 'Introduction: epistemic communities and international policy coordination', *International Organization,* **46** (1), Winter, 187–224.

Haas, Peter M. (ed.) (1993), *Institutions for the Earth: Sources of Effective International Environmental Protection,* New Haven, CT: MIT Press .

Haggard, Stephan (1990), *Pathways from the Periphery: The Politics of Growth in the*

Newly Industrializing Countries, Ithaca, NY: Cornell University Press.

Hall, Peter A. and Rosemary Taylor (1996), 'Political science and the three new institutionalisms', *Political Studies,* **44** (5), December, 936–57.

Harris, Nigel (1986), *The End of the Third World,* Harmondsworth, Middx: Penguin.

Hart, Jeffrey A. (1992), *Rival Capitalists: International Competitiveness in the United States, Japan, and Western Europe,* Ithaca, NY: Cornell University Press.

Held, David (1995), *Democracy and the Global Order: From the Modern State to Democratic Governance,* Cambridge: Polity Press.

Helleiner, Eric N. (1998), 'State power and the regulation of illicit activity in global finance', in Richard Friman and Peter Andreas (eds), *The Illicit Global Economy and State Power,* Lanham, MD: Rowman and Littlefield.

Hirst, Paul and Grahame Thompson (1996), *Globalization in Question? The International Economy and the Possibilities of Governance,* Oxford: Polity Press.

Holloway, John and Sol Picciotto (eds) (1978), *State and Capital: A Marxist Debate,* London: Edward Arnold.

Jessop, Bob (1997), 'The future of the national state: erosion or reorganization? Reflections on the West European case', paper presented at a conference on Globalization: Critical Perspectives, University of Birmingham, 14–16 March.

Johnson, Chalmers (1982), *M.I.T.I. and the Japanese Miracle: The Growth of Industrial Policy, 1925–1975,* Stanford, CA: Stanford University Press.

Kanter, Rosabeth Moss (1993), 'Change masters and the intricate architecture of corporate culture change', in Peter Kabrak (ed.), *The Political Environment of Public Management,* New York: HarperCollins College Publishers, pp. 183–200.

Keck, Margaret E. and Kathryn Sikkink (1998), *Activists Beyond Borders: Advocacy Networks in International Politics,* Ithaca, NY: Cornell University Press.

Kemp, Tom (1983), *Industrialization in the Non-Western World,* Harlow, Essex: Longman.

Kennedy, Paul (1988), *The Rise and Fall of the Great Powers: Economic Change and Military Conflict from 1500 to 2000,* London: Unwin Hyman.

Krajnc, Anita (1999), 'Learning in British Columbia's Clayoquot and Great Bear Rainforest campaigns: from public pressure to global civic politics', paper presented at the Annual Convention of the International Studies Association, Washington, DC, 16–20 February.

Krieger, Joel and Craig Murphy (1998), 'Transnational opportunity structures and the evolving roles of movements for women, human rights, labor, development, and the environment: a proposal for research', Department of Political Science, Wellesley College, MA.

Lahav, Gallya (1999), 'The devolution and privatization of immigration regulation in the European Union: reinvented forms of state control', *Journal of Ethnic and Migration Studies* (forthcoming).

Lowi, Theodore J. (1964), 'American business, public policy, case studies, and political theory', *World Politics,* **16** (4), July, 677–715.

Machin, Howard and Vincent Wright (eds) (1985), *Economic Policy and Policy-making under the Mitterand Presidency, 1981–1984,* London: Frances Pinter.

Mayer, Arno J. (1981), *The Persistence of the Old Regime: Europe to the Great War,* London: Croom Helm.

Maxfield, Sylvia (1997), *Gatekeepers of Growth: The Politics of Central Banking in Developing Countries,* Princeton, NJ: Princeton University Press.

McKenzie, Richard B. and Dwight R. Lee (1991), *Quicksilver Capital: How the Rapid Movement of Wealth Has Changed the World,* New York: Free Press.

Milner, Helen V. (1988), *Resisting Protectionism: Global Industries and the Politics of*

International Trade, Princeton, NJ: Princeton University Press.

Minc, Alain (1993), *Le nouveau Moyen Age,* Paris: Gallimard.

Moore, Barrington Jr (1991), *Social Origins of Dictatorship and Democracy: Lord and Peasant in the Making of the Modern World,* Harmondsworth, Middx: Penguin.

Murphy, Craig (1998), 'Egalitarian social movements and new world orders', paper presented at the Annual Conference of the British International Studies Association, University of Sussex, 14–16 December.

Nature (1996), 'Report stays neutral on deep-sea disposal', *Nature,* **381** (6581), May, 358.

Oakeshott, Michael (1976), 'On misunderstanding human conduct: a reply to my critics', *Political Theory,* **4** (2), August, 353–67.

Olson, Mancur (1965), *The Logic of Collective Action,* Cambridge, MA: Harvard University Press.

Osborne, David and Ted Gaebler (1992), *Reinventing Government: How the Entrepreneurial Spirit is Transforming the Public Sector, from Schoolhouse to Statehouse, City Hall to the Pentagon,* Reading, MA: Addison-Wesley.

Ostrom, Vincent and Elinor Ostrom (1977), 'Public goods and public choices', in E.S. Savas (ed.), *Alternatives for Delivering Public Services: Toward Improved Performance,* Boulder, CD: Westview Press, pp. 7–49.

Ostrom, Vincent, C.M. Tiebout and R. Warren (1961), 'The organization of government in metropolitan areas: a theoretical inquiry', *American Political Science Review,* **55** (3), September, 831–42.

Parsons, Talcott (1964), 'A functional theory of change', in Amitai Etzioni and Eva Etzioni (eds), *Social Change: Sources, Patterns, and Consequences,* New York: Basic Books, pp. 83–97.

Pauly, Louis W. (1997), *Who Elected the Bankers? Surveillance and Control in the World Economy,* Ithaca, NY: Cornell University Press.

Pauly, Louis W. and Simon Reich (1997), 'National structures and multinational corporate behavior: enduring differences in the age of globalization', *International Organization,* **51** (1), Winter, 1–30.

Peters, B. Guy (1997), 'Globalization and governance', paper presented at a conference on Globalization: Critical Perspectives, University of Birmingham, 14–16 March 1997.

Piore, Michael and Charles F. Sabel (1984), *The Second Industrial Divide: Possibilities for Prosperity,* New York: Basic Books.

Polanyi, Karl (1944), *The Great Transformation: The Political and Economic Origins of Our Time,* New York: Rinehart.

Porter, Michael E. (1990), *The Competitive Advantage of Nations,* London: Macmillan.

Portnoy, Brian (1999), 'Alliance capitalism as industrial order: exploring new forms of interfirm competition in the globalizing economy', in Richard Higgott and Andreas Bieler (eds), *Non-State Actors and Authority in the Global System,* London: Routledge.

Prowse, Michael (1992), 'Post-modern test for government', *Financial Times,* 21 April.

Reich, Robert B. (1991), *The Work of Nations: Preparing Ourselves for 21st-Century Capitalism,* New York: Alfred A. Knopf.

Rhodes, R.A.W. (1996), 'The new governance: governing without government', *Political Studies,* **44** (4), September, 652–67.

Riggs, Fred W. (1964), *Administration in Developing Countries: The Theory of Prismatic Society,* Boston, MA: Houghton Mifflin.

Robertson, Roland (1992), *Globalization: Social Theory and Global Culture,* London: Sage.

Rosenau, James N. (1963), *National Leadership and Foreign Policy: A Case Study in Mobilization of Public Support*, Princeton, NJ: Princeton University Press.

Ruggie, John Gerard (1993), 'Territoriality and beyond: problematizing modernity in international relations', *International Organization*, **47** (1), Winter, 139–74.

Rupert, Mark (1995), *Producing Hegemony: The Politics of Mass Production and American Global Power*, Cambridge: Cambridge University Press.

Savitch, H.V. (1998), 'Global challenge and institutional capacity: or, how we can refit local administration for the next century', *Administration and Society*, **30** (3), July, 248–73.

Schattschneider, E.E. [1935] (1974), *Politics, Pressures, and the Tariff*, New York: Arno Press.

Schmidt, Vivien A. (1996), *From State to Market? The Transformation of French Business Government*, Cambridge: Cambridge University Press.

Schmitter, Philippe C. (1974), 'Still the century of corporatism?', in F. Pike and T. Stritch (eds), *The New Corporatism*, Notre Dame; Il: Notre Dame University Press, pp. 85–131.

Schumpeter, Joseph A. (1939), *Business Cycles: A Theoretical, Historical and Statistical Analysis of the Capitalist Process*, New York: McGraw-Hill.

Simon, Herbert A. (1997), *Administrative Behavior: A Study of Decision-making Processes in Administrative Organizations*, 4th edn, New York: Free Press.

Sinclair, Timothy J. (1999), 'The modern Trojan horse: budget deficits and global policy transmission', paper presented at the Annual Convention of the International Studies Association, Washington, DC, 16–20 February.

Spruyt, Hendrik (1994), *The Sovereign State and Its Competitors: An Analysis of Systems Change*, Princeton, NJ: Princeton University Press.

Stone, Diane (1996), *Capturing the Political Imagination: Think Tanks and the Policy Process*, London: Frank Cass.

Stone, Diane (1999), 'Learning lessons, transferring policy and the international movement of ideas', Conference Paper WS/63, European University Institute, Florence, 25–26 March.

Stopford, John and Susan Strange (1991), *Rival States, Rival Firms: Competition for World Market Shares*, Cambridge: Cambridge University Press.

Strange, Susan (1996), *The Retreat of the State: The Diffusion of Power in the World Economy*, Cambridge: Cambridge University Press.

Tarrow, Sidney (1998), *Power in Movement: Social Movements and Contentious Politics*, 2nd edn, Cambridge: Cambridge University Press.

Truman, David B. (1951), *The Governmental Process: Political Interests and Public Opinion*, New York: Alfred A. Knopf.

Vogel, Steven K. (1996), *Freer Markets, More Rules: Regulatory Reform in Advanced Industrial Countries*, Ithaca, NY: Cornell University Press.

Willetts, Peter (ed.) (1982), *Pressure Groups in the Global System: The Transnational Relations of Issue-Orientated Non-Governmental Organizations*, New York: St. Martin's Press.

Williamson, Oliver E. (1975), *Markets and Hierarchies*, New York: Free Press.

Williamson, Oliver E. (1985), *The Economic Institutions of Capitalism*, New York: Free Press.

Znaniecki, Florian [1952] (1973), *Modern Nationalities: A Sociological Study*, Westport, CT: Greenwood Press.

Zysman, John (1983), *Governments, Markets, and Growth: Financial Systems and the Politics of Industrial Change*, Ithaca, NY: Cornell University Press.

Zysman, John (1996), 'The myth of the global economy: enduring national foundations

and emerging regional realities', *New Political Economy*, **1** (1), Summer, 157–84.
Zysman, John and Laura d'Andrea Tyson (eds) (1983), *American Industry in International Competition*, Ithaca, NY: Cornell University Press.

5 The Tyranny of Globalisation: Myth or Reality?

Paul Hirst and Grahame Thompson[*]

INTRODUCTION

When we began to work on the international economy we were open minded on the issue of globalisation (Hirst and Thompson 1996a). But one of the issues that struck us earliest was the lack of a clear definition of the concept – the *word* globalisation existed with many interpretations, but a clear *concept* was missing. A significant problem with discussions of globalisation is that the term tends to expand infinitely its scope of reference. It is employed so loosely that almost anything can be used to illustrate its operation or be included within its embrace. The problem with an expansion and inflation of a term in this way is that if *everything* can be explained by it then clearly *nothing* can be explained by it: it loses its operational effectiveness as an analytical category.

In addition, there is a danger that because the term is used so imprecisely and widely, it is mobilised to justify almost any policy option that policymakers, politicians or business interests wish to press upon their citizens or employees. In general we would argue that globalisation, as a conceptualisation of the current stage of the internationalisation of economic activity, leads to a too hasty denial of the possibilities for effective economic management: it leads to overdiminished expectations as to what can still be done by governments and other agents of governance.

In this chapter we examine the evidence for the existence of a new structural stage of the international economy – a globalised economy – as distinct to previous stages of international capitalism. Two preliminary points should be made about this discussion. The first is that it requires a fairly rigorous definition of what such a new stage of international capitalism might look like. And secondly, it requires us to demarcate what is distinctive about the trends in the present international economy from those typical of, say, the period before the Second World War and particularly during the high Gold Standard period (roughly 1870–1913).

The fact that we have stressed a similarity between many of the features of the present internationalisation of economic activity and the degree of that internationalisation during the high Gold Standard period does not mean that we are arguing nothing has changed. The analysis here will thus concentrate upon what is potentially different about the present period to that of 1870–1913. Since we cannot cover all the pertinent issues involved we concentrate upon the most important and fundamental. These are (1), the effective TRIADisation of the international economy in the present period (and how that might now itself be being partly undermined); (2) the nature and extent of cross-border integrated production; (3) the form of the international financial system; and finally (4) the existence of extended public expenditure, and particularly expenditure on welfare provision, for the continued operation of discrete national welfare systems in a supposedly globalised world.

GLOBALISATION

As far as globalisation has been defined it tends to be used as just another word for the further internationalisation of economic activity, in terms of greater or deeper integration and interdependence. The most widely quoted definition in this style of reasoning emerged from an OECD study of globalisation (OECD, 1992, p. 195): 'Globalisation is being driven by technological change, continued long-term growth in foreign investment and international sourcing, and the recent extensive formation of new kinds of international links between firms and countries. This combination is increasingly integrating national economies and changing the nature of global competition.' This definition of globalisation was recently repeated almost verbatim in the 1997 Annual Report for the European Economy (see European Union, 1997, p. 45).

To us it seemed necessary to provide a clearer definition of globalisation that did not simply imply the extension and deepening of already well-advanced international economic interactions. If globalisation were simply the extension of internationalisation by another name, what was all the fuss about? We thus drew a sharp distinction between what we termed a 'globalised world economy' and an 'inter-nationalised world economy'. If there is something distinctive about the present era – a potential structural shift in the nature of international capitalism – which distinguishes it from previous periods, then something must be said about what the nature of this new phenomenon is, rather than just a continuation of previous trends under a different name (albeit it in an intensified form).

Briefly put an 'inter-nationalised world economy' would be one in which the principal entities remain national economies, or agents that continue to be primarily located in a definite national territory. Although there is increasing integration and enmeshment between these entities, there is a continued relative separation of the 'domestic' arena from the 'international' arena, so that international processes, events and impacts are refracted through national frameworks, policies and processes. This means that an inter-national world economy would be articulated 'upwards', so to speak, from the national actors to the international level. Relatively distinct national economies and nationally embedded actors would be articulated together to form such an inter-national economy. The principal private agents in this kind of an economy would be multinational corporations. These would maintain a clear national base, a nationally formed management style and personnel. They would still be effectively regulated and policed by 'home country' authorities, and continue to operate mainly in respect to their home-base country. The image here, then, would be one of a continued nationally embedded capital.

In contrast to this is a 'globalised world economy'. Here the principle entity is the new global economy itself, which would represent a new structure of disembedded economic relationships. This is an economy that exists 'above' the national economies and agents, autonomously from those national economies, and that bears down upon those economies and actors, stamping them with their particular character and form. It 'enfolds' them within its own dynamic. Thus it is articulated 'downwards'. It would determine what can and cannot be done at the national level, by both public and private agencies. This would be an economy that escapes 'governance' – one typified by unorganised and uncontrollable market forces. The principal private actors here would be transnational corporations. These represent organisations that are disembodied from any national-base. They would source, produce and market genuinely internationally. They would seek competitive advantage and the most secure and largest returns by roaming the globe for cheap but efficient production locations. They would have an internationalised management style and personnel. Thus the image here is one of footloose capital searching the globe for competitive advantage.

These two contrasting images of different types of world economy were presented starkly so as to try to differentiate any new globalised economy from other previously formed sets of internationalised economic relationships. They represent 'ideal types', and are not direct representations of any actual economy. They are constructed to aid analytical enquiry; to help investigate the actual form of the world economy which exists. The internationalisation of economic activity has been going on almost since civilisation began, and certainly since the 1700s. So what is new and distinctive about the present period? That is the question which needs to be addressed, and this requires a specification of the features of a globalised economy as opposed to something else.

We have spent some time on these definitional issues since they are often neglected or misunderstood. These definitions are self-consciously conceptual and deliberately polarised. They have also proved controversial, since commentators have often mistaken these ideal-typical analytical distinctions as measures of actual economies and of globalisation itself. In so doing, however, perhaps unwittingly, other contrasting definitions of globalisation have emerged.

The first of these confuses the analytical distinction just made with a distinction between actual forms of the economic mechanism. It accuses the kind of definition of a globalised economy made above of providing a single 'end-state' for the international system – *the* globalised economy. This is seen as a 'single equilibrium', so to speak – the end result of a series of stages, mechanically unfolding one after another (Goldblatt *et al.,* 1997). By contrast, it is suggested, globalisation is an on-going *process* (or sometimes a set of on-going *practices*), where there may be a number of outcomes, 'multiple-equilibria', depending upon the 'path' by which that process evolves. The present 'phase' of globalisation is thus just one of its many possible forms. The outcome of this approach is to, in effect, revert back to a conception that stresses the increasing intensity and extensivity of the internationalisation of economic relationships. This is a conception explicitly summed up by Lerda: 'Thus ... the growing intensity of flows – of trade, foreign direct investment, short-term capital, technology – which accompanies, reflects and conditions the process of economic globalisation should be interpreted as the acceleration of a historical process whose roots can be discerned in the last century' (Lerda, 1996, p. 67).

The problem with this kind of approach, however, is its relative lack of analytical rigour. To start with the idea of a process is all very well – one that is not, in fact, ruled out by the way we have set up the issue above – but to do any proper analytical work it is always necessary to interrupt such processes and ask where exactly we are in respect to them. This is in effect what our initial definitional activity allowed us to do. In addition, we would argue that all processes tend towards some 'end', even if they never reach it. If not, the notion of 'process' is meaningless. The admission of potential multiple equilibria does not excuse the specification of what those equilibria would consist in, so we are back at the same point from which the accusation of an 'end-state' began.

The second criticism of our definition arises from a different quarter. Our approach emphasises cross-border interactions. In this sense it is fairly conventional. An alternative approach, indeed one that provides an alternative definition of what is the unique feature of the period of 'globalisation', is to suggest that borders are no longer the key feature of the present international system. The 'global' is in the 'local' is one way of putting this. Thus the way globalisation works is to *imbricate* international, and not necessarily cross-border, features at the local level. They become part of the fabric of the local. Features of the commercial world such as accounting conventions, legal frameworks, credit rating measures, ISO 9000 production standards and the like, embody the process of globalisation 'un-noticed' as it were, and do not obviously involve a definite 'flow' of something across a border that can be measured as such. What is distinctive about the present period of globalisation is the emergence of the kinds of processes whereby the international world is increasingly governed by these kinds of private (mostly Anglo-American) commercial practices.

Clearly, this is a feature of the international system, one that gives significant power to those agencies responsible for setting the standards. And many of these are private organisations, though they are not exclusively so. They are a potentially new breed of semi-private organisations that both claim and exercise a public power (Strange, 1996). But what is so new about this situation? Forms of international standard setting have been a feature of the international system at least from the 1870s onwards, when it was the British who were in the position to establish credit ratings, for instance. Before the First World War it was British and Norwegian private classification policies that set the standards for the seaworthiness of commercial shipping, having captured this largely because of the size of their merchant fleets. For all intents and purposes it is the Federal Aviation Agency (FAA) that sets the airworthiness standards for international aircraft, but this was achieved long before the advent of 'globalisation'. And one could go on to multiply these kinds of examples. Thus we remain to be convinced that there is anything unique enough about international standard setting to enable it to operate as the defining feature of a newly globalising economy. Moreover it can be positive if the agencies are reliable, like the *Det Norske Veritas* and such standards facilitate trade by ensuring commonality. Therefore such internationalisation should be seen as part of a world trading system, rather than as an alternative or opposed to it.

We could add other definitions of globalisation that operate along similar lines as these – the idea that it is a 'strategy' for instance, and thus in the *minds* of decision takers, particularly in private businesses. But we would defend our original definitional clarification against all these alternatives because we find it gives the clearest basis on which to begin an empirical investigation into the nature of the contemporary international system. However, there may be a further legitimate and rival claim that speaks for the nature of the international system; that of regionalisation.

REGIONALISATION

Rather than a truly global economy, the recent trends have been towards a regionalised one. But quite how to capture this trend towards regionalisation is subject to debate and is not always consistently formulated. One way is to focus on the *de jure* regional free trade areas (FTAs) that have sprung up since the 1970s, and use these as a basis for looking at the patterns of economic integration they have established. Table 5.1 shows the relative importance of these blocs in 1994 world trade. Some 61 per cent of world trade was accounted for by these regionalised *de jure* trade blocs in the mid-1990s.

Table 5.1 Regional free trade arrangements:share of world trade, 1994 (%)

EU	22.8
Euro-Med	2.3
'Europe' Sub-total	**25.1**
NAFTA	7.9
MERCOSUR	0.3
FTAA	2.6[a]
'Americas' Sub-total	**10.8**
AFTA	1.3
Australia – New Zealand	0.1
APEC	23.7[a]
'Pacific Rim' Sub-total	**25.1**
Total	**61.0**

Notes:
FTAA = Free Trade Area of the Americas
AFTA = ASEAN Free Trade Area
[a] Excludes cross-sub regional totals.

Source: Adapted from: Bergsten, 1996, p. 196.

Furthermore, Figure 5.1 demonstrates that the shares of intra-regional trade in total trade for the FTAs had been increasing during the mid-1990s.

According to Frankel (1997) all these regional arrangements show a bias towards trading between the countries within them – to some extent at the expense of trading outside of their regional bloc. After adjusting for the fundamental determinants of trade such as the size of the countries, their GDP per capita, proximity and common borders between them, trade flows higher than might be expected were found. Thus there would seem to be a 'trade diverting' aspect to regional bloc formation. However, this is not totally at the expense of trade growth generally, since whilst there was a higher than expected growth within blocs, there was also some growth of trade with countries outside of the blocs (but at lower rates). This just means that all the blocs act as discriminating areas in favour of their own members.

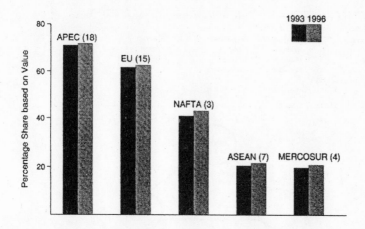

Source: WTO Annual Report 1997, Vol.1, p. 15, adapted from Chart 11.3

Figure 5.1 Share of intra-regional trade of selected regional integration arrangements, 1993 and 1995 (% share based upon value)

Another way of approaching the issue of bloc formation is to concentrate upon the *de facto* construction of blocs, which does not necessarily coincide with their *de jure* existence. This focuses in the first instance upon the consequences of commercial decisions made by firms as to where they conduct their trade and undertake their investments. The results of one such exercise is given in Figure 5.2, where the Triad of the US, the EU and Japan is shown along with the cluster of countries to which they are related in terms of FDI flows and stocks. In fact this is mirrored by trade flows between the countries shown as well, though we concentrate upon investments here (see Hirst and Thompson, 1996a, pp. 63–72).

Figure 5.2 indicates which member of the Triad dominated the inward FDI in particular countries over the period of the late 1980s and early 1990s. It should be remembered that intra-Triad relations alone were responsible for 75 per cent of FDI flows during the 1980s, some 70 per cent of trade in 1992, and a similar percentage of GDP (whereas they accounted for only 14 per cent of the world's population). After the mid-1980s the growth of FDI eclipsed that of trade, so FDI now figures as the central driving force in the international economy (both of these are, however, expanding at a faster rate than is world GDP). For 1970 to 1995 FDI flows to the industrial and developing countries are shown in Figure 5.3.

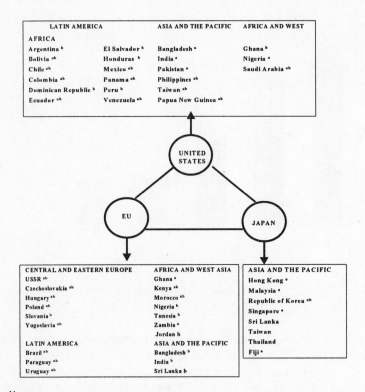

Notes:
a   In terms of average inward FDI flow, 1988-90
b   In terms of inward FDI stock voor 1990

Source: Hirst and Thompson (1996a, figure 3.8, p. 65)

Figure 5.2 Foreign direct investment clusters of Triad members, 1990 (economies on which Triad member dominates inward foreign direct investment stocks/flows)

Although the growth of FDI flows declined somewhat in the early 1990s, and the direction of these flows moved more in favour of the non-Triad countries, the older pattern began to re-establish itself again after 1992. This intra-Triad dominance was reinforced by the important subsidiary flows of investment between the Triad itself and a geographically discrete group of smaller 'clustered' states shown in the square boxes of Figure 5.2. Relatively isolated clusters of main actor and 'client' states were emerging, therefore, which were geographically discrete and stabilising. Thus whilst *intra*-Triad investment relationships were particularly dense, a pattern of further robust *inter*-linkages between each of the Triad members and more marginalised and discrete country clusters was also evident. These country groupings tend to be regionally specific and 'adjacent' to one or other of the Triad members. Further, this testifies to the relative *lack of global integration* in FDI flows and stocks since the boxed clusters indicate a geographical and regional discreteness in the relationships between countries. The direction of FDI relationships is first amongst the Triad countries themselves and then secondly between one or other of the Triad powers and its cluster of 'client' states, rather than between the states shown in the clustered boxes themselves.

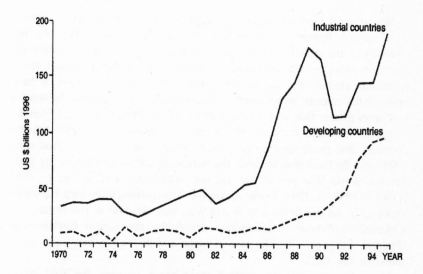

Source: International Finance Corporation, *Foreign Direct Investment*, Washington, DC, 1997 figure 2.4, p.16

Figure 5.3 Real FDI flows to industrial and developing countries, 1970–95 (1996 US$ billions)

In fact, since this analysis was completed there has been some growth of intra-cluster trade and investment relationships, that is, between the countries shown in the square boxes. Attentive readers would have noticed that mainland China is not included among the countries shown in Figure 5.2. But mainland China became the largest single developing country recipient

accumulated stock inherited from the past. This is shown for the years 1980–95 in Table 5.3, expressed as a percentage of GDP.

As might be expected, there has been a growth in the importance of FDI relative to GDP since 1980 – at the world level it has more than doubled from 4.6 per cent to 10.1 per cent. But the absolute levels in 1995 still remain modest for most countries and groupings. The UK is a conspicuous exception amongst the larger advanced countries. At the other end of the spectrum Japan remains largely untouched by inward FDI (and even its outward stock, at 6 per cent in 1995, was modest). It is surely debatable whether a stock of foreign-owned productive activity of around 10 per cent or less of GDP for most of the advanced countries is sufficient as yet to represent such a large MNC presence that it begins to undermine a national economy. It could be argued to have been more important for a small number of rapidly developing countries that have relied upon FDI as the main stimulus to their development strategies, but even this might be challenged (see below).

Table 5.3 Inward FDI stock as a % of GDP (1980, 1985, 1990, 1995)

	1980	1985	1990	1995
World	4.6	6.5	8.3	10.1
Developed economies	4.8	6.0	8.3	9.1
of which: EU	5.5	8.2	10.9	13.4
(UK)	11.7	14.0	22.3	28.5
(Germany)	4.5	6.0	7.4	6.9
USA	3.1	4.6	7.2	7.7
Japan	0.3	0.4	0.3	0.3
Developing Economies	4.3	8.1	8.7	15.4
of which: LA & Caribbean	6.4	10.8	11.6	18.4
(Brazil)	6.9	11.3	8.1	17.8
Asia	3.5	7.3	7.3	14.2
South, East & SE Asia	3.8	6.5	8.7	15.1
Central & Eastern Europe	-	0.1	1.3	4.9

Source: Compiled from UN (1997, annex table B.6)

However, in many ways FDI is not a good measure of the extent of international productive activity. Contrary to common claims FDI is not a measure of the assets held by affiliated firms. Rather, it measures what is going on on the liabilities side of company's balance sheets. FDI flows are made up of changes in the shares, loans and retained earnings of affiliate companies that are operating abroad, though in a number of countries the reporting of FDI does not even include retained earnings. Such earnings have become an important element in the amount of activity conducted abroad (so in this sense, FDI might *underestimate* the extent of this activity in some countries). But in general the FDI measure is likely to *overestimate* this activity. Companies not only massage their liabilities for tax purposes – which has nothing necessarily to do with their ability to produce from their assets – but a major form of FDI liability management, namely the purchase of existing company shares and bonds, also need have no direct relationship to changing the productive capacity of the assets so acquired. If a foreign company acquires an already existing domestic company's liabilities through an acquisition or merger (A&M), but does not alter the asset structure of the acquired company, there is no necessary increase in the productive potential in the country in which it has invested. This would appear as an inward flow of FDI, however. There has been a dramatic growth in the extent of A&M activity internationally, particularly as stimulated by the privatisation programme embarked upon by both the advanced and latterly the developing countries. In 1996 nearly 50 per cent of global FDI flows were made up of cross-border mergers and acquisitions (UN,1997, p. 9) and this is expected to increase as a proportion in the future (ibid., p. 36).

Thus what is needed are new measures of internationalisation that capture more of what is going on on the asset side of companies balance sheets, or which look directly at the extent of productive activity accounted for by foreign affiliates in a country's national income economy as registered in its accounts. But here there are major problems of access to relevant and appropriate information.

In any scrutiny of company accounts, for instance, it is important to recognise what companies are doing on their 'home' territory as at the same time they are investing and operating abroad. FDI flows only capture what companies are 'lending' to their affiliates abroad, not what they are at the same time investing in their home country or territory. Even where there is some assessment of the extent of foreign owned *assets* by MNCs, the companies included are usually those already classified by the extent of their *foreign*-owned assets, thereby prematurely skewing the analysis in favour of the overseas orientation of company activity (see, for example, UN, 1997, table 1.7, pp. 29–31).

In work reported in detail elsewhere we have developed three large-scale cross-sectional data sets designed to circumvent some of these problems (see Hirst and Thompson 1996a; Allen and Thompson 1997; Thompson 1999). The main conclusion drawn from this analysis was that the 'home orientated' nature of MNC activity along all the dimensions looked at (company assets, their sales, subsidiaries and affiliates, and profits) remained significant, even if this is a regionally centred one. It confirms that as much as between two-thirds and three-quarters of MNC aggregate business activity remained home or regionally centred in the early 1990s.

Thus MNCs still rely upon their 'home base' as the centre for their economic activities, despite all the speculation about globalisation. From these results we can be reasonably confident that, in the aggregate, international companies are still predominantly MNCs (with a clear home base to their operations) and not TNCs (which represent footloose stateless companies).

But this is not the end of the necessary adjustments that need to be made to the popular belief that MNCs are now so footloose that they are undermining the continued viability of national economies or national systems of business. We need to supplement this company-based data by looking at the extent of internationalisation in relation to overall national output, and then with that derived directly from national account statistics. This gives some added insights into the true extent of internationalisation.

The data in Table 5.4 provide estimates of the gross product that foreign affiliates were responsible for producing compared to the GDP of various country groupings and the world total.

Table 5.4 Gross product of foreign affiliates as a % of GDP, 1982, 1990 and 1994

	1982	1990	1994
World	5.2	6.7	6.0
Developed countries	5.1	6.7	5.4
European Union	5.7	8.6	7.7
North America	5.1	6.7	5.2
Developing Countries	6.0	7.0	9.1
Latin America & the Caribbean	7.6	9.3	10.3
Asia	5.6	5.9	8.6
South-East Asia	5.0	7.0	9.0
Central & Eastern Europe	0.1	1.1	2.3

Source: UN (1997, adapted from table A4, p. 267)

Note that for the developed countries this only increased from 5.1 per cent in 1982 to 5.4 per cent in 1994 (despite the massive increase in FDI flows over this period); from 6 per cent to 9.1 per cent (that is, an admittedly 50 per cent increase) for the developing countries; and from 5.2 per cent to 6.0 per cent for the world total overall. But these hardly seem dramatic levels or major growth rates for the crucial developed countries where fears of the effects of globalisation are perhaps most pronounced.

Finally, it is worth considering various other detailed attempts to assess the extent of internationalised production as derived directly from national accounts and measures of national output. For the year 1990, for instance, Lipsey, *et al.* (1995) calculated that foreign-based output amounted to only about 7 per cent of overall world output (see also Table 5.4 above), up from 4.5 per cent in 1970 (Lipsey, 1997, p. 2). Although the share was higher in 'industry' (including manufacturing, trade, construction and public utilities) at about 15 per cent in 1990 (up from 11 per cent in 1977), it was negligible in 'services', which amounted to 60 per cent of total world output in 1990. By 1995 foreign-based output was estimated to have increased to 7.5 per cent of total world output, hardly a dramatic and earth-shattering change.

The story of US international firms is interesting in its own right. Their overseas output peaked in 1977 at about 8 per cent of US GDP, and has been declining ever since to about 5.5 per cent in 1995. In manufacturing the production by majority-owned US foreign affiliates was 15.5 per cent of US manufacturing output in 1977, reaching over 17 per cent in 1990, but settling back to 16 per cent in 1995, that is, it has remained almost stable over the past 20 years. In terms of employment the trends have been similar. There was a rapid increase in US firms' employment overseas relative to that at home from 1957 to 1977, but since then the trend has been a decreasing one. In 1994 the foreign manufacturing affiliate employment of US firms remained well below its 1977 level. Most of these decreases in the overseas proportions of US firms' production and employment can be accounted for by the relative decline in the importance of the manufacturing sector in the US economy as a whole. In fact, the story of the internationalisation of the US manufacturing sector has really been one confined to the inward investment side. MNC production in the US as a proportion of GDP rose from almost zero in 1970 to just over 8 per cent in 1995, and in the manufacturing sector from 4 per cent in 1977 to 13 per cent in 1994 (Ramstetter, 1998, figure 8.3, p. 195).

The story of the Japanese economy is almost the reverse of that of the US. There has been virtually no growth in the importance of overseas production to GDP in Japan. Indeed, in terms of directly measured output indicators, the trend has been a declining one (ibid., 1998, figure 8.2, p. 194). On the other hand, Japanese multinationals have been expanding their activities abroad relative to their production at home. For all Japanese manufacturing companies the overseas production ratio doubled from 5 per cent in 1985 to nearly 10 per cent in 1996 (for only those companies with overseas affiliates this ratio also doubled, from about 13.5 per cent to 27.5 per cent over the same period; MITI 1997). Given Japanese overall output growth rates, however, absolute levels of these ratios relative to GDP are low and changes have been modest.

Similar calculations as these for the other advanced countries are not readily available. The broad picture is indicated by the data contained in Table 5.4. But for the Asia-Pacific region as a whole Ramstetter (1998, p. 208) has produced a comprehensive survey along these lines, in particular comparing FDI based indicators with those derived directly from national accounting data, the results of which are worth quoting:

> [The finding that] FDI-based indicators and foreign MNC shares of production often display very different trends, strongly suggests that FDI-related indicators are rather poor indicators of foreign MNC presence. More specifically, since foreign MNC shares of production are clearly more accurate measures of foreign MNC presence, focussing on FDI-related measures apparently leads to significant overestimation of the extent to which MNC presence has grown in the Asia Pacific region since the 1970s.

This remains a salutary warning for all those approaches that stress the simple growth of FDI flows and stocks as indicating to the necessary growth of a global business environment.

A GLOBALLY INTEGRATED FINANCIAL SYSTEM?

Nothing animates the globalisation thesis more strongly than the idea of a globally integrated financial system. This has become the stock in trade of journalists, media pundits, policymakers, politicians, corporate elites and many an academician. But are we really facing such highly integrated capital and money markets as these sources often claim? Clearly there are a number of dimensions to this issue. In some areas there has been an undoubted transformation of the international financial system that has opened up completely new types of financial integration. The spectacular growth of derivative instruments obviously comes to mind.

But we need to look to the more mundane areas of financial integration to see whether the underlying framework for the operation of capital markets has radically changed and internationalised. Money markets are probably more highly integrated than are capital markets. And it is capital markets that most immediately affect the economic prospects for the long-term growth of national economies.

One of the long-established methods of measuring the degree of financial integration between countries relies upon investigating the relationship between national savings and national investment. If there were a completely integrated global financial system domestic investment would not be fundamentally constrained by domestic savings, and the correlation between savings and investment would be broken. But national savings–investment correlations have not unambiguously declined in the 1980s and 1990s, during the period of capital market liberalisation and floating exchange rates. Careful analysis by Bosworth (1993, pp. 98–102) and by Obstfeld (1993, for example, p. 50) shows this not to be the case (despite the less than careful commentary by some others, for example Goldstein and Mussa 1993, p. 25). The persistence of the basic Feldstein–Horioka findings well into a period of financial liberalisation, deregulation and supposed global integration testifies to the continued robust relative autonomy of financial systems, this despite the (sometimes desperate) attempts by conventional economic analysts to prove it otherwise (for example, Bayoumi, 1990). Table 5.5 brings together previous estimates of a simple gross savings–investment equation and adds our own estimates for the period 1991–95.

Table 5.5 Savings and investment correlations, 1900–95

$(I/Y)_i = a + \beta (S/Y)_i + u_i$

	1900–13*	1926–38*	1960–74**	1974–80*	1981–90*	1991–95***
ß	0.774	0.959	0.887	0.867	0.636	0.670
	(0.436)	(0.082)	(0.074)	(0.170)	(0.108)	(0.086)
R^2	0.260	0.940	0.910	0.560	0.640	0.750

Notes:
1 From 1960 data is for 22 main OECD developed economies.
2 Figures in brackets beneath ß coefficients are standard errors.

Sources:
* M. Obstfeld, 'International capital mobility in the 1990s' *NBER Working Paper No. 4534, Cambridge, MA: National Bureau for Economic Research, 1993.*
** M. Feldstein. and C. Horioka. 'Domestic savings and international capital flows', *Economic Journal*, **90**, June, table 2, p. 321.
*** Own estimate.

The ß coefficient can be interpreted as the 'savings retention coefficient' – the proportion of incremental savings that is invested domestically (Feldstein and Bacchetta 1991, p. 206). Thus over the period 1991–95 for every dollar saved in the main OECD countries, 67 cents would have been invested domestically. Clearly the inter-War period and that directly after the Second World War represented the high points of a 'closed' international financial system on this measure. Between 96 per cent and 89 per cent of incremental domestic savings was invested domestically. There was a decline in this ratio during the 1980s and 1990s, but the value of the ß coefficient eased up in the first half of the 1990s. (Most of this decline can probably be attributed to the lagged effects of the collapse in the savings ratio of a single country – the US – after 1979: Frankel, 1991). These coefficients were also lower than that for the Gold Standard period of 1900–13, which is often thought to have been the high point of an 'open' international financial system as well. However, note that the R^2 correlation coefficient has become stronger since 1974–80. All in all, this analysis does not as yet indicate any dramatic change in the relationships between domestic savings and investment during the period of 'globalisation'.

So long as governments continue to target their current accounts and retain some sovereignty within their borders (so that at least the threat of government intervention in cross-border capital movements remains) investors cannot think about domestic and foreign assets in the same way. Different national financial systems are made up of different institutions and arrangements, with different conceptions of the future and assessments of past experience, and thus operating with different calculative modalities. All these features factor into a continued diversity of expectations and outlooks which cannot all be reduced to a single global market place or logic. What is more, even the most committed of the integrationists who have looked at national savings–investment correlations more or less all conclude that the LDCs and most NIEs remain largely out of the frame as far as this form of financial integration is concerned. Thus, even for the integration enthusiasts, there are limits to the extent of the 'globalisation' of financial markets.

Of course, this emphasis on the relationship between domestic savings and domestic investment might seem to reinforce the neoclassical view of investment determination. The critique of this from an essentially post-Keynesian perspective is that the constraint on investment is not savings but the ability to raise finance for investment. In an advanced industrial economy with a developed financial system, credit creation is the key to investment; it is the access to 'liquidity' that determines economic activity, and this is endogenously created.

Formally we would agree with this analysis for mature advanced economies with a developed banking system operating efficiently in an essentially stable financial environment. However, we would emphasise that there are two exceptions to this image. The first is for those societies that remain less developed, that have an *underdeveloped* banking system in particular. The second is for those economies that have an *overdeveloped* financial system typified by speculation and instability. In both these cases, the 'normal' financing system for investment either just does not exist or breaks down in the face of speculative pressures. In addition, we would argue that it is this second case that increasingly typifies the position faced in the advanced industrial countries. In both these cases, however, we are thrown back on to a more 'primitive' conception of what determines investment, namely the brute fact of national savings.

Another way of looking at the importance of domestic resources for investment is via the importance of FDI inflows in the gross fixed capital formation for different economies. This is shown in Table 5.6.

Table 5.6 Share of inward FDI flows in gross domestic fixed capital formation (GDFCF), 1985–95 (%)

	Average 1985–90	1991	1992	1993	1994	1995
World	**5.1**	**3.1**	**3.3**	**4.4**	**4.5**	**5.2**
Developed economies	**5.5**	**3.2**	**3.2**	**3.7**	**3.5**	**4.4**
of which: EU	9.1	5.4	5.5	5.9	5.0	6.8
(UK)	13.7	9.4	9.8	11.0	6.8	13.2
(Germany)	1.6	1.0	0.6	0.4	0.2	1.7
US	5.3	3.1	2.4	4.9	4.8	5.9
Japan	0.2	0.2	0.2	-	0.1	-
Developing economies	**8.0**	**4.4**	**5.1**	**6.6**	**8.0**	**8.2**
of which: LA & Caribbean	11.3	7.8	8.1	7.2	10.3	11.0
(Brazil)	3.1	1.4	3.0	1.3	3.0	4.7
Asia	7.6	3.4	4.2	6.5	7.2	7.5
South, East & SE Asia	9.7	3.8	4.7	7.5	8.3	9.0
Central & Eastern Europe	**1.0**	**0.4**	**0.8**	**7.9**	**5.0**	**5.2**

Source: Compiled from UN (1997, annex table B.5)

What is significant here is the relative *unimportance* of FDI flows in their contribution to domestic investment (even accepting the criticisms of this measure as outlined above). In a number of cases the contribution of FDI to GDFCF actually fell in the mid-1990s from that averaged over the late 1980s.

If we take the Triad alone, the importance of inward and outward FDI flows in relationship to GDFCF is shown for a longer period in Table 5.7 (note the slight discrepancies between these figures and those in Table 5.6). As compared to 1975 the position for the US and the EU in 1995 indicates an increase in the importance of FDI flows, though there has been considerable oscillation in the figures during the intervening years. Japan only shows as important for outflows in 1990 with no obvious longer-term trend. In none of the Triad were inflows or outflows greater than 10 per cent of GDFCF in the 1990s.

It is clear from all these figures – and the analysis of savings–investment correlations discussed above – that economies cannot borrow their way to prosperity via a reliance on FDI. What remains crucial to domestic development strategies is domestic savings, which still account for the bulk of the financial resources available for domestic investment in all advanced and developing economies. Thus it is still the nature of domestic financial systems that is crucial to the long-run developmental success of different economies.

This can be further demonstrated by investigating the cross-border transactions and holdings of bonds and equities between countries and in various domestic financial institutions. As a percentage of GDP the cross-border *transactions* in bonds and equities have escalated since the mid-1970s, as shown in Table 5.8. But if this is looked at from a slightly different angle changes may not appear quite so dramatic.

Table 5.7 Triad foreign direct investment flows, 1975–95 (% of GDFCF)

		1975	1980	1985	1990	1995
US	Inflows	0.9	3.1	2.5	5.1	4.9
	Outflows	5.1	4.0	1.9	2.9	7.8
EU(15)	Inflows	2.6	2.8	2.9	7.0	7.0
	Outflows	2.6	3.6	4.8	9.5	8.3
Japan	Inflows	0.1	0.1	0.2	0.2	0.0
	Outflows	1.1	0.7	1.7	5.1	1.5

Source: 'European Union' (1997, adapted from table 13, p. 49)

For instance, Tables 5.9 and 5.10 give two different sources for the actual *holdings* of foreign bonds and equities in the accounts of institutional investors (not just transactions between countries), expressed as a percentage of their total holdings. The case of Table 5.9 demonstrates a general trend of the growth in importance of foreign securities since 1980 (with the exception of Austria).

The figures for 1993 in Table 5.9 can be compared with those shown for the same year in Table 5.10. In the case of the US there is a significant discrepancy between the data in the two tables for pension funds, though for the other common countries in both tables the figures are reasonably close.

For most countries the foreign securities holdings were in the 10–30 per cent range, with only the Netherlands, Ireland and New Zealand having an over 30 per cent stake. (The dramatically contrasting cases of Hong Kong and Singapore shown in Table 5.10 are discussed in a moment.)

What the figures for 1993 in ·both tables demonstrate, however, is the enormous variation between countries in terms of the importance of foreign holdings. Some financial systems are clearly much more 'open' than others on this measure. Of the G5 countries, the UK and Japan are much more 'open' than are the US, Germany and France.

Table 5.8 Cross-border transactions in bonds and equities[a], 1975–95 (% of GDP)

	1975	1980	1985	1989	1990	1991	1992	1993	1994	1995	1996
United States	4	9	35	101	89	96	107	129	131	135	164
Japan	2	8	62	156	119	92	72	78	60	65	84[b]
Germany	5	7	33	66	57	55	85	171	159	172	200
France		5	21	52	54	79	122	187	201	187	227[c]
Italy	1	1	4	18	27	60	92	192	207	253	468
Canada	3	9	27	55	65	81	113	153	212	189	258

Notes:
[a] Gross purchases and sales of securities between residents and non-residents.
[b] Based on settlement data.
[c] January–September at an annual rate.

Source: Bank of International Settlements, *Annual Report 1996–97*, table V.1, p. 79

Indeed, if we look at this in a slightly different way we continue to see the structural differences between financial systems. Table 5.11 shows the distribution of corporate equity as between different types of shareholder in a range of OECD countries. Apart from indicating the basic well-known differences between the ownership structure of so-called 'insider' and 'outsider' (or 'market-based') financial systems, the table also demonstrates the variation in foreign holdings of shares. Two of the 'outsider' systems (the UK and the US) have amongst the lowest proportions, along with two of the 'insider' group (Germany and Japan). On this classification it is Sweden and France that have the highest measure of 'internationalisation'. The 'big 4' economies of the USA, Japan, Germany and the UK – with 11 per cent or less of their equity stake held abroad in 1996 – can surely hardly constitute a clear case of globalisation.

Table 5.9 Institutional investors' holdings of foreign securities (% of total securities holdings)

	1980	1985	1990	1993
United States[a]				
Private pension funds[b]	1.0	3.0	4.1	7.1
Mutual funds	–	–	4.0[c]	8.0
Japan				
Postal life insurance	0.0	6.7	11.6	12.3
Private insurance companies	8.1	23.2	29.9	22.3
Canada				
Life insurance companies	2.2	2.3	2.4	3.1
Pension funds	6.1	6.6	7.0	10.6
Italy				
Insurance companies	–	–	13.6	12.2
United Kingdom				
Insurance companies[d]	6.3	14.1	14.6	–
Pension funds[e]	10.8	17.3	23.2	–
Australia				
Life insurance companies	–	–	14.0	18.8
Austria				
Insurance companies	14.1	11.6	10.1	9.9
Investment funds	27.0	13.2	18.7	25.1
Belgium				
Insurance companies	5.5	8.6	5.2	–
Netherlands				
Insurance companies	6.9	22.9	20.2	26.0
Private pension funds	26.6	28.1	36.6	36.9
Public pension funds	14.7	9.9	16.6	20.2
Sweden				
Insurance companies	–	1.5[f]	10.5	12.3

Notes:
[a] Per cent of total assets
[b] Tax exempt funded schemes (excluding IRAs)
[c] 1991
[d] Long-term funds
[e] Pension funds exclude central government sector but include other public sector
[f] 1987

Source: Edey and Hviding (1995, table 10, p. 33)

Table 5.10 The internationalisation of pension fund investments

	Stock of assets end of 1993 (US$ billions)	Percent of GNP	Percent international assets – bonds and equities (1993)
US	2908.0	45.5	4
Japan	1752.7	44.6	14
Germany	254.2	13.3	3
UK	726.4	69.6	27
France[a]	199.7	15.5	5
Canada[b]	162.3	28.2	9
Australia	–	–	16
Belgium	–	–	29
Ireland	–	–	35
Switzerland	–	–	6
New Zealand	–	–	34
Hong Kong	–	–	60
Singapore	–	–	0

Notes:
[a] At end of 1991
[b] At end of 1992

Source: HM Treasury Occasional Papers No. 8, 'Overseas Investment and the UK', June 1996. Compiled from Tables A2.1 (p. 24) and A2.3 (p. 26)

From all these figures, what is not clear is that there is any obvious convergence of all the advanced countries to a common openness position. By and large the differences between them seem to have been maintained, indicating the continued variation in the characteristics and structures of their domestic financial systems. Thus, up to the mid-1990s at least, the operation of 'globalisation' did not seemed to have forced the advanced country's domestic financial institutions to fundamentally break with the historical variation in their character, though there had been some increase in their overall internationalisation.

Particular attention is drawn to the figures for Singapore and Hong Kong in Table 5.10. Neither of these countries could be argued to have escaped the full rigours of internationalisation over the recent period. Both have remarkably open economies and have been the centres for similar kinds of 'global integration' forces (in terms of trade openness, for instance, in 1993 the sum of imports and exports to GDP for Hong Kong and Singapore was 252 per cent and 279 per cent respectively). But one had zero foreign participation and the other 60 per cent. Obviously this difference is accounted for by different policy choices. Those who run the Singapore Central Provident Fund (CPF) have decided (or are required) to invest in only domestic financial assets, whereas those who ran the Hong Kong funds have gone for a completely different option (though there is probably some external indirect leakage from the Singapore Fund) (see Ramesh, 1993, for a discussion of the politics of Singapore's CPF).

Table 5.11 Distribution of outstanding listed corporate equity among different categories of shareholders in selected OECD countries (% at year-end 1996)

	United States	Japan	Germany	France	United Kingdom[b]	Sweden
Financial sector	46	42	30	30	68	30
Banks	6	15	10	7	1	1
Insurance companies and pension funds	28	12	12	9	50	14
Investment funds	12		8	11	8	15
Other financial institutions	1	15[a]	–	3	9	–
Non-financial enterprises	–	27	42	19	1	11
Public authorities	–	1	4	2	1	8
Households	49	20	15	23	21	19
Rest of the world	5	11	9	25	9	32
Total	100	100	100	100	100	100

Notes:
[a]　For Japan, pension and investment funds are included in other financial institutions.
[b]　United Kingdom figures are for end 1994.

Source: OECD, *Financial Market Trends,* No. 69, February 1998, Paris: OECD, table 1

Similar comments could be made about the operation of commercial banks. An increase in the importance of foreign assets and liabilities in their balance sheets is evident from Table 5.12, mainly attributed to a growth between 1960 to 1980, since when the positions have tended to stabilise. But there remains a great variation between the economies shown, one largely based upon entrenched historical differences. (There are some exceptions to this, notably in the case of Sweden – not shown in this table, which experienced a rapid growth over almost the entire period 1960–96, to one of the highest in 1996.)

Table 5.12 Foreign assets and liabilities as a % of assets of commercial banks for selected countries, 1960–96

	1960	1970	1980	1990	1996
France					
Assets	–	16.0	30.0	24.9	30.9
Liabilities	–	17.0	22.0	28.6	30.2
Germany					
Assets	2.4	8.7	9.7	16.3	16.0
Liabilities	4.7	9.0	12.2	13.1	12.9
Japan					
Assets	2.6	3.7	4.2	13.9	13.8
Liabilities	3.6	3.1	7.3	19.4	10.6
Netherlands					
Assets	18.4	23.1	33.0	33.5	33.2
Liabilities	7.1	22.2	33.9	31.2	34.1
United Kingdom					
Assets	6.2	46.1	64.7	45.0	47.0
Liabilities	13.9	49.7	67.5	49.3	48.8
United States					
Assets	1.4	2.2	11.0	5.6	2.6
Liabilities	3.7	5.4	9.0	6.9	8.2

Source: IMF, *International Financial Statistics Yearbook*, 1986 and 1997

The final point to make here is to look at the 'bottom line', as it were, of the internationalisation of financial systems by assessing the importance of foreign assets ultimately owned by households as a proportion of their total financial assets. Thus we are still concentrating upon the holdings of only financial assets, but looking at their importance in household wealth. The problem with the figures presented so far is that they do not cover the entire financial system. As Table 5.11 indicated, there are many non-bank and non-financial institutional holdings of financial assets.

These figures are plotted in Figure 5.4 for the end of 1995. A similar variation between countries as the patterns outlined above emerges, and with great diversity amongst them. But only two countries show a foreign percentage of over 15 per cent. Around 10 per cent and below is the norm. Broadly speaking, then, people's financial wealth still remains a domestic affair: it stays at home. What the data in Tables 5.6, 5.7, 5.9, 5.10, 5.11 and 5.12 and in Figure 5.4 indicate is the continued pertinence of domestic policy choices, something rather ignored by the globalisation analysis. We must presume that 'globalisation' has had little impact on these choices in the case of Hong Kong and Singapore, for instance, since both of them have been subject to more or less the same external pressures. The causes are purely 'domestic'. Similarly in the case of the advanced industrial economies: it has been policy choices (and mistakes) that have driven the move towards greater interdependence and internationalisation, as displayed for instance in Table 5.10, not some mysterious process of 'globalisation'. For instance, take the remarks of two commentators who more or less unambiguously welcome the moves towards greater openness and integration:

> In some sense, authorities have suffered the fate of getting what they asked for. They wanted greater participation by foreign investors in their government debt markets, in part to make it easier to finance larger fiscal and external balances. They wanted a more efficient financial system that would erode the power of local monopolies and offer savers a higher rate of return and firms a lower cost of capital. They welcomed innovations that provided a wider range of hedging possibilities against volatile asset prices, and that made it more convenient to unbundle risks. They wanted to regain business that had migrated to the off-shore centres in search of a less restrictive regulatory environment, and to level the playing field against foreign competitors. Much of that has taken place. But along with it has also come the creation of an enormous pool of mobile, liquid capital whose support, or lack of it, can often be the measure of difference in the success of stabilisation, reform, exchange rate, and tax policy. (Goldstein and Mussa, 1993, p. 42)

Despite their complacency, these authors have a point, though, along with them, we are not suggesting here that *everything* was just the result of either deliberate policy choices or mistakes by the authorities.

Similar remarks could be made about other ways of measuring and assessing the degree of international financial integration – real interest rate convergence, equity price movements, off-shore and onshore yields, covered or uncovered interest rate parity, international portfolio diversity, and so on. Again, to quote Goldstein and Mussa (ibid., p. 14):

> Even though there is by now a burgeoning literature that addresses directly the measurement of international capital market integration, it has proven difficult to reach firm and clear conclusions about the degree – if not the trend – of integration. This ambiguity reflects the fact that no single method of measuring the degree of integration is completely free of conceptual and technical difficulties that cloud its interpretation.

Caution remains the order of the day. It is still reasonable to argue, for instance, that short-term interest rates are set nationally, and that even long-term interest rates are fundamentally driven by the decisions of important state authorities, as in the US, Japan and Germany, rather than totally by the anonymous forces of global markets.

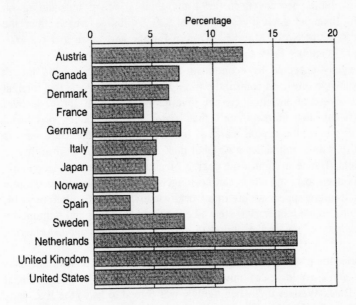

Percentage

Source: Merril Lynch/ *Independent*, 22 December 1997, p. 19.

Figure 5.4 Financial Assets Ultimately Owned by Households Held in Overseas Bonds and Equities at End of 1995 (%)

Even those alternative approaches to ones that concentrate directly or indirectly on financial integration, such as those that stress comparisons of consumption paths between countries, cannot reach an unambiguous conclusion that that financial integration has taken place (Bayoumi and MacDonald 1995).

ARE THE FINANCIAL MARKETS UNGOVERNABLE?

Until the liberalisation of capital movements in the early 1980s governments retained a real power over the financial markets, exchange controls limited external dealing mainly to the facilitation of trade and long-term investment. Now the daily volume of trading on the global markets exceeds $1 trillion - dwarfing the exports of the OECD countries and their daily equivalent GDP (about $40 billion: *The Economist*, 7 October 1995, table 1, p. 6.). In the early 1980s the reserves of the industrialised countries still exceeded the volume of daily foreign exchange dealing, but by 1995 they were less than half that volume. Moreover, in 1994 the total principal outstanding on trading in financial derivatives came to $20 trillion – greater than the combined GDP of North America, Western Europe and Japan in 1993 (*The Economist*, 7 October 1995, table 6, p. 16 and table 15, p. 34).

It is widely accepted by economists that central banks can no longer dictate exchange rates and control the foreign exchange markets, that interest rates and levels of inflation cannot diverge greatly from those deemed appropriate by the markets, and that states are no longer privileged borrowers in domestic capital markets, but are viewed in the same way as municipalities and companies by global markets in terms of their ability to service debt. Hence a significant degree of autonomy in macro–economic policy has been lost, and states can no longer control certain key economic variables. It might appear we are in a world somewhat like that before 1914, but without a stable monetary system like the Gold Standard and without the labour mobility of the earlier period to cushion economies against external shocks.

However, the picture looks a good deal more complicated when one asks 'to what end' would states now try to manipulate the major financial markets? Black Wednesday, when the UK was forced to leave the Exchange Rate Mechanism (ERM) by an uncontrollable wave of selling, is often cited to indicate the new powerlessness of governments. States can no longer directly change prices in the key financial markets and the markets can sanction national polices of which they disapprove. A response might be that states have never been able in the long run to defend exchange rates that are unsupported by real economic performance. For example, Britain devalued in 1966 under the Bretton Woods system, after a two–year struggle to maintain the exchange rate against the dollar. Moreover, in the case of Black Wednesday, the markets took two years to react to the fact of a damagingly over-valued exchange rate. The UK entered in 1990 at an unsustainable target rate of DM 2.95, when British inflation was roughly three times that of Germany.

The British ERM crisis is hardly a demonstration that effective public policies to stabilise exchange rates are impossible. Britain could have entered at a more realistic and sustainable rate, had Chancellor Nigel Lawson not deliberately allowed the pound to appreciate against the Mark, and had inflation been managed more cautiously. Equally, the UK had the option of a devaluation within the ERM, which seems to have been rejected primarily for political reasons. The markets only moved once it was clear that a devaluation was unavoidable. The failure in France of the first Mitterrand government is likewise taken to show that Keynesian expansionary policies of a radical kind are impossible. However, the key questions are whether such radical policies could ever be effective outside a very specific conjuncture, whether such policies exhaust the scope for effective state action, and whether the failure of radical Keynesianism is primarily due to globalisation. Keynes after all was neither in favour of reckless public borrowing nor unaware of the dangers of inflation.

Very high levels of public debt to GDP to finance government spending are ultimately unsustainable, unless borrowing boosts growth significantly and relatively quickly. But this rapid boost to growth is now difficult to achieve; employment and output are far stickier now than they were in the 1930s when significant surplus capacity remained idle, when protectionist tariffs were widespread, and when prices were falling. Boosting domestic demand will now most probably lead to accelerating imports rather than a dramatic rise in domestic production. The reason is that, beyond a modest level of stimulus, additional jobs and output now require significant investment, and are unlikely to come on stream before a policy-induced stimulus to demand has been sourced by foreign importers. Keynesian policies of a radical kind cannot be followed within one medium-sized nation-state. But the reason is less to do with the existence of global markets than with structural changes in the advanced economies. If that is so, borrowing to sustain current expenditure on a large scale and for prolonged periods is clearly foolish, as it results in an accelerating proportion of public revenue supporting interest payments and it drives up the cost of borrowing as the state becomes more indebted.

But this does not mean states have to pursue similar policies in public expenditure, cutting to the lowest level acceptable to integrated financial markets across the globe. At the same time as world capital markets have internationalised and integrated there has been a general tendency for public expenditure to rise in the advanced world. Germany's total government expenditure rose from 32.5 per cent of GDP in 1960 to 49 per cent in 1995. Surprisingly Japan's public expenditure rose too by a similar proportion but from a lower base, from 19.4 per cent of GDP in 1970 to 34.9 per cent in 1995 (Hirst and Thompson, 1996b, table 2, p. 61). In Japan's case this can hardly be because of rising unemployment or welfare spending. Public expenditure seems not to have been mainly driven up by welfare spending: between 1980 and 1990 expenditure on social protection in most of the OECD countries was relatively flat (ibid., table 3, p. 63; OECD, 1994b, table 4.7, p. 151; OECD, 1994a).

Public policy still has a measure of autonomy, provided electorates are willing to pay the price in taxation and see the benefits of spending on infrastructure, training and welfare. What states cannot do is to tax returns to capital punitively or borrow to sustain current consumption for prolonged periods. Levels of public expenditure to GDP vary across the advanced world very considerably and reflect national policy choices. Those variations are not currently diminishing. As *The Economist*, not noted for its hostility to the concept of globalisation, remarked: ' "Wrong" hardly does justice to the claim that market forces have pushed governments into dull conformity on economic policy: the idea is ridiculous' (*The Economist*, 7 October 1995, p. 15).

The huge volumes traded daily on the financial markets and the huge positions built up in the derivatives markets appear to dwarf and dominate the real economy, but one must remember of what these vast sums are actually composed. The main players are financial institutions which utilise both the assets that they can raise in national markets for financial products and their ability to borrow on the strength of these assets, repeatedly to 'churn' large sums through the various international financial markets. Their traders either earn small profit margins by exploiting small and temporary imperfections between the different world market centres, or they establish positions on future market movements, suitably hedged to minimise risk (if they are careful). When a given cycle of trading ends, the borrowed sums are met by market outcomes if trading has been successful, and assets are redeployed. Typically the return on such vast sums is quite modest, although the profits from repeated churning can be large in total.

Institutions have to use these earnings to meet their obligations to depositors, to pensioners, and to life policyholders. International trading thus recycles a substantial portion of its output back into the domestic financial system. Ultimately most of the capital used in these markets is not free-floating, but depends on national capital markets and must be returned into them. This does not mean that the international markets are unproblematic or that they can be easily controlled. People buy financial products such as pensions or life policies to guard against personal risks, often completely unaware that they are fuelling a very risky system of financial dealing. The international financial markets add little to real long-term economic performance that is determined by domestic saving, productivity growth and competitiveness in trade. Yet they have the ability to distribute short-term shocks around the system, and the potential – especially considering the vast obligations in the derivatives market – to produce dangerous instability. The case for regulation and stabilisation is a strong one, but it will work only if the major states are willing to co-operate in order to impose common rules on the system. The Barings and Sumitomo scandals show the dangers of failure in a fragile and interdependent system.

One solution advanced by the leading economist James Tobin is to impose a small turnover tax on short-term financial movements, about 0.5 per cent (Tobin, 1994). This would not deter the financing of trade or direct investment, but it would reduce the viability of repeated 'churning'. Many critics argue that such a tax is impossible, as trading would simply move offshore from those states that imposed it. This ignores the fact that most of the profits of such trading need to be repatriated to meet obligations, although it is true that it would be difficult at present to get most OECD countries to adopt a common regulatory regime. Equally important policy programmes are the widely scouted proposals to reduce the dangers of the derivatives markets both by strengthening external regulation and the procedures within institutions: to restrict the risky over-the-counter trade, to limit market participants to banks, and to oblige players to hold substantial deposits against their positions.

At present such proposals are unlikely to be adopted, but another serious crisis may scare conservative bankers enough to see that they are incurring incalculable and uncontrollable risks, and it might just be possible to get the major states to co-ordinate regulation in that case. Increasingly effective public action to control the economy needs to be co-ordinated between states and, as in the case of trade openness or common economic standards, overseen or implemented by supra-national bodies like the EU or the WTO. Such concerted action does not necessarily weaken states, rather it can strengthen them by stabilising the external economic environment and thus giving them greater scope to pursue national policies, if national elites and electorates are willing. Times have changed, but it would be foolish to talk down the scope of national policy now, particularly by overemphasising the policy autonomy and stand-alone economic sovereignty of states before the 1970s. National economic management in the period 1945–73 depended both on an international economic conjuncture (rapid growth in all the major industrial economies) and on an appropriate structure of international institutions.

There are genuine dangers in the current widespread acceptance of a strong version of the concept of globalisation by key elites. This is not just a fashionable idea; concepts have consequences. The belief that the international economy is now virtually ungovernable and that national policies are powerless before world market forces is now common among politicians, bankers, business leaders and economists. Yet there are urgent economic problems that need to be tackled by extending the agenda and the scope of public governance. Such problems can be tackled by a mixture of appropriate policies and a division of labour in governance between international agencies, interstate agreements and national governments. The first problem is the urgent need to stabilise world financial markets with the aims of containing volatility and preventing the build-up of dangerous levels of exposure in the derivatives markets. The second is to ensure that free trade and foreign direct investment bring some definite benefit to poorer countries. The third is to protect workers in the advanced industrial states against the shocks and risks of an internationalised economy, chiefly by offering adequate welfare and job creation, but also by ensuring a fairer distribution of national income.

Modern capitalism has developed and survived in the advanced countries by catering to the needs of a prosperous broad middle class; it requires high levels of consumption to sustain its output of goods and services. Yet under the rhetoric of responding to international competitive pressures many countries are cutting welfare, attempting to reduce wages, and rendering labour markets more competitive. They are in danger of damaging prosperity by undermining its social foundations (Rodrik, 1997). In the poorer developing countries national elites have accepted the logic of gains from trade, subscribing to the latest GATT treaty. Yet those at the bottom of the income distribution scale often experience few benefits or a worsening of their condition, leading to widespread dissatisfaction with free trade and calls for the localisation of production (Korten, 1995).

The danger of recklessly pursued internationalisation without sufficient regard to its social effects is that there will be revolts against an open international economy in both the advanced and the developing world. In the developing world new protectionist arguments are gaining momentum and span a broad political spectrum. Thus we see environmentalists rejecting long-distance trade between advanced countries as wasteful, trade unionists opposing the threat of accelerating job losses to low-wage countries, and populist business figures turned politician like Ross Perot and Sir James Goldsmith arguing for protection (Lang and Hines, 1993; Greider, 1997; Goldsmith, 1994). So far such movements have not had much political success, yet one should be cautious, given the widespread popular unease in many countries in the EU about the consequences of monetary union.

The option of combining trade openness with extended public governance at both national and international levels, with the aim of combining growth with fairness within and between nations, is a difficult one to argue for in today's climate, dominated as it is by free market economic liberals on the one hand and protectionist populists on the other. Yet it remains essential. Free trade and economic growth are closely correlated in the history of the modern international economy, and protecting workers against the shocks of an open international economy is a condition not only for ensuring political support for free trade but for maintaining the prosperity on which that trade depends. Free trade may require the far greater management both of FDI and of the international financial markets – trade openness and market governance go together. The international economy remains sufficiently concentrated in the key national states for such governance to be possible, if the political will and a measure of international consensus existed.

GLOBALISATION AND THE END OF THE WELFARE STATE?

It is widely believed by the supporters of the concept of globalisation that international competitive processes will force the convergence of public expenditures in general and welfare expenditures in particular towards the lowest possible norm. This will clearly not be with the poorest of the undeveloped countries but with the most successful of the newly industrialising countries. At present public expenditure to GDP ratios vary between 68 per cent in Sweden and 20 per cent in Singapore. Until the recent Asian crisis many western commentators saw countries like Singapore as the model, advocating reducing public expenditures to GDP ratios to 30 per cent (for example, Skidelsky, 1996). One should be careful to compare like with like. Singapore's compulsory pension scheme does not count in public expenditure, whereas Sweden's does. But also, many in the Asian countries are learning the hard lesson, long observable in Europe, that smaller highly internationalised countries require high levels of public expenditure and welfare provision to cushion them against the shocks and risks of international volatility (Katzenstein, 1985; Rodrik, 1997). In South Korea the company-centred welfare system, predicated on growth, is foundering in the face of large-scale unemployment, whilst in Indonesia the poor are thrown to the wolves.

Asia no longer seems a model to be copied. But can developed economies maintain their welfare states as sources of protection against externally generated volatility? One should be careful here to factor out the multiple problems facing European welfare states – an ageing population, high unemployment, high rates of family break up, and the pressures of EU convergence criteria – from internationalisation *per se*. If international competitive pressures are forcing reductions in welfare, then countries with extensive welfare states should be performing less well. In particular, those with 'continental' insurance based systems (Esping-Anderson, 1990) should be encountering even greater constraints than those with more flexible universalist systems. If these propositions are sound, then the Netherlands should represent a kind of crucial experiment. It has very high levels of internationalisation, both in trade and finance. Its ratio of exports and imports to GDP is unusually high at 89.2 per cent and, as Figure 5.4 shows, the Dutch invest a very high proportion of their financial assets abroad (17 per cent) and, as Table 5.9 shows, institutional investors have very high levels of holdings of foreign securities.

Yet Holland has managed to maintain its welfare state, whilst dramatically reducing its unemployment levels to 6.5 per cent in 1996 (comparable to the US), employment growth averaged 1.8 per cent between

1983 and 1993 (the EU average was 0.4 per cent), and it has achieved a rate of growth of GDP between 1991 and 1996 of 2.2 per cent (EU average 1.5 per cent), (Visser and Hemerijck, 1997). How was this possible? Through incomes policies and corporatist concertation, which helped to keep Dutch wage levels competitive. Through active labour market policies – in particular a domestic reduction in disability benefits (which had hitherto been used to get workers out of the labour force). Holland has made strategic cuts in certain aspects of welfare – proving that it is possible for a 'continental' system to adopt to macroeconomic constraints. Yet its welfare state remains substantially intact, extensive and superior to that of countries like the UK, which have deliberately chosen a low-wage, low-skill route to international competitiveness. Moreover, the Dutch example shows that a mixture of vigorous national policy and effective co-operation between the social interests can effect macroeconomic adjustments in a highly internationalised economic environment. Thus if the scope of national policy remains substantial for a small country like the Netherlands, it ought to be available to larger ones as well.

Many bigger countries are in the grip of economic dogma, either an obsession with 'sound money' as in the case of Germany and those rigidly tied to it like France, or in the case of the UK a belief in the inevitability of globalisation and the necessity to reduce the size of the public sector. Hence the scope for policy is restricted by myths rather than by genuinely inescapable internationally competitive pressures. Other countries, like Italy, have faced real problems and are tackling them with considerable energy. Italy's higher ratio of public debt to GDP and its insupportable pension obligations could not be ignored for ever. Surprisingly, given recent political history, industry, organised labour and the state have collaborated to contain wage growth and achieve pension reform (Regini, 1997; Baccaro and Locke, 1996). Perhaps, if the advanced countries need a model for the next century, they would be as wise to turn to Italy as to Singapore.

THE FUTURE AND CONCLUSIONS

The basic point to be drawn from the above analysis is that for the foreseeable future the real character of the international system will be one dominated by the Triad countries and their regional clusters/allies. We have entered a period in which three large economic formations look to have emerged, the relative size and importance of which are indicated in Figure 5.5 and Tables 5.13 and 5.14.

In terms of GDP the EU and US are about equal, with Japan about half as big (though in terms of GDP per capita Japan leads the EU and the US). As far as the shares of world exports of goods are concerned (Figure 5.5; that is, merchandise trade not just 'exports' as in table 5.12), while there has been some convergence, the three blocs seems to have stabilised with the EU at 25 per cent, the US at 20 per cent and Japan at 15 per cent (and falling slightly).

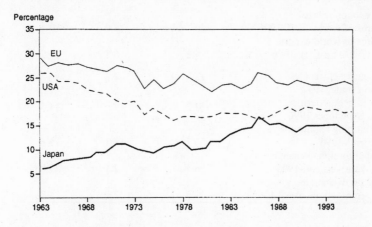

Figure 5.5 Triad shares in world exports of goods

Most of the other data in Tables 5.13 and 5.14 relate to the currency role of the three big countries/blocs. This is important in terms of the future of the international economic and financial system as the euro is introduced at the turn of the century. These data indicate too broadly that: (1) the US dollar still remains the *lingua franca* of the international financial system; (2) that the European currencies have made some inroads into this role, particularly in terms of transactions on foreign exchange and portfolio investments; and finally; (3) that the yen is a relatively unimportant currency for international transactions, but has gained some advantage as a denominator of assets (largely as a consequence of the appreciation of the yen against the dollar and the mark until 1996).

Table 5.13 The United States, Japan and the European Union: relative economic size and relative use of currencies (%)

	United States	Japan	EU15
Relative economic size			
Shares of world GDP, 1996	20.7	8.0	20.4
Shares of world exports			
(ex-intra-EU), 1996	15.2	6.1	14.7
Relative use of currencies[a]			
World trade, 1992	48.0	5.0	31.0
World debt securities,			
September 1996	37.2	17.0	34.5
Developing country debt,			
end-1996	50.2	18.1	15.8
Global foreign exchange			
reserves, end-1995	56.4	7.1	25.8
Foreign exchange			
transactions, April 1995[b]	41.5	12.0	35.0

Notes:

[a]   Shares denominated in currency (or currencies) of country (or EU).
[b]   Shares adjusted for double-counting that arises from the fact that each transaction involves two currencies.

Source: World Bank (1997, table 12, p. 71)

Table 5.14 The international role of the main Triad currencies

(a) Official role

Share of total official currency holdings (%)			
	end 1973	end 1983	end 1995
US dollar	76.1	71.1	61.5
European currencies[a]	14.3	15.8	20.1
of which: German Mark	7.1	11.7	14.2
Yen	0.1	4.9	7.4

Note: [a] *Pound sterling, German mark, French franc, Dutch guilder*

Source: IMF annual reports

Number of currencies linked to:	1983	1994	1994 (% of world GNP)
US dollar	34	25	1.53
European currencies (including the ecu)	18	19	0.25

Source: IMF annual reports

(b) Currency use in international trade

Share of the main currencies as regards use in international trade				
	1980 % of world exports	Inter- nationali- sation ratio[a]	1992 % of world exports	Inter- nationali- sation ratio[a]
US dollar	56.4	4.5	47.6	3.6
German mark	13.6	1.4	15.5	1.4
Yen	2.1	0.3	4.8	0.6

Notes:
[a] Ratio of world exports denominated in currency relative to that country's exports.

Source: European Commission

(c) Transactions on foreign-exchange markets

Breakdown of transactions by currency[a]			
	April 1989	April 1992	April 1995
US dollar	90	82	83
German mark	27	40	37
Yen	27	23	24
Other	56	55	56
Total as %[b]	200	200	200

Notes:
[a] Gross turnover. Daily averages.
[b] Since any transaction on the foreign exchange market involves two currencies, the total of the proportions of transactions involving a given currency is 200%.

Source: BIS, Surveys of activities on foreign exchange markets

(d) Currency in which financial assets and liabilities are denominated

Share of outstanding international bonds			
	end 1981	end 1992	end 1995
US dollar	52.6	40.3	34.2
European currencies	20.2	33.0	37.1
of which: German mark	n.a.	10.0	12.3
Yen	6.9	12.4	15.7

Source: BIS, *International Banking and Financial Activity*

Share of world private portfolio			
	end 1981	end 1992	end 1995
US dollar	67.3	46.0	39.8
European currencies	13.2	35.2	36.9
of which: German mark	n.a.	14.7	15.6
Yen	2.2	6.9	11.5

Sources: BIS, *International Banking and Financial Activity*, and own calculations, External aspects of economic and monetary union', *Euro-Paper No. 1*, European Commission, July 1997, Annex 2, p. 18

The implications of these trends are that the relationship between the US and Europe looks to be becoming the key one for international governance, which will be accelerated as the euro is eventually successfully introduced and becomes a rival to the dollar. This will tend to reinforce the dominance of the two main blocs in the Triad. Thus the future for extended international governance essentially hangs not on global market forces but on the old-fashioned differences of interest between the US, the EU and (to a lesser extent) Japan. This is far from comforting, but it is as well to know from whence one's problems come, and that they are still driven by the classic problem of the divergent interest of states or the political entities that are successors to them, such as the EU. Far from a fully integrating 'globalised world economy', we still inhabit an essentially 'inter-nationalised' one, if one now heavily conditioned by a regionalised Triadic bloc structure.

NOTE

Birkbeck College, University of London and The Open University, UK.

REFERENCES

Allen, J. and G.F. Thompson (1997), 'Think global, and then think again', *Area*, **29** (3), 213–27.

Baccaro, L. and R.M. Locke (1996), *Public Sector Reform and Union Participation: The Case of Italian Pension Reform*, Cambridge, Mass.: MIT, Mimeo.

Bayoumi, T. (1990), 'Savings–investment correlations: immobile capital, government policy or endogenous behaviour?', *IMF Staff Papers*, **37** (2), June, 360–87.

Bayoumi, T. and R. MacDonald (1995), 'Consumption, income and international capital integration', *IMF Staff Papers*, **42** (3), September, 552–76.

Bergsten, C.F. (1996), 'Globalizing free trade', *Foreign Affairs*, **75** (3), June, 105–21.

Bosworth, B. (1993), *Savings and Investment in a Global Economy*, Washington, DC: Brookings Institution.

Edey, M. and K. Hviding (1995), 'An assessment of financial reform in OECD countries', OECD Economics Department, Working Paper no. 154, Paris: OECD.

Esping-Anderson, G. (1990), *The Three Worlds of Welfare Capitalism*, Princeton, NJ: Princeton University Press.

European Union (1997), 'Annual Report for 1997', *European Economy*, **63**, Brussels: European Commission.

Feldstein, M. and P. Bacchetta (1991), 'National savings and national investment', in B.D. Bernheim and J.B. Shoven (eds), *National Savings and Economic Performance*, Chicago: University of Chicago Press/NBER.

Feldstein, M. and C. Horioka (1980), 'Domestic savings and international capital flows', *Economic Journal*, **90** (358), June, 314–29.

Frankel, J.A. (1991), 'Quantifying international capital mobility in the 1980s', in B.D. Bernheim and J.B. Shoven (eds), *National Savings and Economic Performance*, Chicago: University of Chicago Press/NBER.

Frankel, J.A. (1997), *Regional Trading Blocs in the World Economic System*, Washington, DC: Institute for International Economics.

Goldblatt, D., D. Held, A. McGrew and J. Perraton (1997), 'Economic globalization and the nation-state: shifting balances of power', *Alternatives*, **22**, 269–85.

Goldsmith, J. (1994), *The Trap*, London: Macmillan.

Goldstein, M. and M. Mussa (1993), 'The integration of world capital markets', International Monetary Fund Research Department Working Paper (WP/93/95), December, Washington, DC: IMF.

Greider, W. (1997), *One World Ready or Not: The Manic Logic of Global Capitalism*, New York: Simon and Schuster.

Hirst, P.Q. and G.F. Thompson (1996a), *Globalization in Question: The International Economy and the Possibilities of Governance*, Cambridge: Polity Press.

Hirst, P.Q. and G.F. Thompson (1996b), 'Globalization: ten frequently asked questions and some surprising answers', *Soundings*, **4**, Autumn, 47–66.

Katzenstein, P. (1985), *Small States in World Markets*, Ithaca, NY: Cornell University Press.

Korten, D.C. (1995), *When Corporations Rule the World*, West Hartford, CN: Kumarian Press.

Lang, T. and C. Hines (1993), *The New Protectionism*, London: Earthscan.

Lerda, J.C. (1996), 'Globalization and the loss of autonomy by fiscal, banking and monetary authorities', *CEPAL Review*, **58**, April, 65–78.

Lipsey, R.E. (1997), 'Global production systems and local labour conditions', Conference on *International Solidarity and Globalisation*, Stockholm, 27–28, October.

Lipsey, R.E., M. Blomstrom and E. Ramstetter (1995), 'Internationalized production in world output', Working Paper 5385, December, Cambridge, Mass.: NBER.

MITI (1997), *The 6th Basic Survey of Overseas Business Activities*, Tokyo: MITI, March (http://www.jef.or.jp/news/970508.html).

Obstfeld, M. (1993), 'International Capital Mobility in the 1990s', Working Paper No. 4534, November, Cambridge, Mass.: NBER.

OECD (1992), *Industrial Policy in OECD Countries: Annual Review 1992*, Paris: OECD.

OECD (1994a), *Employment Outlook*, Paris: OECD.

OECD (1994b), *Social Protection Database*, Paris: OECD.

Petri, P.A. (1994), 'The East Asian trading bloc: an analytical history', in R. Garnaut and P. Drysdale (eds), *Asia Pacific Regionalism*, Pymble: Harper Educational, pp. 107–24.

Ramesh, M. (1993), 'Social security in Singapore: the state and the changing social and political circumstances', *Journal of Commonwealth and Comparative Politics*, **31** (3), 111–21.

Ramstetter, E. (1998), 'Measuring the size of foreign multinationals in the Asia pacific', in G.F. Thompson (ed.), *Economic Dynamism in the Asia-Pacific: The Growth of Integration and Competitiveness*, London: Routledge, pp. 185–212.

Regini, M. (1997), 'Still engaging in corporatism? Recent Italian experience in comparative perspective', *European Journal of Industrial Relations*, **3** (3), 259–78.

Rodrik, D. (1997), *Has Globalization Gone Too Far?*, Washington, DC: Institute for International Economics.

Skidelsky, R. (1996), 'Welfare without the state', *Prospect*, January, 38–43.

Strange, S. (1996), *The Retreat of the State*, Cambridge: Cambridge University Press.

Thompson, G.F. (1999), 'Where do MNCs conduct their business activity and what are the consequences for national systems?', in S. Quack, G. Morgan and R. Whitley (eds), *National Capitalisms, Global Competition and Economic Performance*, Berlin: De Gruyter.

Tobin, J. (1994), 'Speculator's tax', *New Economy*, 104–9.

United Nations (1997), *World Investment Report 1997: Transnational Corporations, Market Structure and Competition Policy*, United Nations Conference on Trade and Development, New York and Geneva: United Nations.

Visser, J. and A. Hemerijck (1997), *'A Dutch Miracle': Job Growth, Welfare Reform and Corporatism in the Netherlands*, Amsterdam: Amsterdam University Press.

World Bank (1997), *World Economic Outlook, May*, Washington, DC: World Bank.

Index

Abraham, F. 71, 83
acquisitions and mergers, and FDI 151
Adler, M. 47
advocacy groups *see* pressure groups
Alesina, A. 71, 80
Allen, J. 151
Amin, A. 101
Andersen, T.M. 71
Anderson, G. Esping – *see* Esping–
    Anderson, G.
anti-dumping agreement 24–5
Auspitz, J.L. 95
autonomy *see* national sovereignty

Baccaro, L. 172
Bacchetta, P. 155
banks, foreign assets and liabilities
    162–3
Bayoumi, T. 155, 165
Bekaert, G. 59
Bendix, R. 114
Benzie, R. 47
Bergsten, C.F. 144
Betsill, M.M. 125
Bhagwati, J. 72
Biltoft, K. 42
Black, F. 41
Blommestein, H. 42, 44, 58
Blundell-Wignall, A. 51
Bonser-Neal, C. 49
Borio, C. 57
Bosworth, B. 155
Brander, J. 71
Britain *see* United Kingdom
Brown, S.J. 58

capital, taxation of 55, 56
capital flows

speculative, barriers to 59–61,
    168–9
statistics 38–9
volatility 60–61
capital markets *see* financial markets
cause groups *see* pressure groups
Cawson, A. 96
Cerny, P.G. 91, 92, 93, 94, 95, 96, 97,
    99, 105, 110, 119, 124, 128, 129,
    130
Chandler, A.D. 93
Chernow, R. 113, 117–18
Chester, A.C. 44
Claessens, S. 60
Clark, A.M. 125
Clayton, R. 101
collective goods *see* public goods
commodification *see* marketisation
commodity market, model 73–4
communication systems, development
    40–41, 101, 123, 124
competition 14, 25–6
competition states 93–4, 96, 103, 106–7,
    109, 121
competitive advantage 12–13, 15–16,
    104, 107, 141
competitiveness, and social protection
    77, 80, 81, 84–5
computers, development 40–41, 101,
    123, 124
Cooper, I. 49
Coser, L.A. 120
covered interest rate parity 47–8
Cox, R. 96
cross-country consumption, and financial
    market integration 50–51
Crouch, C. 121
Crozier, M. 110

redistributive public goods *see* public
    goods; social protection
Regini, M. 172
regional integration
    concept 144-9
    effects on domestic policies 18-19
    and FDI 145-8
    and multinational enterprises 151-2
    and policy coherence 19-20, 30, 81-5,
        108-9
    social implications 69-70
    and sovereignty 19-20
    statistics 149
    and trade diversion 144-5
    see also free trade
regulation
    of financial markets 61-2, 165-70
    see also deregulation
Reich, R.B. 18, 96, 100, 101
Reich, S. 117
risk management
    and financial market deregulation 61
    and globalisation 53
Robertson, R. 115
Rodrik, D. 2, 59, 80, 170, 171
Rogoff, K. 50, 51, 60
Rosenau, J.N. 90
Rouwenhorst, K.G. 49
Rupert, M. 93

safeguard measures 25-6
Santis, G. de *see* de Santis, G.
savings, institutionalisation of 42-5, 58,
        160-61
savings-investment correlation 51-2,
        154-7, 158
Savitch, H.W. 126
Schattschneider, E.E. 90
Schmidt, V.A. 106
Schmitter, P.C. 96
Scholes, M.S. 41
Schumpeter, J.A. 104
sectional groups *see* pressure groups
securities
    cross-border transactions 39
    see also equities market; foreign
        securities
service sector, trade agreements 9, 26-8,
        32
Shearlock, P. 39

Sikkink, K. 123
Simon, H.A. 110
Skidelsky, R. 171
Smith, A. 104
social agents, for institutional change
        114, 115, 120, 122-6, 128-9
social dumping 69-70
social effects
    of globalisation 55, 72, 169-70
    of regional integration 69-70
social minimum clauses 83-5
social movements *see* transnational
        social movements
social protection
    and competitiveness 77, 80, 81, 84-5
    and employment 79, 81, 82-3, 84
    and globalisation 171-2
    policies
        co-ordination 81-5
        European Community 69-70, 71-2
        model 75-85
    and public expenditure 167
Sørensen, J.R. 71, 73
sovereignty *see* national sovereignty
speculative capital flows, barriers to
        59-61, 168-9
Spencer, B.J. 71
Spruyt, H. 91, 112
standards, international, and
        globalisation 143
states *see* nation-states
Stone, D. 108, 121, 125
Stopford, J. 108
Strange, S. 108, 128, 143
Streeck, W. 121
structural change *see* institutional change
structural form, and institutional change
        110-11, 112-13

Takeda, M. 44
tariffs 23-4
Tarrow, S. 124, 126
taxation
    of capital 55, 56
    see also Tobin tax
Taylor, A.M. 39, 47, 51-2, 54, 56
Taylor, L.W. 48
technological developments
    and growth of financial markets
        40-41, 42